Omnipresence of Intelligent Systems in Modern Society

Editors

Gautam Kumar
Assistant Professor, Department of CSE
National Institute of Technology Delhi
Delhi, India

Aditya Gupta
Thapar Institute of Engineering and Technology
Punjab, India

Gunjan
Assistant Professor, Department of CSE
National Institute of Technology Delhi
Delhi, India

Jayeeta Chakraborty
Assistant Professor, School of Computer Science
KIIT, Bhubaneswar, India

CRC Press
Taylor & Francis Group
Boca Raton London New York

CRC Press is an imprint of the
Taylor & Francis Group, an **informa** business
A SCIENCE PUBLISHERS BOOK

First edition published 2026
by CRC Press
2385 NW Executive Center Drive, Suite 320, Boca Raton FL 33431

and by CRC Press
4 Park Square, Milton Park, Abingdon, Oxon, OX14 4RN

CRC Press is an imprint of Taylor & Francis Group, LLC

Library of Congress Cataloging-in-Publication Data (applied for)

ISBN: 978-1-032-84202-8 (hbk)
ISBN: 978-1-032-87132-5 (pbk)
ISBN: 978-1-003-53104-3 (ebk)

DOI: 10.1201/9781003531043

Typeset in Times New Roman
by Prime Publishing Services

Preface

This book delves into the evolving field of computational intelligence, highlighting its intersection with computer science, AI, and machine learning. It covers recent advancements, theoretical foundations, and practical applications, emphasizing the role of computational algorithms in developing intelligent systems. Topics include visual computing, real-time decision support, and data-driven innovations. Designed for researchers, professionals, and graduate students, the book serves as a comprehensive resource for understanding and applying computational intelligence in real-world scenarios.

What's in the Book?

Chapter 1 entitled "*Machine Learning/Deep Learning in Biometric Systems*" presents a foundational overview of biometric recognition systems, emphasizing their role in security and authentication. It explores both physiological and behavioural biometrics, and highlights how machine learning techniques—such as deep learning, supervised, unsupervised, and reinforcement learning—enhance system performance. Key biometric modalities like face, fingerprint, iris, and gait recognition are discussed, alongside ethical and privacy concerns, setting the stage for future developments in this domain.

Chapter 2 entitled "*Rolling Mean based Real-time Activity Detection and Alert Generation using Deep Learning*" introduces a deep learning-based intelligent surveillance framework using smart CCTV networks for real-time activity recognition. Focusing on detecting robbery, accidents, and fire, the system eliminates the need for additional hardware by leveraging existing IoT-enabled infrastructure. With automatic feature extraction and alert generation, the approach proves to be robust, cost-effective, and more efficient than traditional surveillance methods.

Chapter 3 entitled "*A Triple based Lightweight Authentication Scheme for Smart Grid and Smart Metering System*" explores the development of smart electrical grids to address rising electricity demand and promote energy conservation. It emphasizes the use of predictive algorithms for consumption forecasting and highlights consumer behaviour models like the UTAUT framework to enhance smart meter adoption. Demand Response (DR) programs and big data analytics are shown to reduce peak usage effectively. The chapter also addresses IoT security, proposing a lightweight triple DES-based protocol to safeguard data and ensure system integrity.

Chapter 4 entitled "*A Comparative Analysis of Cloud-Based Education and Skill Development in Smart Cities Context*" examines the role of cloud-based solutions in enhancing smart city education systems. It highlights the benefits of AI-driven customization, flexible services, and hybrid cloud integration in Learning Experience Platforms (LEPs). The study identifies Model 2 as the most effective for real-time, cost-efficient educational delivery, while also addressing challenges related to digital access, data privacy, and usability.

Chapter 5 entitled "*Private Blockchain based Encryption Framework using Computational Intelligence Approaches*" delves into the fusion of private blockchain technology with computational intelligence (CI) to enhance encryption, key management, and intrusion detection. Techniques like neural networks, fuzzy logic, and evolutionary algorithms are explored through real-world applications in healthcare, finance, and supply chains. The chapter also addresses challenges like scalability and privacy, while highlighting future directions including quantum-resistant encryption and IoT integration.

Chapter 6 entitled "*Leveraging AI in Smart Healthcare for future Hospitals: Potential Applications and Challenges*" highlights the transformative potential of integrating Artificial Intelligence (AI) and Internet of Things (IoT) in future healthcare systems. Leveraging advanced technologies like computer vision, natural language processing, and 6G connectivity, it aims to enable faster, more accurate disease detection and real-time health monitoring. The chapter envisions AI-driven healthcare that reduces human error, enhances personalized treatment, and addresses challenges of rising costs and resource scarcity.

Chapter 7 entitled "*Discrete Artificial Bee Colony Optimization Algorithm for Cyber-attack Detection to Mitigate Credential Stuffing in Cyber Defense*" focuses on cybersecurity, particularly defending against credential stuffing attacks—where reused login credentials are exploited. It introduces a discrete artificial bee colony optimization algorithm to enhance protection mechanisms. The proposed approach shows significant improvements in network resilience, with a 24% increase in alive nodes and a 32% extension in network lifetime.

Chapter 8 entitled "*Qryptographix: Quantum Image Encryption via Random Gates*" presents a novel image encryption framework using quantum gates, implemented via Qiskit. Addressing the threat quantum computing poses to classical encryption, the study demonstrates how quantum circuits can secure image data. Experimental results affirm the approach's effectiveness, marking a step forward in quantum cryptography and secure communication for the quantum era.

Chapter 9 entitled "*Handling Missing Data in Healthcare with Fuzzy Clustering Imputation*" addresses the challenge of missing data in healthcare by applying computational intelligence techniques for data imputation. It focuses on fuzzy clustering, which allows flexible data grouping to enhance imputation accuracy. The method proves effective in improving predictive modeling and supporting reliable, data-driven healthcare decisions.

Chapter 10 entitled "*A Novel Weighted Ensemble Approach for Improved Brain Tumor Detection and Classification*" introduces a deep learning-based weighted ensemble model for the accurate detection and classification of brain tumors. Addressing the limitations of traditional diagnostic methods, the proposed model achieves high performance—99.90% in detection and 95.02% in classification. The approach demonstrates strong potential to aid medical professionals in early, precise diagnosis and improved patient outcomes.

Chapter 11 entitled "*Glioma Brain Tumour Grade Detection using Clinical Feature, Molecular Feature and ConvLSTM Network*" presents a ConvLSTM-based deep learning approach for glioma brain tumor grade detection using clinical and molecular data. Feature selection via random forest narrows down to 17 key predictors, enabling a model that achieves 99.40% accuracy and a 0.993 F-score. The method outperforms existing techniques, offering a reliable tool for accurate glioma grading to guide patient treatment.

Chapter 12 entitled "*Machine Learning for Ocular Disease Detection in Fundus Images*" explores the synergy between medical imaging and bioinformatics to enhance image analysis and interpretation. By leveraging feature extraction, statistical analysis, and machine learning, it advances diagnostics and personalized treatment across various diseases. The chapter also discusses challenges like data privacy and algorithmic bias, while highlighting future prospects including AI, radiomics, and explainable models for transformative healthcare.

Contents

List of Contributors

Aditya Verma
Department of CSE, COEP Tech., Pune, India

Aleena Swetapadma
School of Computer Engineering, KIIT deemed to be University, Bhubaneswar, India

Alok Kumar Jagadev
School of Computer Engineering, KIIT Deemed to be University, Bhubaneswar, India

Amit Joshi
Department of CSE, COEP Tech., Pune, India

Anil Kumar Swain
School of Computer Engineering, KIIT deemed to be University, Bhubaneswar, India

Anjali Vaish
School of Computer Engineering, KIIT deemed to be University, Bhubaneswar, India

Ankit Kumar Jain
Department of Computer Engineering National Institute of Technology Kurukshetra, India

Ankita Mohan
School of Computer Engineering, KIIT Deemed to be University, Bhubaneswar, India

Ankur Mittal
National Institute of Technology, Delhi

Anshul Kulkarni
Department of CSE, COEP Tech., Pune, India

Brijesh Raj Swain
PG Department of medicine, IMS & Sum Hospital, SOA University, Bhubaneshwar, India

Chandrashekhar Azad
Department of Computer Science and Engineering, National Institute of Technology, Jamshedpur, India

Gautam Kumar
Department of Computer Science and Engineering, National Institute of Technology, Delhi, India

Harish Gavel
Department of Computer Science and Engineering, National Institute of Technology, Jamshedpur, 831014, India

Hitesh Mohapatra
School of Computer Engineering, KIIT Deemed to be University, Bhubaneswar, India

Indumathi N.
Department of Computer Science and Engineering, Rajalakshmi Institute of Technology, Chennai, India

Jahanvi Singh
School of Computer Engineering, KIIT Deemed to be University, Bhubaneswar, India

Jayeeta Chakraborty
School of Computer Science and Engineering, KIIT Bhubaneswar

Ketan Anand
Department of AI & ML Sreenidhi Institute of Science and Technology, Hyderabad

Kirti Baliyan
Computer Engineering Department, NIT Kurukshetra

Kritika Upadhyay
Department of Electronics & Communication Engineering National Institute of Technology, Delhi, India

Mahery Ranaivoson
Analyst Developer Data Platform, Beneva, Quebec Canada

Mahesh K. Singh
National Institute of Technology, Delhi

Manisha Bharti
Department of Electronics & Communication Engineering National Institute of Technology, Delhi, India

Manoj Kumar
Department of Electronics & Communication Engineering National Institute of Technology, Delhi, India

Mohit Zanwarb
Department of CSE, COEP Tech., Pune, India

Naliniprava Behera
School of Computer Engineering, KIIT deemed to be University, Bhubaneswar, India

Pabbisetti Satya Gouri Aruna Sri
Department of Internet of Things, Koneru Lakshmaiah Education Foundation, Vaddeswaram

Pabitra Mohan Khilar
National Institute of Technology, Rourkela

Priyanka Ahlawat
Computer Engineering Department, NIT Kurukshetra

Priyanka Ahlawat
Department of Computer Engineering National Institute of Technology Kurukshetra, India

Ramkumar K.
Department of Computer Science and Engineering, Rajalakshmi Institute of Technology, Chennai, India

Sahil Sahani
School of Computer Engineering, KIIT Deemed to be University, Bhubaneswar, India

Santosh Kumar Birthriya
Department of Computer Engineering National Institute of Technology Kurukshetra, India

Santosh Kumar Swain
School of Computer Engineering, KIIT Deemed to be University, Bhubaneswar, India

Satya Subham Nayak
School of Computer Engineering, KIIT deemed to be University, Bhubaneswar, India

Satyakam Nayak
School of Computer Engineering, KIIT Deemed to be University, Bhubaneswar, India

Somasundari P.
Department of Computer Science and Engineering, Rajalakshmi Institute of Technology, Chennai, India

Srinivasan M.L.
Department of Computer Science and Engineering, Rajalakshmi Institute of Technology, Chennai, India

Subhashish Nayak
National Institute of Technology, Rourkela

Sumit Kumar
Department of CSE, Haridwar University, Roorkee

Suraj Sawant
Department of CSE, COEP Tech., Pune, India

Syed Ali Hussain Rizvi
Department of Computer Science and Engineering, National Institute of Technology, Delhi, India

I
VISUAL COMPUTING

DOI: 10.1201/9781003531043-1

Chapter 1

Machine Learning/Deep Learning in Biometric Systems

*Mahesh K. Singh** and *Ankur Mittal*

Abstract

Biometric recognition systems have become most popular and trustworthy systems for organizations of all sizes. This chapter provides a comprehensive overview of biometric systems and recent trends, including fundamental concepts, physiological and behavioral traits, and their applications in security, authentication, and identification. It highlights the role of machine learning (ML) algorithms and in enhancing the efficiency, accuracy, and adaptability of biometric systems. Various ML methods, including deep learning, supervised learning, unsupervised learning, and reinforcement learning, are integrated with biometric systems, fingerprint recognition, voice verification, and iris and retina recognition verification, are also explored using ML methods like SVMs, Hidden Markov Models (HMMs), and deep neural networks. The chapter concludes with a summary of key attributes of different biometric recognition systems and discusses future prospects, especially privacy and ethical issues.

National Institute of Technology, Delhi.

* Corresponding author: ksmahesh@nitdelhi.ac.in

DOI: 10.1201/9781003531043-2

1.1 Introduction

Biometric recognition is a highly effective method for identifying individuals based on unique biological features and behavioral features. Almost every country employs biometric recognition systems for its citizens. For instance, India's Aadhar Card system uses fingerprints and iris scans to verify identities. These distinct features provide a reliable means of identity verification. During the COVID-19 pandemic, only methods that allowed for distance-based recognition were used. Biometric recognition is also widely utilized across various industries to verify employees entering the workplace. It involves the use of anatomical, physiological, and behavioral characteristics to identify individuals, with the primary goal of providing a secure, efficient, and user-friendly method for identity verification. There are various methods of biometric recognition: facial, iris, fingerprint, retina, hand geometry, ear shape, signature, gait, and voice. Facial recognition analyzes facial features, considering the contribution of teeth, skin, lips, hair, face shape, mouth, eyebrows, cheekbones, and jawline. Iris recognition leverages the unique patterns found in the eye's colored ring, making it suitable for high-security areas and financial institutions. The classification of inputs of biometric recognition systems is shown in Figure 1.1. And it has physiological and behavioral properties. Fingerprint recognition utilizes the distinctive patterns of ridges and valleys on an individual's fingertips and is used for smartphones, biometric attendance, and forensic investigations. Gait recognition observes the unique way a person walks and is employed in surveillance and security systems. Signature recognition examines the unique manner in which a person signs their name, including pressure and speed. Voice recognition analyzes vocal characteristics such as pitch, tone, and rhythm. The Process of biometric recognition is shown in Figure 1.2. We cannot give the biometric input directly to the feature extraction module because every input has some noise associated with it. The noise is removed from the biometric input with the help of a preprocessing

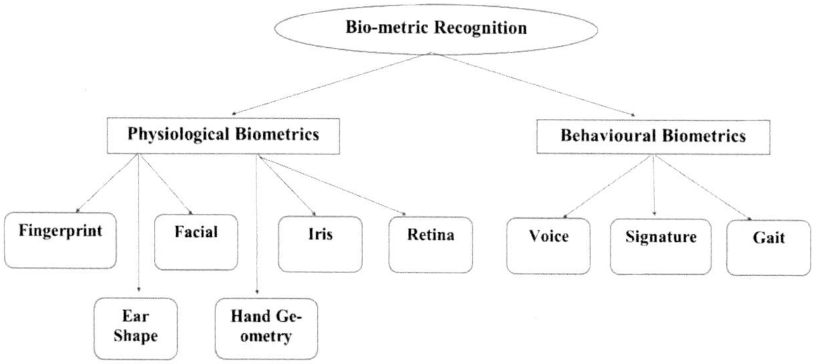

Figure 1.1: Biometric recognition methods.

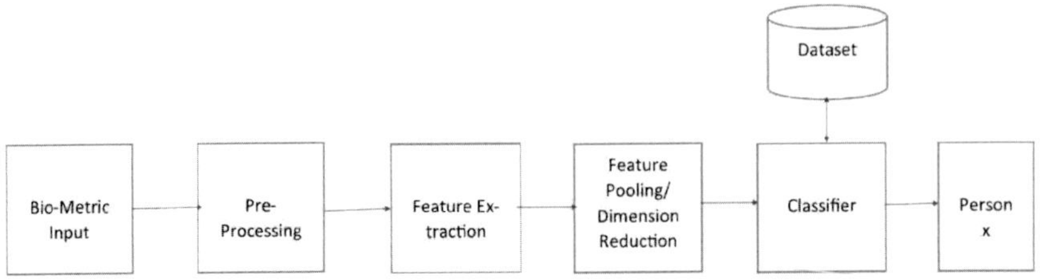

Figure 1.2: Biometric process.

module. There are various application fields for biometric recognition, such as security and access control at airports and military installations. It can also assist with forensics and criminal identification. It can also be used as passwords for mobile phones, laptops, door locks, etc., and for banking transactions, bank lockers. The combination of AI and ML is enhancing the ability to process and analyze biometric data, making systems more robust and reliable. Biometric systems are security technologies designed to identify or authenticate individuals by analyzing their distinctive physiological or behavioral traits. Biometric information systems can be classified into identification and verification systems. A verification system confirms an individual's identity based on their claimed identity, while an identification system determines an individual's identity from a database of registered individuals without needing the person to declare their identity.

Fingerprints are widely recognized as reliable biometric traits used in various applications, including identity verification and identification for building access, mobile devices, and contactless payment systems. Unlike passwords, fingerprints are convenient as they cannot be forgotten, making them an attractive alternative for verification processes. In law enforcement, fingerprints are crucial for identification due to their uniqueness and consistency throughout a person's life. Most current systems rely on contact fingerprints, which require physical contact with a sensor. This method can lead to issues such as contamination from previous users' latent fingerprints, resulting in poor-quality images and potential hygiene risks, especially highlighted during the COVID-19 pandemic. To overcome the limitations of contact fingerprint systems, contactless fingerprint recognition systems have been developed [20]. These systems eliminate physical contact, thus addressing contamination and hygiene concerns. Contactless fingerprint systems can capture more detailed images using high-resolution cameras, which can enhance the quality of the captured data and inspire new applications.

The authors introduce an innovative indexing method designed to efficiently categorize and retrieve protected biometric templates. This method is adaptable, working independently of specific biometric traits and cancelable biometric systems. It can integrate diverse biometric data types, including facial, fingerprint, and iris information, while maintaining individual privacy. The experimental findings indicate that the system developed in this work can substantially decrease computational load by about 57% when incorporating up to three different types of biometric features for indexing and by 53% when indexing up to two types [15]. This efficiency is achieved without sacrificing biometric performance at high-security levels, highlighting an advantage over conventional approaches.

The author introduced a multimodal biometric recognition system tailored for an IoT Blockchain environment. This system seamlessly combines various biometric traits such as palmprint, iris, face, and periocular features. This multiple model combined approach enhances the security and accuracy of the biometric recognition procedure, as different traits provide complementary information. The research highlights the importance of efficient feature extraction algorithms tailored to every biometric trait. The extracted features are converted into cancelable biometric formats to improve the security and privacy of the stored templates. However, this chapter also acknowledges potential security issues associated with cancelable biometrics, such as vulnerability to database and channel attacks [17]. For addressing the identified security concerns, the chapter introduces the AT technique as a Bio-Cryptographic method. This technique is noted for its effectiveness in encryption and decryption processes without compromising information, thereby enhancing the security of biometric data.

The author proposed a lightweight joint biometric authentication scheme, SELBA. SELBA is designed to utilize both fingerprint features and facial recognition for user identification. This dual approach enhances the security and reliability of the authentication process. The scheme employs a Local Binary Pattern (LBP) feature description operator and ciphertext retrieval methods for ensuring the privacy of biometric features during authentication [3]. This is crucial for maintaining confidentiality and relevance in biometric recognition. A significant contribution of SELBA is the introduction of a cancelable mechanism. This allows users to revoke and update their biometric templates if they are compromised, addressing the critical issue of biometric data being immutable once leaked.

Figure 1.3 presents various biometric identification methods, such as fingerprints, iris, face, and voice, based on their performance across different criteria. The performance is categorized into three possible ranges: Minimum (Min), Intermediate, and Maximum (Max). Experimental results indicate that SELBA has a low computational cost while maintaining reasonable authentication accuracy. However, it is noted that its accuracy is slightly lower compared to schemes based on Convolutional Neural Networks (CNNs), which have higher computational overheads.

Biometric \ Criteria	Universality	Permanence	Distinctiveness	Collectivity	Performance	Acceptability	Circumvention
Fingerprints	Intermediate	Max	Max	Intermediate	Max	Intermediate	Intermediate
Finger Vein	Intermediate	Max	Max	Max	Max	Max	Intermediate
Face	Max	Min	Intermediate	Max	Min	Intermediate	Intermediate
Iris	Max	Max	Max	Intermediate	Max	Intermediate	Max
Voice	Intermediate	Intermediate	Intermediate	Max	Intermediate	Max	Max

Figure 1.3: Biometric method.

Aim

- Enhance security to prevent unauthorized access and reduce fraud.
- Improve Accuracy for reliable identification and minimize errors.
- Enhance convenience for quick and efficient results.
- Address specific needs of various sectors like health, law enforcement, financial services and travel and immigration.

1.2 Machine Learning Methodology in Biometric Systems

1. Facial Recognition: Convolutional Neural Networks (CNNs), FaceNet and DeepFace.
2. Fingerprint Recognition: CNNs, SVMs and Random Forests.
3. Voice Recognition: Deep Neural Networks (DNNs), Hidden Markov Models (HMMs), RNNs and LSTMs.
4. Iris Recognition: CNNs, Gabor Filters.
5. Gait Recognition: RNNs and LSTMs, CNNs.
6. Signature Recognition: Dynamic Time Warping (DTW), CNNs and SVM.

1.3 Discussion About Methodologies

1.3.1 Convolutional Neural Network

Convolutional neural networks belong to the category of deep learning that has been exceptionally effective for involving image classification and object recognition. CNNs are especially effective for biometric recognition because they can adaptively and automatically acquire spatial feature hierarchical structures from input images.

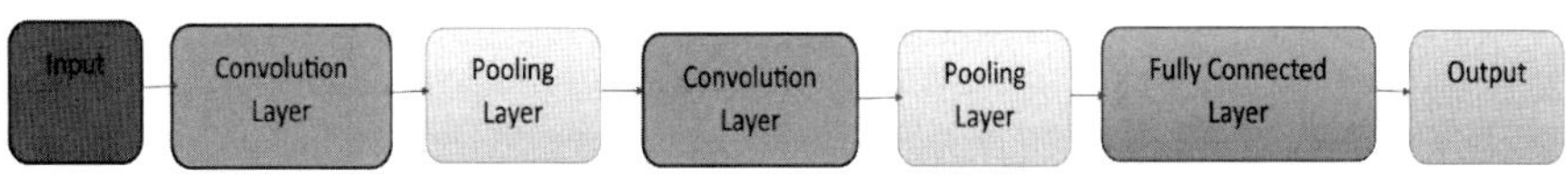

Figure 1.4: Convolutional neural networks.

Figure 1.4 shows the complete process of CNN discuss below.

- Convolution layers - A convolutional layer is used to detect features from the input image or video. It can use different sizes of kernels (1×1, 2×2, 3×3, 5×5, 7×7, etc.) for detecting the features.
- The kernel consists of small matrices that slide over the input image matrices to detect patterns. Each kernel activates when it detects a specific feature like edges, textures, etc., in the input image.
- A 3×3 kernel as shown in Figure 1.5, has some weights, as depicted in the figure above. These weights can be learned by the CNN during training without any human intervention.
- Striding is used to control the movement of the filter over the image, while padding adds borders to the input to control the output size.
- For the activation function, ReLU (Rectifier Linear Unit) is used. ReLU provides non-linearity to the input, setting all negative values to zero.
- There are two popular pooling methods: max pooling and average pooling. Max pooling selects the maximum pixel within a window, while average pooling computes the average pixel value within a window.

W_{11}	W_{12}	W_{13}
W_{21}	W_{22}	W_{23}
W_{31}	W_{32}	W_{33}

Figure 1.5: kernel/Filter (3×3).

- Fully connected layers, also known as dense layers, are used for classification and object detection.

Applications of CNNs in Biometric Recognition:

a. **Facial Recognition** - Facial recognition systems identify individuals by analyzing distinct facial features such as the eyes, nose, and mouth. These systems extract specific patterns from these features to accurately distinguish and verify identities.

b. **Fingerprint Recognition** - This identifies minute points and ridge patterns to match fingerprints.

c. **Iris Recognition** - This analyzes the unique patterns in the iris for identification.

d. **Gait Recognition** - It captures and analyzes the walking patterns from video frames.

The author emphasizes the growing need for alternative biometric systems due to the increasing fraudulent use and legal issues associated with human biometric authentication. This highlights the importance of exploring non-human biometric options to protect sensitive information. The performance of a deep learning technique, specifically Convolutional Neural Networks (CNN), for recognizing and identifying wood and leaf biometric patterns has been successfully demonstrated [18]. This approach shows promise in providing a reliable method for biometric authentication. Using this approach experimental results indicate that the proposed system is both feasible and effective. The accuracy values achieved during testing were above 96% for both the validation and test sets, showcasing the system's high reliability and practicality in real-world scenarios.

The author introduced two multimodal authentication systems (sequential and parallel) that utilize Convolutional Neural Networks to combine ECG and fingerprint data at different levels of merging, as shown in Figure 1.6. These systems effectively address common issues found in unimodal systems, such as loss of au-

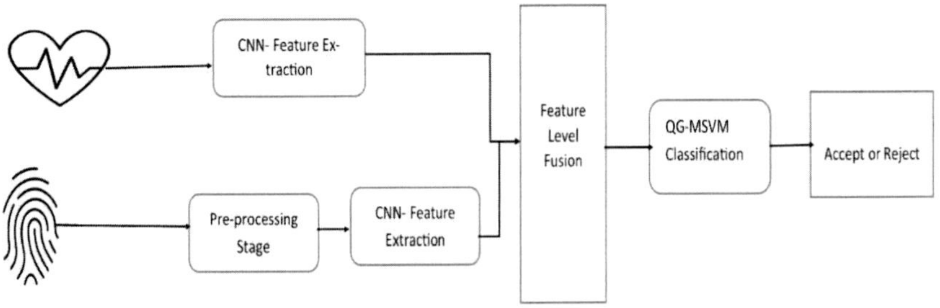

Figure 1.6: Multimodal biometric fusion system.

thentication accuracy and vulnerability to spoof attacks. CNN was employed for feature extraction from both biometrics, and an enhanced Bio-Hashing approach was implemented to safeguard the features obtained, thereby enhancing authentication accuracy [6]. The study proposed an internal fusion method that combines significant features from each biometric modality, leading to improved authentication accuracy. The experimental results indicated that the proposed unimodal systems for fingerprint and ECG authentication yield acceptable results when compared to other methods.

The author describes the DeepEyedentificationLive model significantly outperforms previous methods in oculomotor biometric identification by processing both controlled stimuli and the resulting binocular gaze responses. This model effectively determines embeddings of gaze sequences while simultaneously detecting presentation attacks. The model achieves lower error rates for identification and identity verification compared to prior works, demonstrating its reliability in detecting replay attacks. The study emphasizes that increasing the data volume, training population size, and number of sessions enhances model performance, indicating that more data generally leads to better outcomes. By analyzing high-frequency, low-velocity micro-movements in a dedicated sub-network, DeepEyedentificationLive can automatically detect unique micro-movement characteristics that differ among individuals [13]. This capability is crucial as it allows the model to function without requiring user-specific calibration. The research highlights the potential of using eye movements for quick and non-intrusive identification across various applications. Eye movements are accessible to a large portion of the population and can complement existing biometric systems, making them more robust against challenges posed by colored contact lenses or facial coverings.

1.3.2 FaceNet

FaceNet, introduced by Google researchers in 2015, is a face recognition system that utilizes ZF-Net and an Inception module to produce high-quality face mappings from images. FaceNet employs an end-to-end learning architecture, particularly using 1×1 convolutions to reduce the number of parameters. As illustrated in Figure 1.7, a batch of images is processed through the deep learning architecture, and the output is fed into L2 Normalization. These embeddings are subsequently processed through a loss function to determine the loss as shown in Figure 6.

Triplet loss will help the model to enforce a margin between faces of different identities.

The findings introduce Low-FaceNet, a unique face recognition-driven low-light image enhancement network that integrates multiple modules to enhance low-

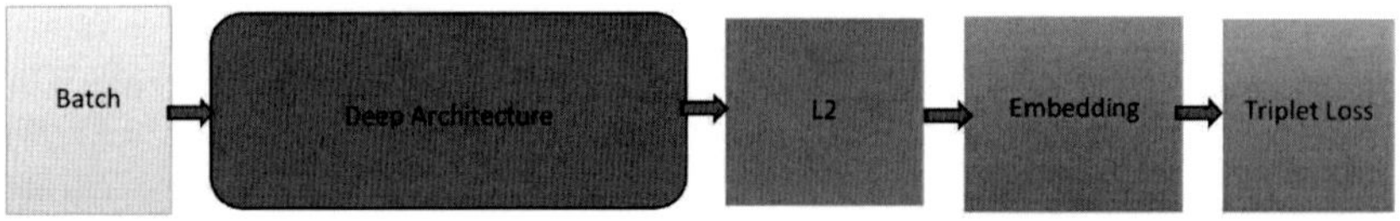

Figure 1.7: FaceNet architecture.

light images while improving face recognition accuracy. This framework is designed to work under a unified deep learning paradigm, which is a significant advancement over traditional methods that treat these tasks separately. It demonstrates that enhancing underexposed images can significantly improve recognition performance, suggesting that these two tasks can promote each other effectively [4]. Low-FaceNet effectively utilizes semantic information to ensure consistent and smooth illumination across images. This capability is crucial for maintaining natural exposure levels and avoiding overexposure in certain areas, which can occur when semantic information is not considered.

1.3.3 Support Vector Machine (SVM)

SVM are a powerful set of supervised learning methods popularly used for regression, classification and outlier detection. Support Vector Machines (SVMs) are known to be highly effective in high dimensional spaces.

Fundamentals of SVM:

- The SVM's goal is to maximize the margin, which is the distance between the closest points for each class and hyperplane. This distance represents the support vectors. SVMs achieve better generalization while maximizing the margin.
- SVM is the commonly used method for binary classification. It classifies the data into two classes, with the decision boundary defined by support vectors.
- For multiclass classification, SVM uses a one-vs-one or one-vs-all approach, training multiple binary classifications and then combining them.
- SVM is used for regression and is known as support vector regression (SVR), predicting a continuous value instead of a class label.

The author proposed a biometric system using Fiber Bragg Gratings (FBGs) to identify foot features achieving 86% accuracy with the SVM algorithm across various stepping patterns [5]. This robust system withstood different pressures and foot positions, indicating its potential for applications like postural analysis and gait monitoring beyond mere identification.

1.3.4 Random Forests

Random forest algorithms create multiple decision trees by randomly selecting data points and features. For predictions, the algorithm combines the results of all the trees outputting the most common outcome, akin to a majority vote as shown in Figure 1.8.

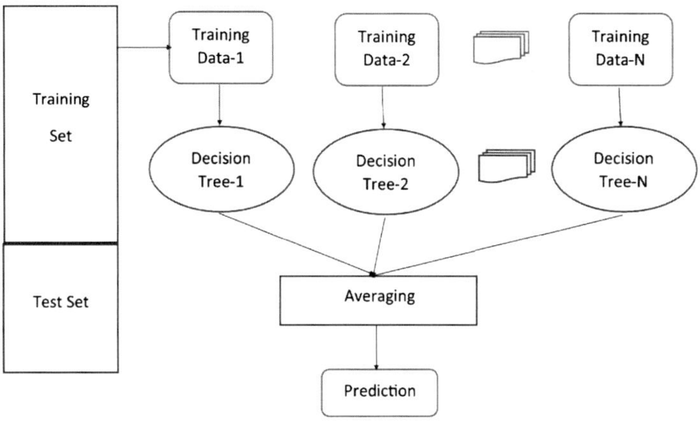

Figure 1.8: Random forest method.

The paper emphasizes the importance of merging feature extraction and statistical modeling processes under a unified objective function, which enhances model discriminability and effectiveness in face recognition tasks. A novel discriminative training criterion, developed from statistical hypothesis test theory, is introduced. This criterion maximizes the confidence in accepting the hypothesis that observations belong to the target HMM state, which is crucial for improving the accuracy of face recognition systems. The MC-HMM (Maximum Confidence Hidden Markov Modeling) framework is developed, which integrates a transformation matrix to derive distinctive facial characteristics [1]. This integration is significant for achieving robust performance in face recognition applications. The findings suggest that the MC-HMM framework not only improves recognition accuracy but also reduces the dimensionality of features making it more effective for face recognition tasks.

1.3.5 Hidden Markov Models (HMM)

A Hidden Markov Model (HMM) is a statistical framework that describes systems with unobservable states evolving over time. Each hidden state generates observable outcomes, with defined probabilities for for state transitions and symbol generation. HMMs effectively model uncertainty and temporal dependencies, making them useful in fields like finance, bioinformatics, and speech recognition.

A new approach to face recognition is introduced, which specifically addresses faces with multiple poses, in contrast to traditional methods that primarily focus on frontal faces or mug shots. The method clusters face into pose categories and uses Embedded Hidden Markov Models (EHMM) to break down facial appearances into subject-specific and pose-oriented components, referred to as SSPO components [8]. SSPO is an integrated method that merges pose-specific facial components with a novel classification technique, demonstrating superior performance in face recognition compared to traditional methods.

1.3.6 RNN

A Recurrent Neural Network (RNN) is an artificial neural network ideal for sequential data, commonly used in speech recognition and natural language processing (NLP). RNNs remember past inputs to influence future outputs excelling in tasks like predicting the next word in a sentence or recognizing speech patterns. However, they struggle with lengthy sequences, which frameworks like Gated Recurrent Units (GRUs) and Long Short-Term Memory (LSTM) networks help to address.

Using ML-enhanced iris and retinal images for biometric recognition offers highly accurate and secure identity verification. EfficientNet for feature extraction and CAE for classification achieve superior results [12]. Combining CNN and RNN models captures intricate patterns, enhancing security and reliability for applications like healthcare, mobile device verification, access control, and border control.

Biometric recognition uses unique physiological and behavioral traits in time-series data to identify individuals. Deep learning algorithms offer effective classification and feature extraction, making them suitable for ECG-based identification [10]. The study highlights the novel use of unidirectional and bidirectional RNNs, especially the BGRU model, for biometric identification.

Handwritten signature verification, crucial in research area, uses two main methods: off-line (ink on paper) and on-line (electronic devices capturing temporal sequences) [16]. Despite advancements, traditional methods like SVMs, HMMs, and Dynamic Time Warping remain prevalent. Deep learning is less common in on-line verification due to difficulties in acquiring large-scale datasets and the lack of standard experimental protocols.

1.3.7 LSTM

Long Short-Term Memory (LSTM) Networks are deep learning architectures designed for sequential data, allowing information to persist over time. They excel at time series prediction and natural language processing by effectively capturing long-term dependencies, making them ideal for sequence prediction tasks.

With increasing demand for information security, ECG-based biometric systems are gaining attention. These biometric systems are used in mobile devices, healthcare, and continuous authentication, especially in healthcare due to their reliability and resistance to alteration [7]. The proposed system employs a hierarchical LSTM model with an attention mechanism to capture multiscale temporal variations in ECG signals, improving identification and verification performance.

Eye movement biometric systems are offer benefits like liveness detection and continuous authentication, making them ideal for multimodal systems. However, commercial viability is limited due to treating it as a closed-set classification task and lacking diverse datasets [9]. This study aims to overcome these limitations by training a CNN with exponentially dilated convolutions and multi-similarity (MS) loss, validated on the GazeBase dataset, which comprises recordings from 322 participants over 37 months.

Biometric Authentication (BA) uses unique physiological traits for identity verification, applied in secure transactions, data protection, and access control. Photoplethysmography (PPG) signals, easily captured by smart devices, are crucial for biometric authentication, providing accessible data [2]. The paper highlights the role of classification algorithms like k-Nearest Neighbor (kNN), Support Vector Machine (SVM), neural networks (NN), and decision tree-based methods (boosting and bootstrap aggregation) in improving identification accuracy and enhancing decision-making in biometric systems.

1.3.8 Gabor Filters

Biometrics identifies individuals using unique characteristics like fingerprints or voice patterns to enhance security and efficiency. The chapter discusses an automated fingerprint identification system that utilizing a Gabor filter-based coefficient map. It detects the fingerprint core by analyzing pixel neighborhoods, improving accuracy [19]. The image divided into quadrants around the core, extracting texture orientation in three Gabor filter directions. Results highlight the Gabor filter's effectiveness in high-quality fingerprint image identification and its potential in biometric applications.

The chapter presents a new online signature verification method that enhances speed and accuracy by analyzing local temporal shifts using Gabor filter phase outputs. The method generates a normalized and quantized phase profile to create a fixed-size signature code, effectively utilizing morphological and temporal dissimilarities for improved verification, leveraging Gabor filter phase relationships [11].

Device compatibility in online biometric signature validation is challenging with various devices like pen tablets, smartphones, and PDAs in banking and commercial applications. The study considered mobile and access control scenarios to replicate real conditions, where users signed while standing and holding the device in one hand [14].

1.4 Conclusion & Future of Biometrics Systems

In conclusion, implementing biometric systems with machine learning enhances accuracy, efficiency, and security. ML algorithms excel at identifying complex patterns in biometric data like fingerprints, facial features, and iris patterns, ensuring precise identification and verification processes. ML models adapt over time improving performance and reducing errors. Deep learning further refines the system's ability to handle variations in biometric inputs, such as lighting changes or slight alterations.

However, implementing these systems requires careful consideration of privacy and ethical concerns. Secure storage and handling of biometric data are crucial to protect privacy and prevent misuse. Transparency in data use and consent mechanisms are vital for maintaining trust and compliance. The synergy between biometrics and machine learning offers great potential for secure access, identity verification and enhanced user experience. Continued advancements in ML and data security will solidify the role of biometric systems in our digital world.

The future of biometric systems with ML is transformative, offering high accuracy and security across various applications. Advanced deep learning models and multimodal systems enhance accuracy, security, and robustness. Real-time applications benefit from edge computing and cloud integration. Self-learning systems and personalization further improve these systems. AI integration enables emotional and behavior analysis and fraud detection. Privacy and ethical issues must be addressed due to the confidential nature of biometric data.

References

[1] J.-T. Chien and C.-P. Liao. Maximum confidence hidden markov modeling for face recognition. *IEEE Transactions on Pattern Analysis and Machine Intelligence*, 30(4):606–616, April 2008.

[2] S. L. Gonzaga de Oliveira and J. Teixeira de Assis. A methodology for identification of fingerprints based on gabor filter. *IEEE Latin America Transactions*, 4(1):1–6, March 2006.

[3] H. Wang et al. Joint biological id : A secure and efficient lightweight biometric authentication scheme. *IEEE Transactions on Dependable and Secure Computing*, 20(3):2578–2592, May-June 2023.

[4] Y. Fan et al. Low-facenet: Face recognition-driven low-light image enhancement. *IEEE Transactions on Instrumentation and Measurement*, 73:1–13, 2024.

[5] N. S. Girão, M. Muller, and L. V. R. de Arruda. A new biometric identification system based on plantar pressure. *IEEE Sensors Journal*, 23(15):16900–16906, August 2023.

[6] M. Hammad, Y. Liu, and K. Wang. Multimodal biometric authentication systems using convolution neural network based on different level fusion of ecg and fingerprint. *IEEE Access*, 7:26527–26542, 2019.

[7] D. Jyotishi and S. Dandapat. An ecg biometric system using hierarchical lstm with attention mechanism. *IEEE Sensors Journal*, 22(6):6052–6061, March 2022.

[8] P.-H. Lee, G.-S. Hsu, Y.-W. Wang, and Y.-P. Hung. Subject-specific and pose-oriented facial features for face recognition across poses. *IEEE*

Transactions on Systems, Man, and Cybernetics, Part B (Cybernetics), 42(5):1357–1368, October 2012.

[9] D. Lohr, H. Griffith, and O. V. Komogortsev. Eye know you: Metric learning for end-to-end biometric authentication using eye movements from a longitudinal dataset. *IEEE Transactions on Biometrics, Behavior, and Identity Science*, 4(2):276–288, April 2022.

[10] H. M. Lynn, S. B. Pan, and P. Kim. A deep bidirectional gru network model for biometric electrocardiogram classification based on recurrent neural networks. *IEEE Access*, 7:145395–145405, 2019.

[11] J. M. E. López, A. H. Celdrán, F. Esquembre, G. M. Pérez, and J. G. Marín-Blázquez. A supervised ml biometric continuous authentication system for industry 4.0. *IEEE Transactions on Industrial Informatics*, 18(12):9132–9140, December 2022.

[12] L. A. Maghrabi, M. Altwijri, S. S. Binyamin, F. S. Alallah, D. Hamed, and M. Ragab. Secure biometric identification using orca predators algorithm with deep learning: Retinal iris image analysis. *IEEE Access*, 12:18858–18867, 2024.

[13] S. Makowski, P. Prasse, D. R. Reich, D. Krakowczyk, L. A. Jäger, and T. Scheffer. Deepeyedentificationlive: Oculomotoric biometric identification and presentation-attack detection using deep neural networks. *IEEE Transactions on Biometrics, Behavior, and Identity Science*, 3(4):506–518, October 2021.

[14] B. L. Ortiz, J. W. Chong, V. Gupta, M. Shoushan, K. Jung, and T. Dallas. A biometric authentication technique using smartphone fingertip photoplethysmography signals. *IEEE Sensors Journal*, 22(14):14237–14249, July 2022.

[15] D. Osorio-Roig, L. J. González-Soler, C. Rathgeb, and C. Busch. Privacy-preserving multi-biometric indexing based on frequent binary patterns. *IEEE Transactions on Information Forensics and Security*, 19:4835–4850, 2024.

[16] R. Tolosana, R. Vera-Rodriguez, J. Fierrez, and J. Ortega-Garcia. Deepsign: Deep on-line signature verification. *IEEE Transactions on Biometrics, Behavior, and Identity Science*, 3(2):229–239, April 2021.

[17] S. Umer, A. Sardar, R. K. Rout, M. Tanveer, and I. Razzak. Iot-enabled multimodal biometric recognition system in secure environment. *IEEE Internet of Things Journal*, 10(24):21457–21466, December 2023.

[18] W. Yan, J. Tang, and S. Stucki. Design and implementation of a lightweight deep cnn-based plant biometric authentication system. *IEEE Access*, 11:79984–79993, 2023.

[19] Jonghyon Yi, Chulhan Lee, and Jaihie Kim. Online signature verification using temporal shift estimated by the phase of gabor filter. *IEEE Transactions on Signal Processing*, 53(2):776–783, February 2005.

[20] X. Yin, Y. Zhu, and J. Hu. A survey on 2d and 3d contactless fingerprint biometrics: A taxonomy, review, and future directions. *IEEE Open Journal of the Computer Society*, 2:370–381, 2021.

Chapter 2

Rolling Mean-based Real-time Activity Detection and Alert Generation using Deep Learning

Syed Ali Hussain Rizvi,[a] *Gautam Kumar*,[a,*] *Jayeeta Chakraborty*[b] and *Mahery Ranaivoson*[c]

Abstract

Securing and monitoring various places like shopping stores, traffic, industries, and homes is crucial. IoT-enabled devices and sensors are widely used for, but integrating expensive sensors and processors increases complexity and costs. Detecting abnormalities in large videos requires significant human effort. This study develops an intelligent surveillance framework using CCTV networks and deep

[a] Department of Computer Science and Engineering, NIT Delhi, India.

[b] School of Computer Science and Engineering, KIIT Bhubaneswar.

[c] Analyst Developer Data Platform, Beneva, Québec Canada.

* Corresponding author: gautamkumar@ieee.org

DOI: 10.1201/9781003531043-3

learning for automatic feature extraction. The model identifies three types of daily mishaps: robbery, accident, and fire. 'Smart' CCTV cameras detect events in real-time, generate alerts, and notify authorities without additional hardware. Tested on actual CCTV footage, the system proves more reliable, robust, and cost-effective than existing techniques.

2.1 Introduction

Nowadays, CCTV-based video surveillance systems are essential for factories, home automation, and public spaces like airports, government offices. Standard cameras are widely used in public to monitor traffic, and human interactions, and deter violence and disasters ([1]). There are many advantages to using CCTV cameras for surveillance. For example, during the London nail bombs assault in 1999, surveillance cameras played a crucial role in identifying the culprits.[1] CCTV has also been used to identify criminals in high-profile cases such as the Boston Marathon bombing in April 2013 and the Charlie Hebdo attack in January 2015.[2] With rising security concerns and crime rates worldwide, the video surveillance industry is expanding rapidly. Development technologies for intelligent monitoring systems has become essential for disaster detection, crime prevention ([19, 21, 15]), and preserving industrial and public safety ([22]). The Carnegie Endowment for International Peace (CEIP)[3] reported that out of 176 countries, 44% countries use advanced surveillance to monitor individuals or systems. Around 75 countries employ AI-based advanced techniques to enhance administration efficiency. However, immediate event detection and response remain challenging supervision is needed, especially at night. These security systems are costly, require substantial memory to store videos, and need continuous human effort to monitor surveillance areas via CCTV cameras. In cases of crimes like robbery, the police often can't get instant information and the crime's location, causing delays in administrative actions. While recorded videos can help police identify culprits, reviewing them is time-consuming. Similarly, in traffic accidents and fires delayed information to emergency services like ambulances and fire brigades often leads to loss of lives ([9, 17]).

This study aims to automate surveillance process by eliminating manual supervision of CCTV footage. The proposed framework creates a cost-effective intelligent surveillance system that enables CCTV cameras to recognize events in real-time and instantly alert authorities with the event location. Therefore, the proposed system operates independently of third parties or control rooms to inform local administrations. Figure 2.1 illustrates the event recognition and alert generation framework for both existing and proposed systems. In this study, we

[1] https://www.bbc.com/news/uk-england-london-47216594.
[2] https://www.bbc.com/news/magazine-30793614.
[3] https://carnegieendowment.org/2019/09/17/global-expansion-of-ai-surveillance-pub-79847.

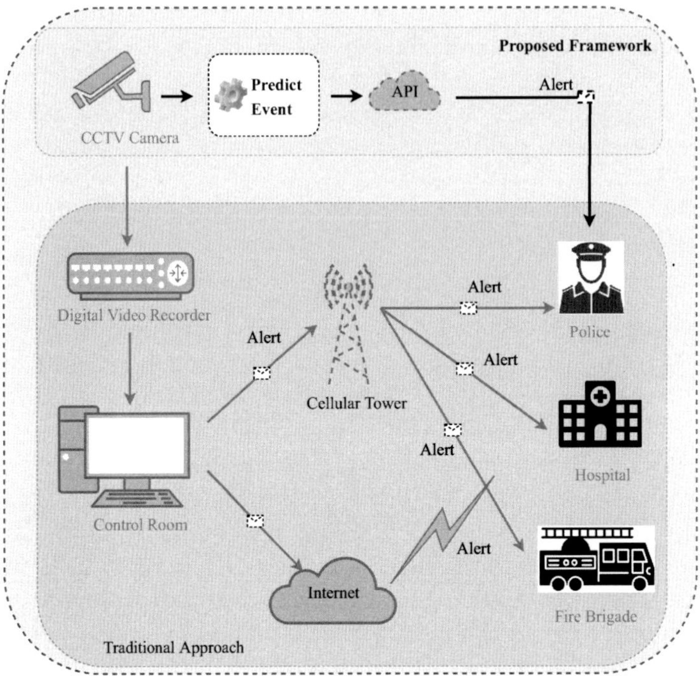

Figure 2.1: Traditional and proposed framework of real-time activity identification and alert generation.

provide a novel database collected from various internet sources, made publicly available for further experimentation and standardization. The proposed method augments image samples and trains the ResNet50 deep model after preprocessing. It employs the rolling average window principle to efficiently generate alert messages. The framework uses the Twilio API (trial version) to send alerts authorities for further action.

The rest of the paper is structured as follows: Section 2.2 details existing methods and algorithms for recognizing mishaps, while Section 2.3 proposes an approach for intelligent video surveillance. It covers dataset collection, pre-processing, data augmentation, model training, and testing with actual CCTV footage. Section 2.4 presents simulation results and analysis, comparing with state-of-the-art techniques. Finally, Section 2.5 concludes the study.

2.2 Literature Review

Surveillance and monitoring are continuous processes requiring operators to watch each camera stream continuously, which is time-consuming and exhausting. The system is ineffective and costly, especially with the increasing number of

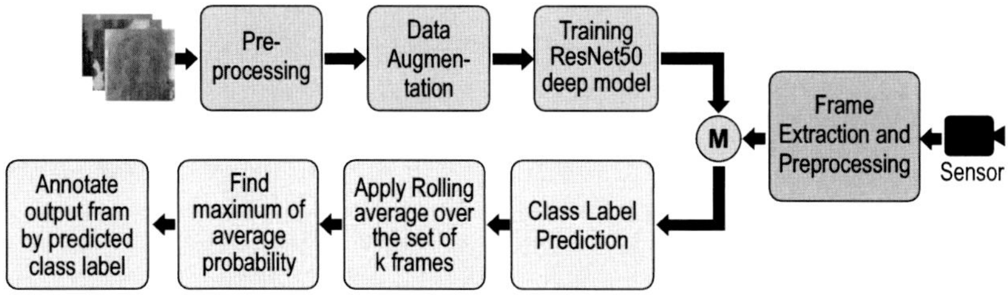

Figure 2.2: Block diagram of the proposed method.

global locations to monitor. One goal of intelligent surveillance systems is to reduce security officers' workload by automatically analyzing video streams. Motion detection and tracking help identify suspicious object movements. Following these techniques, [15] proposed a method for object movement detection during surveillance. The proposed method counts people in the surveillance area, uses face recognition to detect unauthorized access, and tracks the real-time movement of objects like smartphones, and laptops. The system generates an alert messages using the Twilio API, sending notifications via SMS, WhatsApp, email, and call. Similarly, [8] proposed a kernel-based method to track moving objects and obtain their trajectory. Histogram features are used to analyze robbery events by detecting suspicious object movements between two individuals. Experiments found this approach robust and accurate in identifying robberies in a surveillance environment. [10] proposed an IoT-based intelligent video surveillance system by integrating software and hardware. The system uses OpenCV for movement recognition and human activity recording, and generates an alarm to notify the concerned person via SMS through the GSM module. The system's hardware architecture of the system is supported by the Arduino boards and Raspberry Pi. Although effective, the hardware makes it complex and costly. Traffic accidents and fires in homes, offices, and industries are other common mishaps. The rise in urbanization and expanding transportation networks have made road safety a critical concern, leading to more accidents and causing various damages and fatalities. Often, accident victims can't pinpoint their exact location to call for police or ambulance assistance. Hence, there's a need for an intelligent surveillance system that can detect accidents and automatically notify local authorities via SMS. For this purpose, [3] used a self-powered wireless sensor to develop a fully automatic real-time surveillance system. [25] proposed an IoT-based framework that can detect an accident and send a notification immediately. The system integrates sensors and a micro-controller within the vehicle. When an accident is detected, the sensors trigger an SMS notification via GSM to the concerned person. Many researchers have conducted similar studies, available in the literature ([24, 30, 7, 33, 18, 32]). However, these models rely on hardware, raising development and maintenance costs. Fire can occur due to a short circuits, cooking equipment, or smoking materials. Early fire detection in buildings is crucial, with some detectors serving as the first line of defense. These devices sometimes fail to detect smoke or generate alarms and can't communicate with other devices in that environment. Several studies have focused on early fire detection using multi-sensors, with some integrating costly sensors and hardware like Arduino Uno and Raspberry Pi for efficiency and accuracy ([23, 27, 14, 2, 6]).

Current algorithms and techniques for event detection are effective. However, as we develop smart and safe cities to enhance people's quality of life, it's essential to further advance surveillance systems with cutting-edge advanced AI techniques. Existing technologies often require costly hardware like multi-sensors, Arduino and Raspberry Pi, making the architecture complex, expensive, and maintenance-intensive. With CCTV cameras widely used for surveillance, this study aims to add intelligence to these cameras without additional hardware enabling event detection and automatic notifications.

2.3 Proposed Methodology

Deep learning algorithms are one of the most preferred and recommended techniques for classification and recognition problems. Unlike traditional methods, which extract hand-crafted features, convolutional neural networks (CNN) automatically extract discriminating and dominating patterns.

A variety of deep architectures have been proposed in the literature such as AlexNet, VGG, GoogleNet, SqueezeNet [16, 26, 28, 13] and many more. Among them, VGG gained popularity among researchers because of its simple and deep-layered architecture. However, as the network depth increases, accuracy saturates and rapidly deteriorates, known as the degradation problem ([29]).

To solve the vanishing gradient problem in a deep convolutional network, ResNet [11] uses residual blocks. During deep model training, the primary objective is to acquire knowledge of the residual function $F(X)$. If the network can effectively learn the difference between the input and output, it has the potential to enhance overall accuracy. When backpropagation is performed, two paths exist for the

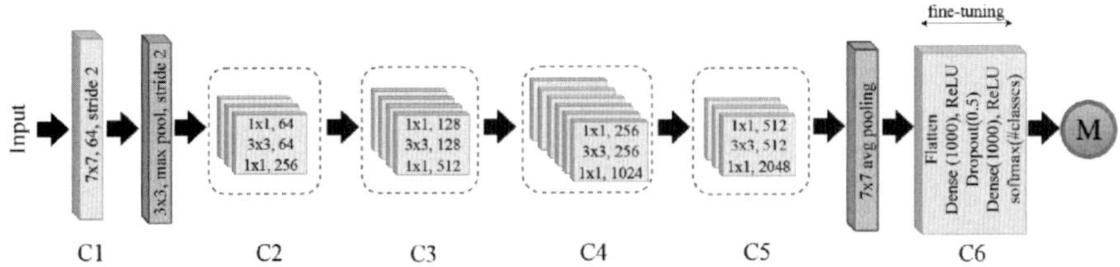

Figure 2.3: Architecture of fine-tuned ResNet50, where 'M' represents the trained model.

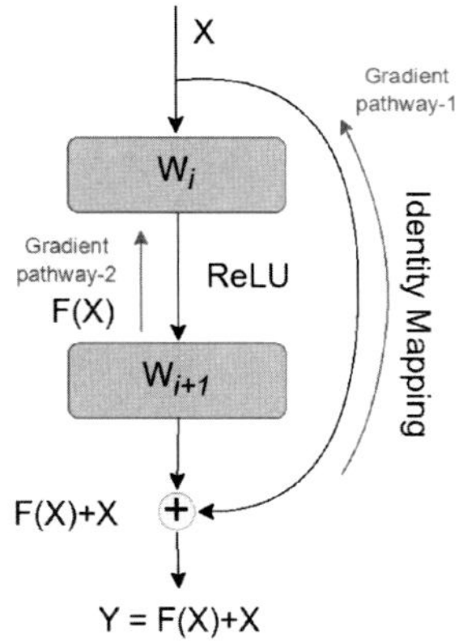

Figure 2.4: Gradient pathways in ResNet.

gradients to propagate toward the input layer while passing through a residual block. The first pathway is the identity mapping route, while the second is the residual mapping route, as shown in Figure 2.4.

If X represents the input to the residual block, Y denotes the output then it can be mathematically computed as

$$Y = F(X, \{W_i\}) + X \tag{2.1}$$

where $F(X, \{W_i\})$ depicts the residual block. Residual block contains weight layers (W_i) and term $F(X, \{W_i\})$ for two weight layers can be written as

$$F(X, \{W_i\}) = W_2 \sigma(W_1 X) \tag{2.2}$$

where σ represents the ReLU activation function. Once the computed gradients pass through Gradient Pathway-2, they encounter two weight layers, W_1 and W_2, within the residual function $F(X)$. The kernels in these weight layers are updated, and new gradient values are calculated. However, for the initial layers, these newly computed values may become small or vanish entirely. To prevent this from happening, the shortcut connection (identity mapping) is introduced. This allows the gradients to bypass the weight layers and pass directly through Gradient Pathway-1, as shown in the previous diagram. As a result, the computed gradients retain their original values without encountering any changes. Transfer learning and fine-tuning techniques are used to avoid overfitting/underfitting and speed up the training process. The performance of the model is tested on actual CCTV video clips. The alert message is generated and notified to the concerned person using Twilio API. There are numerous APIs available for transmitting messages. Twilio offers better features and service at low cost or with a free limited trial. Therefore, we used a Twilio trial account to send alerts in this study.

The main contribution is applying rolling average principles to predict class labels accurately and generate alerts efficiently. Figure 2.2 shows the complete block diagram of the proposed method.

2.3.1 Transfer Learning and Fine-tuning

There are fifty convolutional layers stacked in the ResNet50 architecture. These layers can be divided into blocks. The first block (say C1) contains 64 filters with a kernel size of 7×7. This layer accepts an input image of 224×224 and generates an output tensor of $112 \times 112 \times 64$. Block C2 consists of 3 layers, each with 64 filters of size 3×3 reducing the image dimension to 56×56. Convolution block C3 has three layers (1×1, 128; 3×3, 128; and 1×1, 512), repeated four times, totaling twelve layers. Similarly, convolution blocks C4 and C5 contains three layers each, repeated six and three times, resulting in eighteen and nine layers, respectively. After each convolution block, the input image resolution decreases while the number of filters increases. The output tensor dimension from the final convolution block is 7×2048. Figure 2.3 summarizes the convolutional layers and kernel sizes. The final layer is a fully connected layer with 1000 nodes and the Softmax function. In this study, the network architecture is fine-tuned by freezing all internal layers except the last one. The fully connected layer is enhanced with a Dense layer of 1000 nodes, a Dropout layer that drops connections of 50% of connections between two dense layers, and a Softmax function with the required number of classes. The fine-tuned architecture is shown in Figure 2.3. For transfer learning, ResNet50 model pre-trained on the ImageNet ([16]) dataset is reused.

2.3.2 Rolling Mean or Moving Average

The idea of rolling mean (also rolling average) is utilized to decrease the predicted label flickering effect. It is also referred to as the running average and is often used to decrease output fluctuations in time series data ([31]). For example, if there are n data points such as $d_1, d_2, ..., d_n$ then simple average (SA) of over the last k data points can be calculated by Equation 2.3 ([4]).

$$SA_k = \frac{1}{k} \sum_{j=n-k+1}^{n} d_j \tag{2.3}$$

In rolling average, for calculating the next average $SA_{k,next}$ over the same window of size k, a new value d_{n+1} is introduced into the sum, and the old value d_{n-k+1} drops out. This process continues for all data points.

In this study, each frame from a live video stream is considered a data point and input to CNN. The model predicts its class label and probability, storing these values in a Queue of size $k = 64$, suitable for applying the rolling mean algorithm. The average rolling technique is then applied over 64 frames. Therefore, if f_j presents the number of frames where $j = 1,...,k$ and c_i denotes the number of classes where $i = 1,2,...,n$ then the predicted probability of a class for a particular frame can be represented by $p_{c_i}^{f_j}$. The maximum of the average probability over the set of 'k' frames can be calculated by p_{c_i} as shown in Equation 2.4.

$$p_{c_i} = max\left(\frac{1}{k}\sum_{j=1}^{k}\left(p_{c_1}^{f_j}, p_{c_2}^{f_j}, ..., p_{c_n}^{f_j}\right)\right) \tag{2.4}$$

Based on the calculated value of p_{c_i} and the threshold value (Th), an output frame is labeled as a detected event or as 'Normal'.

Algorithm 1 Algorithm to reduce 'prediction flickering'.

Result: Reduced flickering effect in the output video
while live video stream is ON **do**
    Loop over all frames in the video;
    Pass each frame to the Deep model (M) as input;
    Classify each frame individually and independently and store it in the Queue;
    Repeat the above steps for k frames and calculate their average;
    Calculate P_{c_i}, i.e., maximum of average probabilities over the set of k frames;
    if $P_{c_i} > Th$ **then**
        Annotate output frame by predicted label and corresponding probability;
        Generate an alert message whenever predicted label changes;
    else
        Output frame is annotated as 'Normal' along with corresponding probability;
    end if
end while

Therefore, if the maximum average probability over the set of 'k' frames is $> Th$, then the algorithm annotates the output frame by the predicted label and corresponding predicted probability. The system generates an alert message for every change in the predicted labels; else, it is annotated as 'Normal' along with the corresponding probability. The complete working process of this module is summarized in Algorithm 1.

2.4 Simulation and Results

A deep model is trained by the database consisting of images and videos of events under consideration. Crime scene videos are collected from various websites for training and performance evaluation[4,5,6,7]. However, for robust evaluation, a large number of images having similar representations are also used. Each image offers diverse scenarios for evaluating the proposed method. Performance is assessed using statistical parameters from the confusion matrix. This section discusses the simulation and results in detail.

The collected database has three classes: 'Robbery', 'Accident', and 'Fire'. During crimes like robbery or attempted murder criminals often hide their identity with cloth or masks and may carry weapons such as guns or knives. The 'Robbery' class includes 1000 images of similar representations. The 'Accident' class consists of 887 images of crushed vehicles involved in accidents. The 'Fire' class comprises 990 images of burning buildings or houses. The collected database and source code are publicly available for further research and standardization[8]. Figure 2.5 shows sample images: the first row (a-e) depicts crime scenes, the second row (f-g) shows accidents, and the third row (k-o) displays buildings on fire.

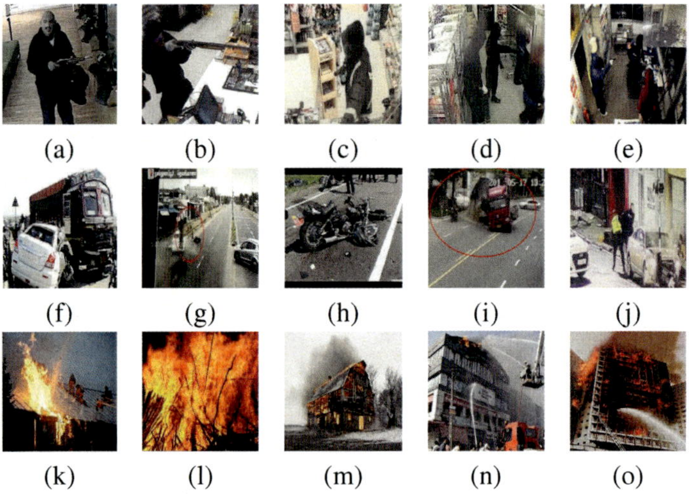

Figure 2.5: Sample images from the database.

[4]https://www.fresnobee.com/news/local/crime/article222309205.html.

[5]https://indianexpress.com/videos/news-video/cctv-footage-of-car-accident-on-nizambad-hyderabad-national-highway-2/.

[6]https://www.ndtv.com/india-news/surat-coaching-centre-fire-tyres-for-seats-made-fire-spread-fast-official-2043311.

[7]https://www.bbc.com/news/uk-40301289.

[8]https://github.com/gautamkumarjaiswal/videoClassification.

Database samples of varying spatial resolutions uniformly scaled to 224×224 pixels before being fed into CNN for training. Data augmentation improves the model's generalization property and reduces overfitting, or underfitting ([20]). Five transformations are applied during augmentation: rotation (30 degrees clockwise and counterclockwise), zoom (out by 0.15), shift (height and width by 0 to 0.2), shear - it applies horizontal and vertical shear by a scale of 0.15, and lastly, images are flipped horizontally.

The database is split into training and validation sets in an 80:20 ratio. The ResNet50 architecture is trained for 120 epochs, sufficient to saturate validation loss. Stochastic Gradient Descent (SGD) ([5]) a popular deep learning optimizer, is used. Unlike simple Gradient Descent, SGD trains the model using one sample from the database per iteration. With less data per iteration, it fits easily in memory, speeding up the training process ([12]). Experiments are conducted on a computer system with 16 GB RAM and an NVIDIA GeForce GT 1030 GPU. Model performance is evaluated using precision, recall, f-score, and accuracy.

2.4.1 Experiments with Proposed Method

CCTV footage and video clips of robberies, road accidents, and building fires are collected and processed by CNN. The algorithm extracts each frame, resizes it to 224×224, and passes it to the trained model, which classifies each image and predicts class labels and probabilities. The model's output video experiences prediction flickering, causing frequent label changes. To address this, the rolling average principle, explained in Section 2.3, is applied. This significantly reduces the flickering. To minimize false positives, the threshold is set to 80%, found suitable empirically. The alert message can be customized per user requirements, including the store/building address and geolocation. Figures 2.6, 2.7 and 2.8 show screenshots of the output video. Figure 2.6 shows a 'Robbery' prediction label with its probability and the corresponding alert message on a cellphone. Figures 2.7 and 2.8 display predictions for 'Accident' and 'Fire' with their probabilities and alert messages. The Twilio SMS API, implemented using REST architecture in Python is used to send these alerts[9]. If the input doesn't match any of the three classes, it labels the output frame as 'Normal' (Figure 2.9) without generating an alert message.

The algorithm's accuracy is measured in two ways: (a) the number of frames predicted positive during CCTV video testing, and (b) statistical parameters from the confusion matrix. If an event's input video clip has a total of 'N' frames and 'k' frames are predicted positive, accuracy is measured by $Acc_{event} = \frac{k}{N}$. The CCTV footage of the robbery consists of 572 frames; among them, 309 frames are actually predicted as robbery. Therefore, the prediction accuracy of the model

[9]https://www.twilio.com/docs/libraries/python.

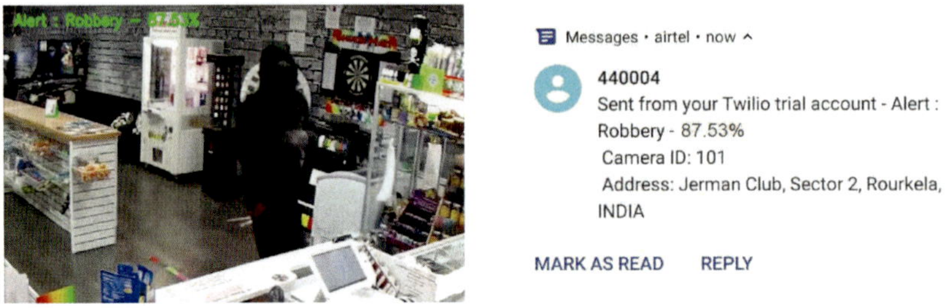

(a) (b)

Figure 2.6: Snapshot of (a) Annotated output frame and (b) Alert notification.

(a) (b)

Figure 2.7: Snapshot of (a) Annotated output frame and (b) Alert notification.

(a) (b)

Figure 2.8: Snapshot of (a) Annotated output frame and (b) Alert notification.

is calculated as 54.02%. Similarly, out of 74 frames of an accident video clip, 40 frames are positively predicted, and 194 frames are labeled as 'Fire' from 206 frames of a fire video clip. Therefore, the resulting accuracy of the model is found to be 54.05% and 94.17% for accident and fire, respectively. The resolution of test videos for robbery and accident is 360p, while for fire, it is 720p. Therefore, accuracy may increase if the surveillance CCTV camera is of high quality and records high-resolution videos.

Figure 2.9: Snapshot of output frame annotated as 'Normal' along with it's probability.

Table 2.1: Comparison of the proposed method with state-of-the-art solutions.

Method	Classes	Precision (in %)	Recall (in %)	F-Score (in %)	Accuracy (in %)
AlexNet ([16])	Robbery	92.24	93.80	92.50	90.82
	Accident	86.80	87.40	87.10	87.24
	Fire	93.20	91.40	92.33	93.10
	Average	**90.75**	**90.87**	**90.64**	**90.56**
VGG16 ([26])	Robbery	94.30	94.20	94.20	92.34
	Accident	89.10	92.44	90.82	92.60
	Fire	96.00	93.26	95.62	94.39
	Average	**93.13**	**93.30**	**93.54**	**93.32**
ResNet50 ([11]) + Fine-tuning and Rolling Average (proposed method)	Robbery	94.82	95.30	95.10	95.80
	Accident	93.80	92.00	92.20	92.20
	Fire	95.60	95.10	95.20	95.30
	Average	**94.74**	**94.13**	**94.16**	**94.40**

Further, the performance of the proposed method is evaluated using precision, recall, f-score, and accuracy as presented in Table 2.1. For comparison purposes, the same metrics are also evaluated for AlexNet and VGG16. The results are also analyzed by interpreting the receiver operating characteristic (ROC) curve and precision-recall curve as shown in Figures 2.10 and 2.11, respectively.

Analysis of Results

From the analysis of the confusion matrix, it is noticed that the trained model can classify input images into Robbery, Accident, and Fire with an accuracy of 95.80%, 92.20%, and 95.30%, respectively. Based on the results of the confusion matrix, performance parameters are calculated and shown in Table 2.1. Since precision measures the relevance of favorably classified classes the results presented in the table, help conclude that the proposed method can more accurately acknowledge each class, which is nearly 94% for Robbery, 93.80%

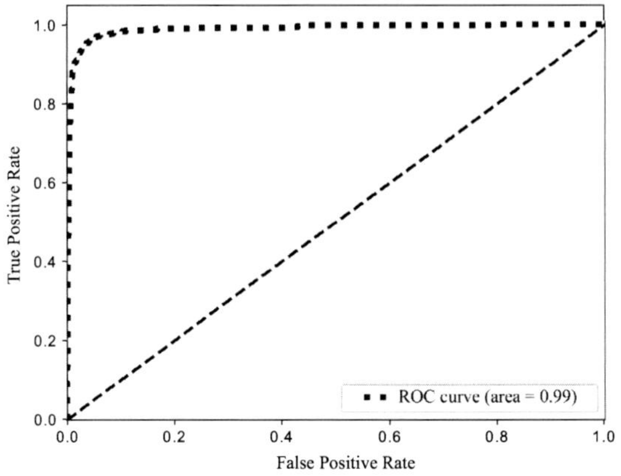

Figure 2.10: Receiver operating characteristic curve.

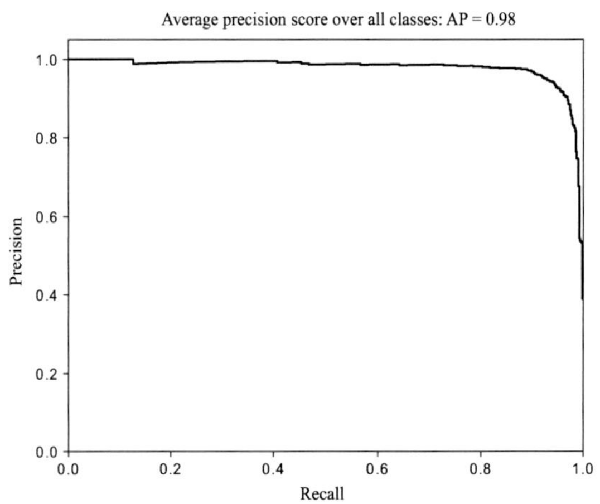

Figure 2.11: Precision-Recall curve.

for Accident, and around 95.60% for Fire. Recall (or sensitivity) measures the % of a positive prediction made by the model. The model achieves 95.30% recall the Robbery class 92.01% for Accident, and 95.10% for Fire. The F-score, representing the balance between precision and recall, is 95.10% for Robbery, 92.20% for Accident, and 95.21% for Fire. Overall, the model classifies these events with 94.82% accuracy. The average value of all statistical parameters are summarized in Figure 2.12. Figure 2.10 presents the relation between True Positive Rate (TPR) and False Positive Rate (FPR), which is also known as the ROC curve. Researchers often use these curves to show the ability of a model to separate classes among themselves. A higher value of the Area Under the Curve (AUC) presents two classes well separated, while an AUC value close to zero

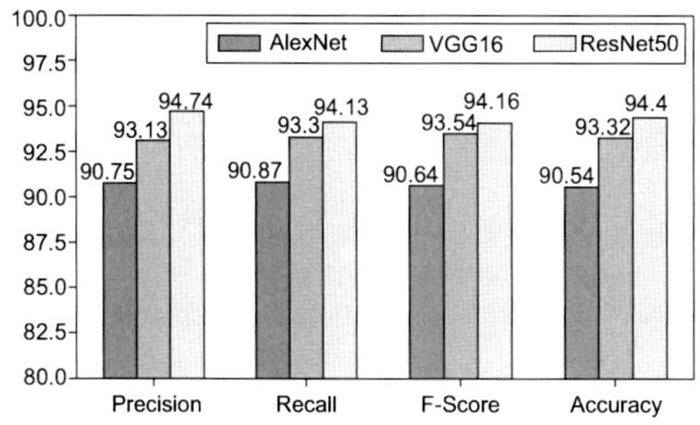

Figure 2.12: Average value of the statistical parameters measured.

presents the worst performance. We found AUC = 0.99, which means the developed system has excellent separability. A classifier is said to be ideal if it does not make any prediction error. These classifiers have average precision (AP) or Area under the curve (AUC-AP) equal to 1 or close to 1. The studied model produces $AP = 0.99$, which means the developed system has minimum prediction error.

2.4.2 Comparison with State-of-the-Art Methods

The performance of the proposed method is compared with state-of-the-art solutions. Standard and well-known deep learning architecture AlexNet and VGG16 are trained using transfer learning and fine-tuning. From the confusion matrix analysis, individual class classification accuracy produced by AlexNet is found to be 90.82%, 87.24%, and 93.10% for Robbery, Accident, and Fire, respectively, while overall classification accuracy of the model by combining all classes, is calculated as 90.56%. For VGG16, the classification accuracy is measured as 93.32% while individual class classification accuracy is 92.34%, 92.60%, and 94.39% for Robbery, Accident, and Fire classes, respectively. On the other hand, the overall accuracy of the proposed method is found to be 94.82%. Statistical parameters are calculated from the outcomes of the confusion matrix and compared in Table 2.1. The findings show that the proposed method produces significant improvement in performance compared to AlexNet and VGG16.

2.5 Conclusion

Rising incidents of robbery, accidents, and fire, along with investigation and relief delays, have shown that current surveillance methods are ineffective, complex, and costly. This study develops an intelligent surveillance framework using CCTV cameras, training deep models on actual footage to recognize events like Robbery, Accident and Fire. The method uses the average rolling principle for instant alerts and notifications. Preliminary tests show significant accuracy improvement and automatic alerts without human/sensor support. This application is effective for traffic monitoring, home/office/industrial security, and surveillance.

Future work will involve extensive testing, including operational analysis and comparisons with standard camera systems and NIR sensors. Improvements will focus on a more sophisticated decision module and a mechanism for selecting threshold values.

References

[1] Yair A. Andrade-Ambriz, Sergio Ledesma, Mario-Alberto Ibarra-Manzano, Marvella I. Oros-Flores, and Dora-Luz Almanza-Ojeda. Human activity recognition using temporal convolutional neural network architecture. *Expert Systems with Applications*, 191:116287, 2022. DOI: 10.1016/j.eswa.2021.116287.

[2] Md Saifudaullah Bin Bahrudin, Rosni Abu Kassim, and Norlida Buniyamin. Development of fire alarm system using Raspberry Pi and Arduino Uno. pages 43–48, 2013. DOI: 10.1109/ICEESE.2013.6895040.

[3] Walid Balid and Hazem H Refai. On the development of self-powered IoT sensor for real-time traffic monitoring in smart cities. In *IEEE SENSORS*, pages 1–3. IEEE, 2017. DOI: 10.1109/ICSENS.2017.8234157.

[4] Eric Booth, Jeff Mount, and Joshua H Viers. Hydrologic variability of the cosumnes river floodplain. *San Francisco Estuary and Watershed Science*, 4(2), 2006. DOI: 10.15447/sfews.2006v4iss2art2.

[5] Léon Bottou. Large-scale machine learning with stochastic gradient descent. In *Proceedings of COMPSTAT'2010*, pages 177–186. Springer, 2010. DOI: 10.1007/978-3-7908-2604-3_16.

[6] Fengju Bu and Mohammad Samadi Gharajeh. Intelligent and vision-based fire detection systems: A survey. *Image and vision computing*, 91:103803, 2019. DOI: 10.1016/j.imavis.2019.08.007.

[7] Antonio Celesti, Antonino Galletta, Lorenzo Carnevale, Maria Fazio, Aime Ĺay-Ekuakille, and Massimo Villari. An IoT cloud system for traffic monitoring and vehicular accidents prevention based on mobile sensor data processing. *IEEE Sensors Journal*, 18(12):4795–4802, 2017. DOI: 10.1109/JSEN.2017.2777786.

[8] Chi-Hung Chuang, Jun-Wei Hsieh, and Kao-Chin Fan. Suspicious object detection and robbery event analysis. In *16th International Conference on Computer Communications and Networks*, pages 1189–1192. IEEE, 2007. DOI: 10.1109/ICCCN.2007.4317981.

[9] Shashi Gandhar, Kirti Sharma, Nakul Verma, Divyam Goel, and Yuvraj Shubham. A real-time solar powered fire detection system. *Journal of Information and Optimization Sciences*, 43(1):85–92, 2022. DOI: 10.1080/02522667.2022.2039460.

[10] Sonali P Gulve, Suchitra A Khoje, and Prajakta Pardeshi. Implementation of IoT-based smart video surveillance system. In *Computational intelligence in data mining*, pages 771–780. Springer, 2017. DOI: 10.1007/978-981-10-3874-7_73.

[11] Kaiming He, Xiangyu Zhang, Shaoqing Ren, and Jian Sun. Deep residual learning for image recognition. In *Proceedings of the IEEE conference on computer vision and pattern recognition*, pages 770–778, 2016. DOI: 10.1109/CVPR.2016.90.

[12] Wenwu He and Yang Liu. To regularize or not: Revisiting SGD with simple algorithms and experimental studies. *Expert Systems with Applications*, 112:1–14, 2018. DOI: 10.1016/j.eswa.2018.06.026.

[13] Forrest N Iandola, Song Han, Matthew W Moskewicz, Khalid Ashraf, William J Dally, and Kurt Keutzer. Squeezenet: AlexNet-level accuracy with 50x fewer parameters and¡ 0.5 MB model size. *arXiv preprint arXiv:1602.07360*, 2016.

[14] Razib Hayat Khan, Zakir Ayub Bhuiyan, Shadman Sharar Rahman, and Saadman Khondaker. A smart and cost-effective fire detection system for developing country: an IoT based approach. *International Journal of Information Engineering and Electronic Business*, 12(3):16, 2019. DOI: 10.5815/ijieeb.2019.03.03.

[15] Fatimah Khodadin and Sameerchand Pudaruth. An intelligent camera surveillance system with effective notification features. *International Journal of Computing and Digital Systems*, 9(6):1251–1261, 2020. DOI: 10.12785/ijcds/0906022.

[16] Alex Krizhevsky, Ilya Sutskever, and Geoffrey E Hinton. Imagenet classification with deep convolutional neural networks. *Advances in neural information processing systems*, 25:1097–1105, 2012.

[17] C. L. Lai, J. C. Yang, and Y. H. Chen. A real time video processing based surveillance system for early fire and flood detection. In *2007 IEEE Instru-*

mentation & Measurement Technology Conference IMTC 2007, pages 1–6, 2007. DOI: 10.1109/IMTC.2007.379190.

[18] Xueping Liu, Yibo Li, and Qing Shen. Real-time action detection and temporal segmentation in continuous video. *The Imaging Science Journal*, 65(7):418–427, 2017. DOI: 10.1080/13682199.2017.1361664.

[19] Khan Muhammad, Jamil Ahmad, and Sung Wook Baik. Early fire detection using convolutional neural networks during surveillance for effective disaster management. *Neurocomputing*, 288:30–42, 2018. DOI: 10.1016/j.neucom.2017.04.083.

[20] Luis Perez and Jason Wang. The effectiveness of data augmentation in image classification using deep learning. *arXiv preprint arXiv:1712.04621*, 2017.

[21] Eric L Piza, Brandon C Welsh, David P Farrington, and Amanda L Thomas. CCTV surveillance for crime prevention: A 40-year systematic review with meta-analysis. *Criminology & Public Policy*, 18(1):135–159, 2019. DOI: 10.1111/1745-9133.12419.

[22] Tomi D Räty. Survey on contemporary remote surveillance systems for public safety. *IEEE Transactions on Systems, Man, and Cybernetics, Part C (Applications and Reviews)*, 40(5):493–515, 2010. DOI: 10.1109/TSMCC.2010.2042446.

[23] F. Saputra, M. A. Rasyid, and Bey Aryo Abiantoro. Prototype of early fire detection system for home monitoring based on wireless sensor network. *International Electronics Symposium on Engineering Technology and Applications (IES-ETA)*, pages 39–44, 2017. DOI: 10.1109/ELECSYM.2017.8240373.

[24] Arif Shaik, Natalie Bowen, Jennifer Bole, Gary Kunzi, Daniel Bruce, Ahmed Abdelgawad, and Kumar Yelamarthi. Smart car: An IoT based accident detection system. In *Global Conference on Internet of Things (GCIoT)*, pages 1–5. IEEE, 2018. DOI: 10.1109/GCIoT.2018.8620131.

[25] Shivani Sharma and Shoney Sebastian. IoT based car accident detection and notification algorithm for general road accidents. *International Journal of Electrical & Computer Engineering (2088-8708)*, 9(5), 2019. DOI: 10.11591/IJECE.V9I5.PP4020-4026.

[26] Karen Simonyan and Andrew Zisserman. Very deep convolutional networks for large-scale image recognition. *arXiv preprint arXiv:1409.1556*, 2014.

[27] Robert Sowah, Abdul R. Ofoli, Selase Krakani, and Seth Fiawoo. A web-based communication module design of a real-time multi-sensor

fire detection and notification system. pages 1–6, 2014. DOI: 10.1109/IAS.2014.6978416.

[28] Christian Szegedy, Wei Liu, Yangqing Jia, Pierre Sermanet, Scott Reed, Dragomir Anguelov, Dumitru Erhan, Vincent Vanhoucke, and Andrew Rabinovich. Going deeper with convolutions. In *Proceedings of the IEEE conference on computer vision and pattern recognition*, pages 1–9, 2015.

[29] Andreas Veit, Michael J Wilber, and Serge Belongie. Residual networks behave like ensembles of relatively shallow networks. *Advances in neural information processing systems*, 29:550–558, 2016.

[30] Jules White, Chris Thompson, Hamilton Turner, Brian Dougherty, and Douglas C Schmidt. Wreckwatch: Automatic traffic accident detection and notification with smartphones. *Mobile Networks and Applications*, 16(3):285–303, 2011. DOI: 10.1007/s11036-011-0304-8.

[31] Zheng Yi and Fan Liangzhong. Moving object detection based on running average background and temporal difference. In *International Conference on Intelligent Systems and Knowledge Engineering*, pages 270–272. IEEE, 2010. DOI: 10.1109/ISKE.2010.5680866.

[32] P WT Yuen and Mark Richardson. An introduction to hyperspectral imaging and its application for security, surveillance and target acquisition. *The Imaging Science Journal*, 58(5):241–253, 2010. DOI: 10.1179/174313110X12771950995716.

[33] Zhigang Zhu, Guangyou Xu, Bo Yang, Dingji Shi, and Xueyin Lin. VISATRAM: A real-time vision system for automatic traffic monitoring. *Image and Vision Computing*, 18(10):781–794, 2000. DOI: 10.1016/S0262-8856(99)00046-3.

II SMART SYSTEMS AND IOT

DOI: 10.1201/9781003531043-4

Chapter 3

A Triple Based Lightweight Authentication Scheme for Smart Grid and Smart Metering System

*Priyanka Ahlawat** and *Kirti Baliyan*

Abstract

The hunt for new renewable energy sources has been more severe due to the rising demand for electricity and the diminishing traditional energy stocks. Developing an affordable electrical infrastructure is vital to bridge the energy demand-supply gap, encourage energy conservation, and discourage energy-intensive device usage during peak hours. Achieving these goals requires accurate and efficient algorithms for electricity consumption prediction, considering weather conditions and static characteristics influencing user acceptance and technology adoption. The integration of environmental awareness in the UTAUT model has

Computer Engineering Department, NIT Kurukshetra.

* Corresponding author: priyankaahlawat@nitkkr.ac.in

DOI: 10.1201/9781003531043-5

improved residential consumers' acceptance of smart meters. Implementing Demand Response (DR) programs can effectively reduce system peaks and result in substantial annual savings, focusing on a small percentage of customers who account for the majority of price responses. Researchers have validated the effectiveness of such strategies with data from over 5567 households. A smart electrical grid can meet the increasing demand for electricity, promote energy conservation, and reduce peak-hour energy usage. This requires widespread acceptance of innovative technologies and the utilization of big data analytics. Additionally, addressing security challenges in IoT systems is crucial. Incorporating lightweight triple DES security strength into a password-based key agreement protocol can prevent sensitive data leakage and mitigate various attacks, ensuring the security and integrity of IoT systems.

3.1 Introduction

Authentication is crucial for securing smart grids, IoT systems, and smart metering systems [18]. Within the vast realm of the Smart Grid, the Internet of Things and the Smart metering System hold a crucial position. However, the wireless nature of these sensor networks introduces additional challenges due to the expanded attack surface, providing adversaries with more opportunities to exploit weaknesses in authentication protocols and gain unauthorized access to sensitive information [17]. Despite the importance of authentication, wireless sensor networks increase vulnerabilities due to their expanded attack surface. Authentication protocols face challenges in ensuring robust mutual authentication among users, gateways, and sensors [1]. This complexity is due to various attacks that compromise secure authentication and session agreement. The traditional power grid relies heavily on non-renewable energy sources, but there is a shift towards sustainable energy like solar power [5]. This evolution involves integrating distributed renewable energy, bi-directional transmission, and microgrids [6]. However, issues such as load monitoring and communication infrastructure remain challenges. Smart meters provide real-time data, improving load optimization and grid efficiency [16]. Additionally, the big data from smart meters offers insights for system planning and customer energy behavior. In conclusion, lightweight triple DES security enhances IoT systems by preventing data leakage and mitigating attacks. This study aims to improve authentication and mutual authentication stages within wireless sensor networks, ensuring better security and integrity in IoT systems.

In summary, the concept of smart grids has existed for some time. IoT based smart grid infrastructure is given in Figure 3.1.

With recent technological advancements, it is feasible to construct intelligent grids that integrate distributed and utility-scale renewable energy generation, bi-

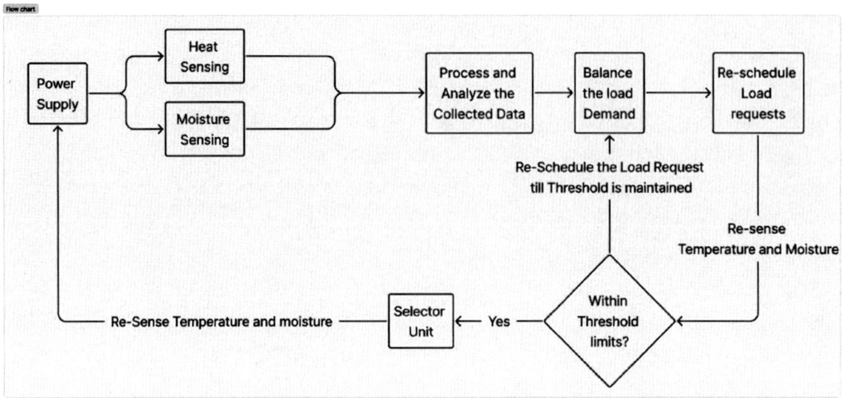

Figure 3.1: Temperature and Moisture based smart load balancing power supply using IoT sensors.

directional transmission, and microgrids [10]. The utilization of smart meter data and big data analytics presents an opportunity to optimize grid load, anticipate power outages, and negotiate pricing with end-users, ultimately leading to a more sustainable and reliable energy infrastructure. Figure 3.2 shows the IoT based smart grid architecture.

3.2 Motivation

The motivation for this chapter arises from the critical need to ensure the security of IoT modules and the integrity of the datasets they collect. With the increasing use of advanced detection systems in power systems, vast and complex datasets provide valuable insights into system functioning and planning. However, ensuring the security of these datasets during the data collection phase is paramount, as any attack or manipulation can have significant consequences. This chapter aims to address this challenge by providing security solutions for resource-constrained devices, focusing on mitigating physical attacks, including sensor capture, gateway impersonation, and MitM attacks. Developing a new protocol is necessary because existing cryptosystems do not meet essential constraints. Additionally, safeguarding Sensor Networks deployed in critical domains to protect the integrity of collected information is vital. Identifying and mitigating protocol weaknesses in Sensor Networks is a crucial challenge. Using advanced detection systems and big data in power systems offers opportunities for improved decision-making, load optimization, real-time information for customers, anticipation of power outages, and pricing negotiation. Leveraging big data can enhance overall efficiency and sustainability, enabling well-informed decisions about energy production and use.

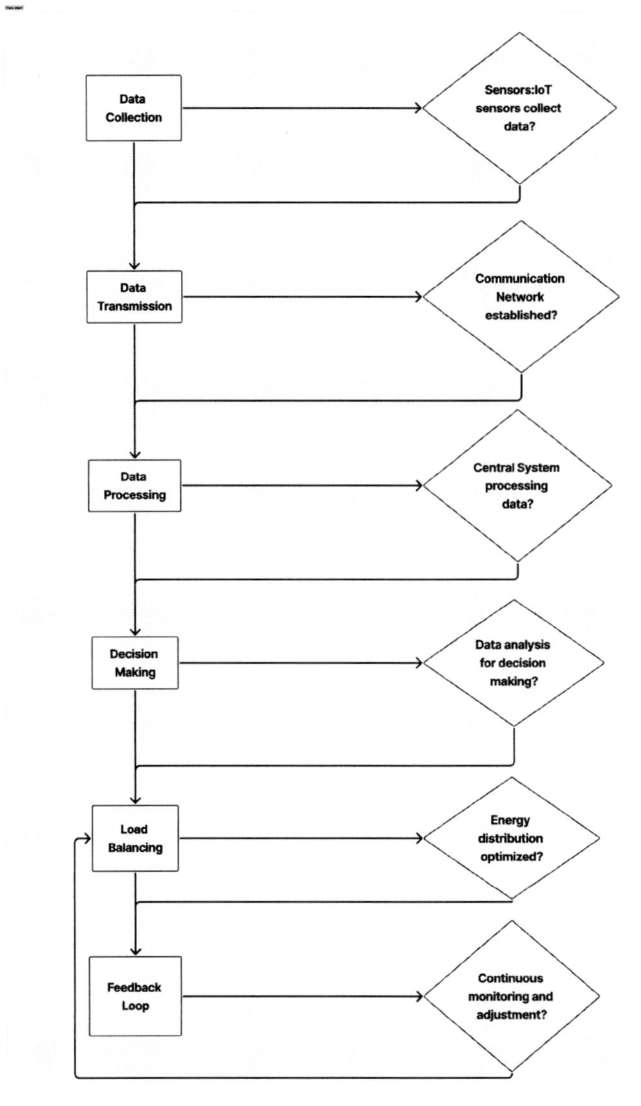

Figure 3.2: IoT based smart grid architecture.

3.3 Literature Survey

The utilization of advanced detection systems in power systems has led to the accumulation of vast datasets, offering valuable insights into system functioning and planning [13]. Ensuring the security of these datasets during data collection is paramount, as attacks on IoT modules, especially at the perceptron layer, can exploit vulnerabilities and compromise network privacy [4]. Security measures must be implemented to prevent replay attacks, selective data packet forwarding, MitM attacks, and sensor capture attacks [4]. Addressing security concerns in constrained devices involves considering limitations like battery consumption, storage, and communication capabilities [18]. Existing cryptosystems may not meet all constraints, emphasizing the need for new protocols [18]. Group rekeying techniques based on member join history enhance IoT security by focusing on scalable multi-group key management [5, 17]. Sensor networks in various applications require protection against adversarial attacks, posing significant challenges in identifying and mitigating protocol weaknesses [6]. Efficient key management schemes for IoT-based healthcare systems [8] and smart grids [9] address specific security demands, while lightweight schemes cater to resource-constrained IoT devices [14]. Authentication mechanisms relying on user knowledge, possession, and inherent characteristics establish secure access and transactional requests [4]. Robust security measures are essential for protecting innovative home applications and identifying potential threats against smart devices and apps [6, 15]. Ensuring the acceptance and successful deployment of IoT-based smart meters involves addressing privacy, data security, and energy-saving knowledge concerns [1]. Efficient key management in smart grids and Advanced Metering Systems emphasizes energy economy and scalability. Similarly, distributed key management approaches in agricultural IoT networks ensure secure communication while optimizing energy consumption [19]. Secure multicast design schemes like the LKH tree enhance key management efficiency in IoT environments [7]. Energy-efficient key management schemes provide secure communication in IoT-based healthcare systems, minimizing energy consumption in resource-constrained environments [8]. Lightweight key management strategies for IoT-based smart grids balance security and efficiency [14]. Developing efficient key management schemes, group rekeying protocols, and lightweight authentication mechanisms plays a vital role in IoT security. Future research should focus on mitigating attacks like sensor node impersonation, gateway impersonation, and MitM attacks, and comparing protocol effectiveness in terms of time, cost, efficiency, space, and security [16]. [3] highlight a novel neural network approach for wind speed forecasting. Meanwhile, [11] survey IoT security trends, detailing evolving protocols. [12] emphasize robust IoT security frameworks, and [10] explore the zero trust model's role in IoT risk mitigation. Collectively, these studies offer valuable insights for improving renewable energy predictions and securing IoT systems against emerging threats.

3.4 Existing Authentication Schemes

In addition to the existing authentication schemes, [2] suggested a technique to provide mutual authentication and offer protection from significant assaults. However, it was later found that the protocol lacked adequate mutual authentication and was open to sensor capture attempts. This protocol's seven stages comprised the initialization/system setup, user registration, sensor node registration, login, and key agreement phases. They also included the Rabin cryptosystem in their plan for safe key generation and transmission between users and the wireless sensor network via monitoring gateway nodes. Despite their best efforts, concerns were raised about the protocol's vulnerability to cryptographic flaws due to its reliance on the Rabin cryptosystem.

Scheme 1: The existing authentication schemes, such as the one proposed by [2] consist of several phases responsible for ensuring secure communication between users and the wireless sensor network via gateway nodes. These phases include:

1. Initialization/System Setup: This phase involves initializing the system and setting up the necessary parameters and configurations for secure communication. It has tasks such as establishing trust between the user and the gateway nodes.
2. User Registration: In this phase, users must register with the system. This typically involves providing their credentials, such as username and password, and verifying their identity to gain access to the network.
3. Sensor Node Registration: During this phase, network sensor nodes must be registered with the system. This includes assigning unique identifiers to each sensor node and securely associating them with the user and gateway nodes.
4. Login: Once the user and sensor nodes are registered, the login phase allows users to authenticate themselves to gain access to the network. This may involve using credentials, such as username and password, or other authentication mechanisms like biometrics or smart cards.
5. Key Agreement: This phase establishes secure session keys between the user and the sensor nodes for secure data transmission. Several cryptographic techniques are used to guarantee the confidentiality and integrity of the exchanged keys, including key exchange protocols.

Scheme 2: The authentication schemes, including the Rabin cryptosystem, involve different phases to establish secure communication between users and the wireless sensor network. These phases include:

1. Initialization/System Setup: In this phase, the Rabin cryptosystem initializes by generating system parameters (prime numbers, modulus) to compute public and private keys. These parameters must be securely stored and shared among authorized entities.
2. User Registration: Individuals provide their credentials (usernames, passwords) to access the wireless sensor network. The system verifies their

identity and assigns a unique identifier, ensuring only registered users can access the network.

3. Sensor Node Registration: During this phase, each sensor node is assigned a unique ID and public key ensuring secure communication between users and authorized sensor nodes.
4. Login: Registered users can log in using their credentials or cryptographic mechanisms. The process verifies the user's identity through authentication protocols, ensuring secure network access for further interactions.
5. Key Agreement: This phase is vital for secure communication between users and sensor nodes. Session keys are generated and exchanged, then used to encrypt and decode data during communication. The Rabin cryptosystem ensures the secure generation and exchange of these session keys, maintaining data confidentiality and integrity.

3.5 Problem Overview

Amin and Biswas's IoT authentication technique has critical security flaws, making it vulnerable to sensor capture attacks, gateway forgeries, and sensor node forgeries. These attacks can compromise the protocol's feasibility, security features, and mutual authentication, resulting in failed robust security. A significant concern is physically tampering with sensors using hardware tools, exposing sensitive information like sensor IDs, secret keys, and configurations. If a symmetric key is used and a sensor is compromised, an attacker can hijack the entire session using the sensor's key, identical to the gateway's and the user's key (Figure 3.3). This compromises the system's security. Another vulnerability is the algorithm's susceptibility to sensor capture attacks, where attackers capture a sensor node, gain system administrator privileges, and share sensor IDs secretly. By sniffing network packets and leveraging security flaws, attackers can deduce sensor IDs and private keys, leading to session hijacking and sensor forgery. The Rabin cryptosystem used in the protocol also introduces issues like chosen ciphertext and factorization attacks, compromising data confidentiality and integrity. To address these vulnerabilities, it is crucial to explore alternative encryption algorithms and cryptographic techniques that provide robust security, and ensure mutual authentication within the IoT network.

3.6 Proposed Methodology

The proposed work introduces a novel, cost-effective authentication scheme for IoT security. It uses the triple DES symmetric cryptosystem to ensure secure communication and generate session keys. Triple DES's robust encryption capabilities enable a three-factor authentication and session key generation mech-

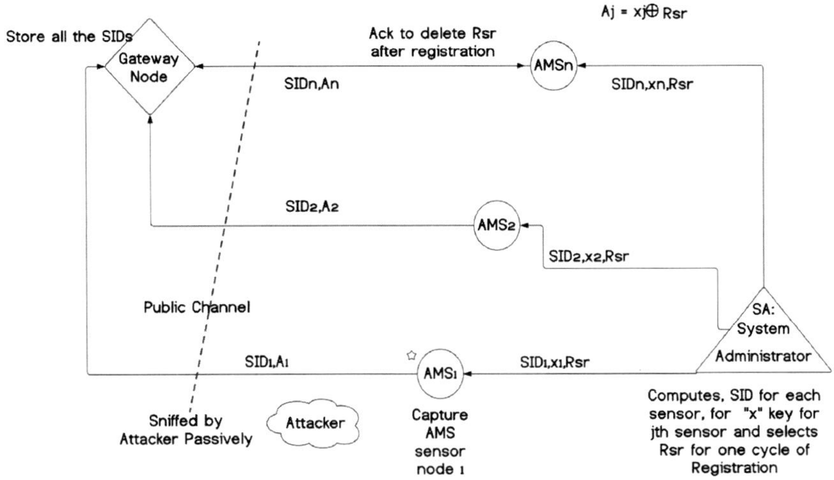

Figure 3.3: Sensor capture attack occurring in Amin and Biswas's algorithm.

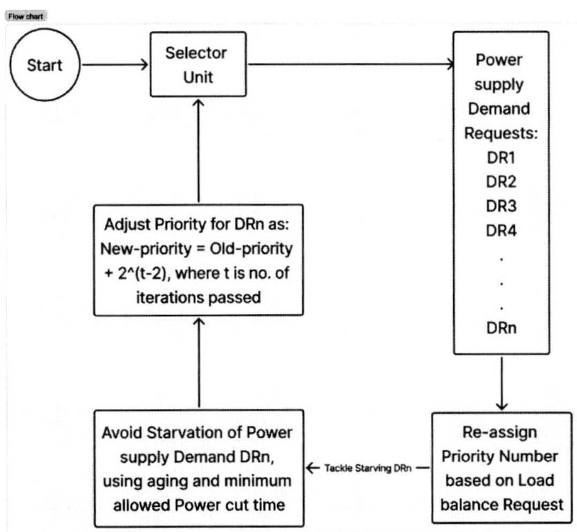

Figure 3.4: Smart Grid and Smart Metering System.

anism. The scheme also incorporates random nonces and fuzzy verifiers to enhance unpredictability with a probabilistic approach.

The proposed work aims to handle unpredictable attack vulnerabilities often found in self-proclaimed secure algorithms. Mechanisms will be designed to detect and mitigate vulnerabilities, ensuring the effectiveness of the authentication scheme. Additionally, optimization efforts will focus on improving message efficiency, complexity, and security, providing a more efficient and reliable approach

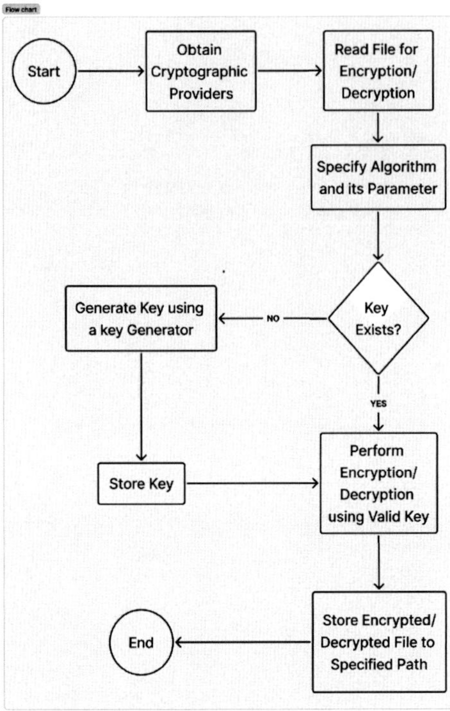

Figure 3.5: General flow of protocol.

to securing IoT communications. Figure 3.5 depicts the proposed authentication scheme incorporating several vital elements to ensure secure communication in IoT modules. By utilizing a symmetric cryptosystem, the scheme establishes a strong foundation for secure data exchange and session key generation. By requiring multiple factors for authentication, the three-factor authentication and session key generation protocol enhances system security. To achieve robust encryption, the scheme leverages the triple DES algorithm. This ensures that the transmitted data remains confidential and protected from unauthorized access. Additionally, the scheme introduces random nonces and fuzzy verifiers, adding an extra layer of unpredictability to prevent potential attacks. One of the primary objectives of the proposed scheme is to address the vulnerabilities often present in self-proclaimed secure algorithms. The scheme aims to provide a reliable and effective solution for securing IoT communications by designing mechanisms to detect and mitigate these vulnerabilities.

Our suggested technique encrypts and decrypts data using the fast triple DES algorithm. A private key pair is created during the encryption stage, and a public key is produced from it. Decryption is performed by applying modular arithmetic using the ciphertext and modulus. The protocol addresses two different

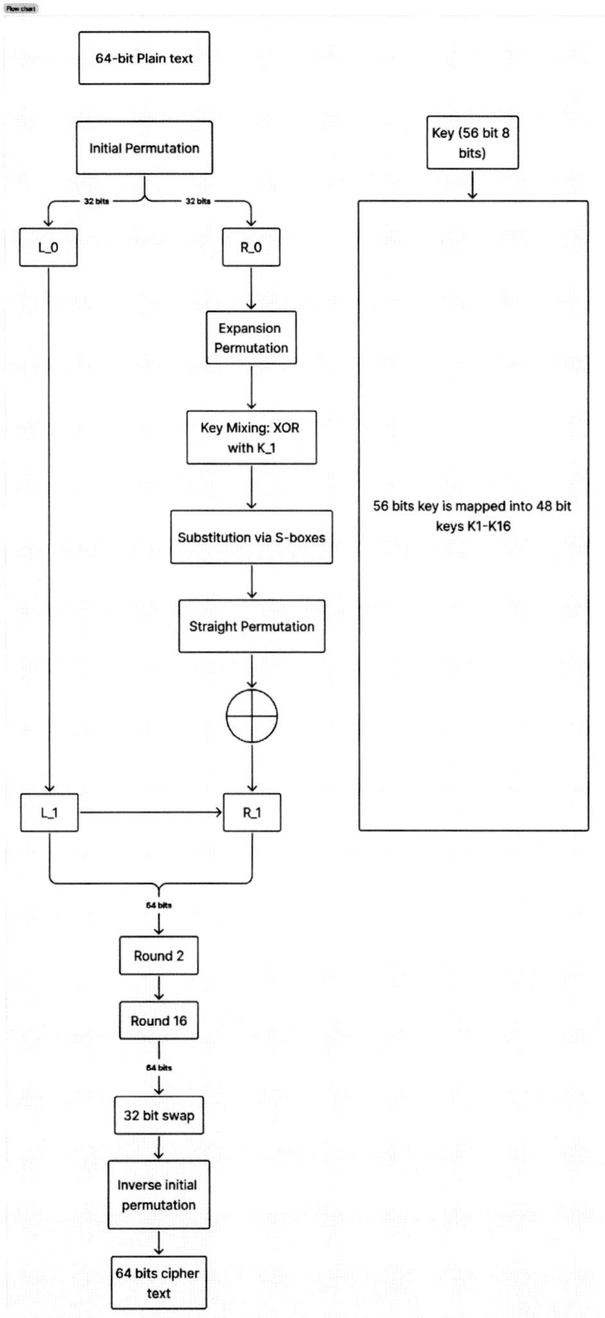

Figure 3.6: The Encryption/Decryption algorithm's flow.

cases. When the user and the accessed sensor(s) are in the same cluster and are managed by the same home gateway node, Case 1 is handled. In Case 2, the protocol addresses circumstances where the sensor(s) are operated by a Foreign gateway node rather than the user's home gateway node. Both cases involve nine phases, but we focus on discussing the five major phases in detail, omitting the unchanged phases.

Case 1, where a single home gateway node serves as the home gateway cluster for both the user and the accessible sensor(s):

The following steps are taken to handle the scenario:

1. Initialization: To create a secure connection, the initialization step comprises the user and the sensor(s) exchanging the appropriate data. This includes exchanging authentication credentials, such as usernames and passwords, encryption keys, and establishing a secure communication channel using protocols like Transport Layer Security (TLS).
2. User Authentication: The home gateway node requests the user's login credentials from the user for validation. The gateway node verifies the user's identity by cross-referencing the supplied credentials with a trusted user database or authentication server. The user is granted access to the cluster if the authentication is successful.
3. Sensor Authentication: Once the user is authenticated, they send a request to access the sensor(s) within the same cluster. The home gateway node performs sensor authentication by verifying the sensor(s) credentials. This may involve checking the digital certificates or shared keys between the gateway and the sensors to ensure their authenticity.
4. Key Generation: Upon successful authentication of the user or sensor(s), a session key is generated using the lightweight triple DES algorithm. The user's public key and the home gateway node's private key create a secure, shared secret throughout the key creation process. The data sent back and forth between the user and the sensor(s) is encrypted and decrypted using this session key.
5. Secure Communication: The session key enables secure communication between the user and the sensor(s) within the same cluster. All data transmitted between them is encrypted using the lightweight triple DES algorithm, ensuring confidentiality and integrity. The encrypted data is decrypted at the receiving end using the same session key to access the original information.

Case 2: Protocol response when sensor(s) are managed by a different (foreign) gateway node than the user's home gateway node:

1. Initialization: A secure communication channel is established between the user's home and foreign gateway nodes involving the exchange of cryptographic keys (public keys and certificates) to ensure secure and authenticated communication. It also includes the exchange of necessary information for subsequent authentication and key generation processes.

2. User Authentication: The user provides credentials to their home gateway node, which verifies the identity either by checking its trusted user database or consulting an authentication server. If successful, the user is deemed legitimate, and the home gateway node continues with the process.

3. Foreign Gateway Authentication: The home gateway node authenticates the foreign gateway node responsible for the user's desired sensor. This step ensures that the foreign gateway node is trustworthy, typically by verifying its digital certificate, checking a signature from a reputable authority, or confirming a shared key. This mutual authentication establishes trust between the two gateway nodes.

4. Sensor Authentication: After authenticating the foreign gateway node, the home gateway node requests access to the sensor(s) on behalf of the user. The foreign gateway node then authenticates the sensor(s), possibly by verifying shared keys or digital certificates. This ensures that the user communicates with legitimate and authorized devices.

5. Key Generation: After successful authentication, the lightweight triple DES algorithm generates a session key using the user's public key and the foreign gateway node's private key. The user and the foreign gateway node securely exchange the session key to establish a secure communication channel for data between the user and the sensor(s) via the foreign gateway node.

6. Secure Communication: Users can interact securely with sensors through the foreign gateway node using a session key. The lightweight triple DES technique encrypts data between the user and the foreign gateway node, and between the foreign gateway node and the sensors, ensuring data confidentiality and integrity, preventing unauthorized access and tampering.

The final permutation in the authentication scheme is achieved after 16 rounds of processing, as illustrated in Figure 3.7. Each round involves operations like substitution, permutation, and key mixing to transform the data, ensuring confusion and diffusion. The output of each round becomes the input for the next continuing this process for all 16 rounds. After the 16th round, a final permutation operation

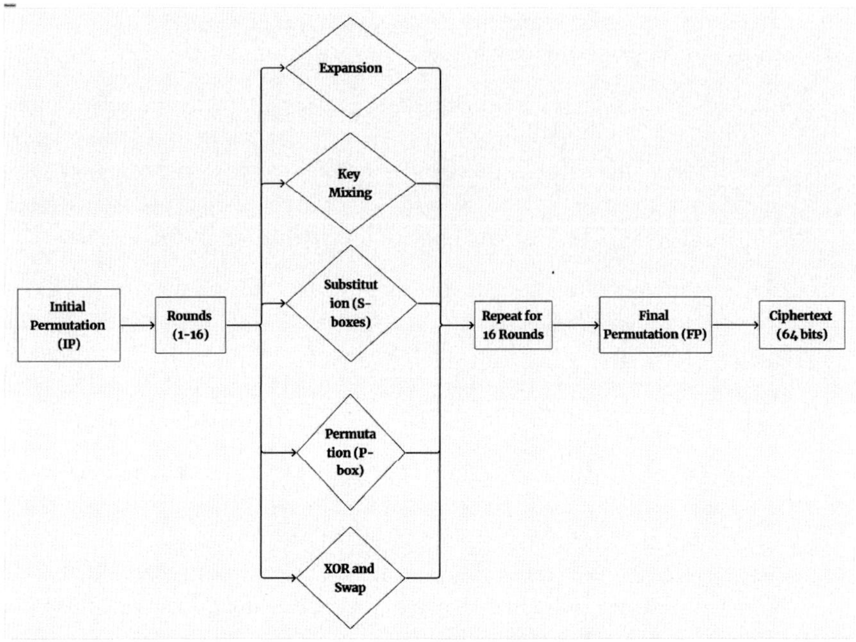

Figure 3.7: Process of obtaining final permutation.

shuffles the bits according to a predefined pattern to achieve the desired output. This ensures a secure and unique final permutation for the processed data. By performing 16 rounds of operations followed by a final permutation, the proposed authentication scheme achieves the desired cryptographic properties and enhances overall network security.

3.7 Error Calculation

In the algorithm's mathematical background, each round's encryption or decryption process is defined by the following formulas:

$$L_n = R_{n-1} \tag{3.1}$$

$$R_n = L_{n-1} + f(R_{n-1}, K_n) \tag{3.2}$$

where,

L: The left half of the block, beginning with L_0 after the initial split.
R: The right half of the block, beginning with R_0 after the initial split.
n: Indicates the round number, starting with 0 after the initial split of the block.
f: Refers to the F function, a specific algorithmic function.
K_n: Represents the subkey for round n.

These formulas show how the block's left and right halves are transformed in each round. The previous round's left half becomes the current round's left half, while the right half is determined by adding the F function applied to the right half and the corresponding subkey for that round.

The algorithm encrypts or decrypts the input block by iteratively applying these formulas iteratively for the specified rounds. The F function's implementation and subkey derivation may vary based on the algorithm's variant and design choices.

3.8 Results and Discussion

This section provides a comprehensive analysis of the proposed algorithm, highlighting its strengths, limitations, and potential areas for improvement. It aims to give an understanding of the algorithm's performance, security, and practicality in IoT networks.

3.8.1 Server-Side Encryption/Decryption

The server-side encryption/decryption process begins with the server receiving plaintext data from the client. The data is divided into blocks, and an encryption algorithm is applied using a secret key for each block. The encrypted data is stored securely on the server. During decryption, the encrypted data is retrieved from storage, and the decryption algorithm is applied using the same secret key. The decrypted data is then sent back to the client.

3.8.2 Client-Side Encryption/Decryption

For client-side encryption/decryption, the client starts by dividing plaintext data into blocks and applying the encryption algorithm using the secret key. The encrypted data is then securely transmitted to the server for storage. During decryption, the client retrieves the encrypted data from the server and applies the decryption algorithm using the same secret key, obtaining the decrypted data for further processing or display to the user.

3.8.3 Encryption/Decryption using Lightweight Triple DES

The encryption/decryption process involves both server-side and client-side operations, with each party applying security measures throughout the algorithm. This ensures the secure transformation of data, enhancing the overall operation of the cryptographic system.

3.8.4 Security in Smart Grid or Smart Metering Systems

The Scheme's security in the smart grid or smart metering system depends on the secure transfer of private data between the sender and receiver. The vulnerability of the existing authentication procedures compromises the security of the smart grid or smart metering system. Two significant attacks are addressed in our proposed method:

1. **Preventing Gateway Impersonation Attack:** With the help of our protocol, the adversary in a smart grid or smart metering system cannot pretend to be the Gateway node. To do so, the adversary must calculate a protected value, denoted as 'X', sent during the authentication process. Without this value, the adversary cannot compute 'X'. Our protocol utilizes a hash-based algorithm and timestamps, making it impossible for the adversary to gain any helpful information from previous authentication sessions. The system administrator securely guards the secret key and other protected information necessary to compute 'X', making it infeasible for the adversary to obtain them. Additionally, the computational complexity of decrypting the ciphertext further strengthens the protocol's security against this attack.

2. **Avoiding Sensor Node Impersonation Attack:** By examining prior exchanged messages an, attacker might attempt to impersonate a Sensor node in the smart grid or smart metering system. They need to compute a value "Y" to succeed, but our approach safeguards the information required for this computation. Similar to the gateway impersonation attack analysis, the adversary lacks the necessary skills and materials for successful impersonation. Our protocol enhances the overall security of the smart grid or smart metering system by providing improved defense against these attacks.

3.8.5 Efficiency Comparison

Time delays at sensor nodes, gateways, and user terminals were measured as part of the evaluation. The comparison table shows the efficiency of current schemes,

Table 3.1: Comparison among the proposed and existing schemes.

Attack Type	Existing Protocols	Proposed Protocols
Type II SSLA Attack.	Insecure	Secure
Gateway Impersonation Attack	Insecure	Secure
Sensor Node Impersonation	Insecure	Secure
Sensor Node Capture Attack	Insecure	Secure

Table 3.2: Comparison analysis in terms of time cost efficiency of the proposed scheme.

Protocol	Total Time Cost for User (Ui)	Total Time Cost for Gateway Node (GWN)	Total Time Cost for Sensor Node (Sj)	Overall Total Time Cost
Das's Protocol	10Thash	10Thash	5Thash	25Thash
Li et al.'s Protocol	6Thash+2TSED	8Thash+5TSED	6Thash+1TSED	18Thash+10TSED
Amin and Biswas's Protocol	13Thash	14Thash	5Thash	32Thash
Rabin Cryptosystem	9Thash	9Thash	8Thash	26Thash
Amutha & Latha's Protocol	8Thash+3TMOD	12Thash+3TSQRT	6Thash+26Thash+ TMOD+TSQRT	27Thash+TMOD+ TSQRT
Proposed Protocol	7Thash+2TMOD	11Thash+2TSQRT	5Thash+25Thash+ TMOD+TSQRT	25Thash+TMOD+ TSQRT

the proposed scheme, and the Rabin Cryptosystem. The proposed protocol offers is more time-efficient, enhancing smart grid and metering system performance by reducing computational loads on users and network nodes.

The Rabin Cryptosystem offers lower time costs for users and gateway nodes but slightly increases costs for sensor nodes. Das's Protocol incurs higher overall time costs due to uniform computational loads. Li et al.'s Protocol adds cryptographic operations, raising time costs, particularly for gateway nodes. Amin and Biswas's Protocol, though secure, has the highest overall time cost, making it less efficient for time-sensitive applications. Amutha & Latha's Protocol has higher time costs across all nodes, emphasizing the efficiency of the proposed protocol.

3.8.6 Performance Analysis

The proposed protocol significantly improves time cost efficiency while balancing both computational and cryptographic security. It is suitable for real-time applications in IoT-based smart grids and Advanced Metering Systems. The reduced computational load on network nodes also enhances energy efficiency, crucial for resource-constrained IoT devices.

3.9 Conclusion and Future Scope

In conclusion, smart meter analytics and IoT security research have paved the way for future advancements. The analysis of smart meter data and the application of machine learning techniques have shown promise in accurately predicting energy consumption and identifying energy-saving opportunities. Further improvements can be made by leveraging recent data sets, advanced processing methods, and incorporating static features. In the realm of IoT security, the proposed authentication scheme based on lightweight triple DES has addressed the constraints and security requirements of constrained devices. However, future research should focus on enhancing key-sharing mechanisms, conducting comprehensive security analyses, and exploring alternative encryption algorithms and cryptographic techniques to develop more efficient and secure authentication schemes.

Exploring novel approaches for efficient and secure data transmission, privacy preservation, and anomaly detection will enhance IoT security. By emphasizing these research areas, we can unlock the full potential of smart meter analytics and IoT security, leading to improved energy management, sustainability, and resilience in IoT networks.

In summary, the findings from this research provide a strong foundation for future advancements in smart meter analytics and IoT security. We can contribute to a more sustainable and secure future by addressing challenges and exploring new possibilities.

Smart meter analytics aims to increase efficiency by utilizing current data sources and processing techniques such as parallel processing and column storage. Incorporating a more comprehensive range of static features and exploring higher-dimensionality processing can potentially enhance forecast results for energy consumption. It is necessary to investigate streaming algorithms and real-time analytics for smart meter data now that high-frequency meters are available. Creating a comprehensive time series analytics benchmark for diverse applications can provide valuable insights for better household energy management, promoting sustainability and efficiency. In IoT security, future research should focus on improving key sharing mechanisms to enhance security without increasing complexity. The effectiveness of the suggested protocol can be improved by doing a thorough security examination of it against different threats. Exploring alternative lightweight encryption algorithms and cryptographic techniques can lead to more efficient and secure authentication schemes for IoT modules. Moreover, investigating novel approaches for secure data transmission, privacy preservation, and anomaly detection will contribute to the overall improvement of IoT security. Emphasizing these research areas will foster enhanced protection and resilience in the rapidly expanding landscape of IoT networks.

References

[1] G.A. Alkawsi, N. Ali, and Y. Baashar. An empirical study of the acceptance of iot-based smart meter in malaysia: The effect of electricity-saving knowledge and environmental awareness. *IEEE Access*, 2020.

[2] R. Amin and G. P. Biswas. A secure light weight scheme for user authentication and key agreement in multi-gateway based wireless sensor networks. *Ad Hoc Networks*, 36:58–80, 2016.

[3] N. Amjady and S. P. Gharehpetian. Hourly wind speed forecasting using a new hybrid forecasting approach based on neural networks. In *17th International Conference on Harmonics and Quality of Power (ICHQP)*, pages 390–396, 2016.

[4] Mahmoud Ammara, Giovanni Russello, and Bruno Crispo. Internet of things: A survey on the security of iot frameworks. *Journal of Information Security and Applications*, 2019.

[5] M. Benmalek and Y. Challal. eskami: Efficient and scalable multigroup key management for advanced metering infrastructure in smart grid. In *IEEE Trustcom/BigDataSE/ISPA*, 2015.

[6] E. Fernandes, J. Jung, and A. Prakash. Security analysis of emerging smart home applications. In *Proceedings of the 37th IEEE symposium on security and privacy*, 2016.

[7] S. M. Hussein, Ramos, and Bermejo. Distributed key management to secure iot wireless sensor networks in smart-agro. *Sensors*, 2020.

[8] R. Kumar, S. Kumar, and R. S. Anand. An energy-efficient key management scheme for iot-based healthcare systems. *Journal of Ambient Intelligence and Humanized Computing*, 2021.

[9] C. Liu, X. Liu, J. Zhang, L. Ren, and W. Dou. Efficient authentication scheme for smart grid in iot environment. *IEEE Transactions on Industrial Informatics*, 2021.

[10] C. Liu, R. Tan, and Y. Wu et al. Dissecting zero trust: research landscape and its implementation in iot. *Cybersecurity*, 7:20, 2024.

[11] Rachit, S. Bhatt, and P. R. Ragiri. Security trends in internet of things: a survey. *SN Applied Sciences*, 3:121, 2021.

[12] T. Rajmohan, P. H. Nguyen, and N. Ferry. A decade of research on patterns and architectures for iot security. *Cybersecurity*, 5:2, 2022.

[13] M.A.A. Rakib, M.M. Rahman, and M.A. Rahman. Iot based controlling of power grid. *European Journal of Engineering and Technology Research*, 2021.

[14] A. Sharma, S. Sharma, R. K. Sharma, and S. L. Maskara. A lightweight key management scheme for internet of things (iot)-based smart grid. *Journal of Ambient Intelligence and Humanized Computing*, 2021.

[15] A.K. Sikder, G. Petracca, and H. Aksu. A survey on sensor-based threats and attacks to smart devices and applications. *IEEE Communications Surveys and Tutorials*, 2021.

[16] Y. Sun, S. Yin, J. Liu, and L. Teng. A certificateless group authenticated key agreement protocol based on dynamic binary tree. *International Journal of Network Security*, 2019.

[17] M. Tiloca and G. Dini. Grep: A group rekeying protocol based on member join history. In *IEEE Symposium on Computers and Communication (ISCC)*, 2016.

[18] M. Tiloca, G. Dini, and K. Rizki. Group rekeying based on member join history. *International Journal of Information Security*, 2020.

[19] H. Zhang, S. Y. Shi, and Q. Shi. Design of key management scheme for secure multicast based on lkh tree. *Computer Engineering and Design*, 2019.

Chapter 4

A Comparative Analysis of Cloud-Based Education and Skill Development in Smart Cities Context

Ankita Mohan, Jahanvi Singh, Sahil Sahani, Satyakam Nayak, Hitesh Mohapatra, Alok Kumar Jagadev* and *Santosh Kumar Swain*

Abstract

Smart cities enhance convenience in education for schools, students, and parents through new technologies. The use of cloud applications enables cost-efficient data transfer and supply, automation, and glossary articulation. However, digital access and skill gaps indicate the need for inclusive workforce development. Similar issues are present in Web 2.0 for education, where data protection and privacy must be balanced with usability and development. This chapter discusses various cloud-based education models, finding that Model 2 is the most effective due to AI based customization and flexible services, simplifying the management of Learning Experience Platforms (LEPs) without rewriting applications for hybrid cloud integration. This study highlights the efficiency, affordability

School of Computer Engineering, KIIT Deemed to Be University, Bhubaneswar, India.

* Corresponding author: hiteshmahapatra@gmail.com

DOI: 10.1201/9781003531043-6

and growing trend of using real-time cloud-based education solutions in smart cities. Updated databases can be accessed to foster cooperation and enhance work performance.

4.1 Introduction

In smart cities, which utilize advanced technologies for urban improvement, cloud-based education is seen as shaping the future of learning. The key benefits of cloud computing—scalability, personalization, collaboration, cost-effectiveness, and sustainability—are essential for successful educational initiatives in these cities. These features support diverse learners' success and adapt the educational environment to societal changes. However, cloud-based education's cost-effectiveness and sustainability come with challenges, such as ensuring accessibility, affordability, and opportunities for upskilling and reskilling for all learners.

Rapid technological advancements have transformed urban living significantly. Smart cities use cutting-edge technologies to address urban problems while promoting sustainability, efficiency, and inclusivity. Cloud computing plays a crucial role in these cities, enabling innovative cloud-based solutions for education [26]. These cloud-based educational programs offer flexible learning options that accommodate learners' interests and needs without the constraints of specific locations or times [17].

This flexibility accommodates diverse schedules, removing barriers related to infrastructure, time, and geography. Cloud-based education is a radical shift from traditional models, making education more democratic and accessible regardless of socio-economic status, empowering people from all backgrounds [13]. In the dynamic urban landscape where labor market needs change frequently cloud solutions provide workers with essential skills. These programs foster a culture of continuous learning and innovation through personalized, interactive, and collaborative experiences. In smart cities, characterized by diversity and inclusivity, cloud education promotes social mobility and economic empowerment, enabling active community participation.

Individualized learning environments, teamwork, innovation, and continuous learning are key areas [18]. Cloud-based education has helped bridge the digital divide. Cloud-based education has helped bridge the digital divide, enhancing student collaboration and delivering personalized experiences, positively impacting socio-economic growth. This chapter presents a comparative study of current initiatives, guiding stakeholders in creating inclusive, resilient, and sustainable urban environments [4]. The advancement of cloud technology in education proves that learning frameworks can revolutionize education and are essential for the development of smart cities.

The integration of cloud technology marks a fundamental shift toward more accessible, efficient, and collaborative learning environments [19]. This approach reveals cloud technology's potential to unlock the full capacity of education, paving the way for boundless, inclusive learning deeply embedded in smart cities. In these dynamic urban landscapes, cloud-based education plays a crucial role in bridging the digital divide and fostering collaboration and innovation. By delivering personalized learning experiences tailored to individual needs, cloud technology enhances performance and positively impacts socio-economic growth.

By evaluating current initiatives, stakeholders can gain insights into creating inclusive and sustainable urban environments. The transformative power of cloud technology in education underscores its importance in revolutionizing learning frameworks and growing inclusive instructional environments deeply included into the fabric of smart cities. Cloud-based platforms offer extensive educational resources, applications, and data analytics tools, allowing educators to tailor learning experiences to individual student needs, learning styles, and skill gaps [9]. These platforms track student progress in real-time, identify areas needing additional support, and recommend supplementary materials or adjust learning pace.

This approach moves beyond a "one-size-fits-all" model, catering to diverse learners in a smart city. Additionally, cloud-based platforms foster collaboration and innovation, connecting students and educators across the city throughout a smart city to connect, collaborate, and percentage know-how. Collaborative learning environments can be fostered through on-line forums, virtual classrooms, and real-time communication tools. These not only build a sense of community but also expose students to diverse perspectives and encourage innovation through collaborative problem-solving. Imagine students from different schools in a smart city, working together on projects leveraging cloud-based tools to share information, conduct research, and present findings [6]. The rapid development of smart cities, characterized by interconnected technologies and data-driven solutions, necessitates reevaluating educational frameworks. Traditional classrooms struggle to meet the dynamic needs of urban learners, while cloud-based education transforms learning landscapes within smart cities. This approach highlights the potential of cloud technology to revolutionize education, making learning boundless, inclusive, and integral to smart urban living.

Enabling Educators & Simplifying Processes: By reducing administrative burdens and streamlining academic processes, cloud technology enables teachers to spend more quality time with their students. Cloud-based grading tools quickly assess student progress, making administrative tasks more efficient. Additionally, online professional development opportunities help educators stay updated with relevant knowledge & technology.

Creating Inclusive Learning Spaces: Cloud technology can equitably provide educational resources within a smart city [27]. Students in underserved areas or geographically isolated areas can access learning opportunities online from any internet-connected device. Additionally, cloud platforms offer text-to-speech conversion and closed captioning, making education accessible for disabled students.

Smart City Infrastructure Integration: Cloud-based real-time data from traffic and environmental sensors contributes to an integrated smart city ecosystem. This data can be incorporated to promote critical thinking. Imagine a simulation where students use live traffic data to create an optimized transportation system for their smart city. This approach enhances education by fostering collaboration and problem-solving skills in a cloud-based context [21].

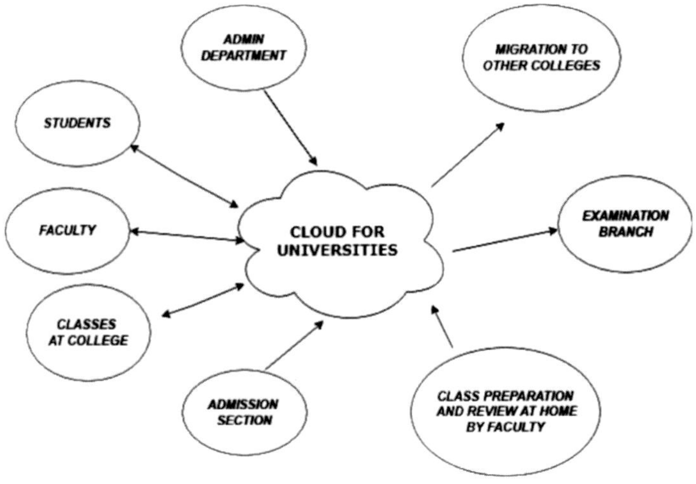

Figure 4.1: Role of cloud computing in education at universities.

4.1.1 Research Gap

Research Gap 1: Properly managing bigdata in smart cities is essential, as it involves high-speed, diverse data forms that are challenging to store, process, and analyze. Efficient management requires technologies for real-time processing and analysis, providing valuable insights for accurate decision-making in urban domains [11]. Innovative methods are needed to handle voluminous, high-speed unstructured or semi-structured data, ensuring smooth functioning of applications and services based on such analytics, transforming them into operational systems.

Research Gap 2: Strengthening data protection is crucial as smart cities rely on innovative technologies to optimize urban services and improve quality of life.

Managing Big Data in smart cities raises privacy, hacking, and security challenges. Solutions include deploying encryption, authentication, and access control for data storage, transmission, and processing. New approaches are needed for privacy preservation and managing multiple stakeholders in smart cities [22].

Research Gap 3: Enhancing Information Processing Efficiency: Smart cities require insights from increasing data volumes. Current big data platforms face scalability and performance issues with diverse data sources and complex computations. Research focuses on optimizing with techniques specific to smart city applications, including algorithms, data structures and processing methods [7]. The goal is to improve data processing speed decision-making, services, and resource usage. Scalability and Performance Limitations: Current systems struggle with large data sets and intensive analysis needed in smart cities, constraining real-time analysis and decision making. Heterogeneous Data Sources: Smart cities gather data from sensors, social media and mobile devices, which can be unstructured, semi-structured, and challenging to integrate and analyze with conventional methods.

Research Gap 4: Cloud Skills Management: Creating trusted assessment tools and methods for validating skills in cloud education and smart cities is crucial [26]. Traditional assessment may not effectively capture the diverse skills needed in today's dynamic workplace. Effective assessments include theoretical and relation-based assessments, objective and performance assessments, employment-based competencies, project-based assessments and performance expectations-based assessments [2]. These tools are essential for promoting the relevance of educational programs to market conditions and improving learners' employment prospects in the modern digital economy [23].

4.2 Literature Review

Recently, the smart cities have been promoted as solutions to challenges from urbanization and global sustainability. Smart cities integrate advanced technologies to improve transportation, energy management and public services [9]. Education has shifted from being peripheral to central in smart city frameworks, preparing citizens for digital life [27]. It provides the knowledge, skills, and competencies needed to use emerging technologies, driving innovation and economic development. Additionally, education fosters lifelong learning and adaptability to changing threats. The new age will require not only thinkers and charity workers but also to efficiently use emerging technologies revolutionizing our cities. Cloud technology exemplifies using broadband internet for maximal service in smart cities [21]. It is fundamental to digital transformation across various industrial environments.

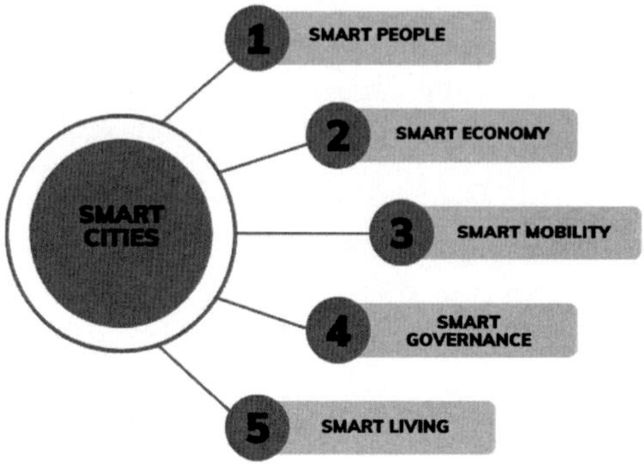

Figure 4.2: Relationship and evolution of smart cities.

Cloud computing fosters features like smart mobility, governance and living standards in the precinct of a smart city [5]. It allows development of smart transportation systems, helps city planning and execution work efficiently to improve quality of life along with sustainability. The data used to manage traffic flow, energy consumption and governance processes is analyzed by cloud-based systems, providing insights into making smart cities more efficient. When devising strategies for incorporating information technology into smart city initiatives, considering the benefits of different cloud-based services is essential. Infrastructure-as-a-Service (IaaS), Platform-as-a-Service (PaaS), and Software-as-a-Service (SaaS) offer valuable tools for enhancing smart city management and functionality [10]. Figure 4.2 illustrates the core components and evolution of smart cities, emphasizing smart people, economy, mobility, governance, and living standards. While cloud computing's role may not be explicitly depicted, it significantly supports these pillars by enabling data analysis, optimization, and efficient resource management within smart city frameworks [28].

Table 4.1 presents a concise summary of the three main types of cloud-based services, along with representative examples for each category. Firstly, Infrastructure-as-a-Service (IaaS) empowers users to initiate and manage various resources such as processes, data storage systems, and networks for building installed Infomedia. Leading examples of IaaS providers include Amazon Web Services (AWS), Microsoft Azure, and Google Cloud Platform (GCP), which offer a foundational layer for users to construct and oversee their virtual infrastructure flexibly. Secondly, Platform-as-a-Service (PaaS) provides users access to platforms and Infomedia for creating, testing, and deploying new applications and services without the need to manage underlying infrastructure [15]. Google App Engine, AWS Elastic Beanstalk and Azure App Service are all examples of PaaS which allow developers to focus on application-development eliminating infrastructure complexities. Software-as-a-Service (SaaS): Customers can ac-

Table 4.1: Summary of three categories of cloud-based services and their examples.

Category	Description	Examples
Infrastructure-as-a-Service (IaaS)	Infrastructure-as-a-Service (IaaS) allows users to initiate processes, set up data storage systems, establish networks, and allocate various resources for creating installed Infomedia.	Examples include Amazon Web Services (AWS), Microsoft Azure, and Google Cloud Platform (GCP)
Platform-as-a-Service (PaaS)	Platform-as-a-Service (PaaS) provides users with the opportunity to utilize the platform and Infomedia for creating, testing, and allocating new supplements.	Examples include Google App Engine, AWS Elastic Beanstalk, and Azure App Service
Software-as-a-Service (SaaS)	Software-as-a-Service (SaaS) offers clients the option to utilize additional features from providers operating on cloud-based infrastructure.	Examples include Google BigTable, Amazon SimpleDB, Salesforce, and Dropbox.

cess software applications hosted on cloud infrastructure and these are executed without any installation & maintenance [31]. SaaS solutions cover services like database management, customer relationship management and file storage which run in the cloud. Some SaaS providers are Google BigTable, Amazon SimpleDB, Salesforce or Dropbox [29]. Table 4.1 summarizes these cloud-based services to provide a sense of what they do and who the big players are in each category.

Cloud technology has significantly transformed the landscape of educational delivery and management within institutions, providing educators and learners with unparalleled flexibility and accessibility. The future of cloud-based solutions offers numerous high-end tools and services for educationalists, administrations & learners. From cloud-based learning management systems to collaborative productivity suites, these tools have transformed the education industry helping organizations automate processes and enhance collaboration as well as bring online personalized experiences. Using the scalability and cost-effectiveness of cloud computing, cloud providers enable educational institutions to move beyond barriers associated with implementing higher education initiatives at a scale needed for smart cities [8].

Cloud-fueled education is essentially the idea of learning ecosystems using cloud to design new-age, lively and interactive educational spaces. A large variety of tools, platforms, and services created to enable teaching and learning across multiple types of educational contexts are part of these ecosystems. Examples include cloud-based learning management systems (LMS), online collaboration tools, interactive multimedia content like images, videos, etc., and data analytics platforms that enable tracking resource users. This structured system enables educators to offer individualized learning experiences, effectively track student progress, and analyze data for informed instructional decisions. Cloud technology helps educational institutions overcome time and space barriers, providing ubiquitous access to resources and fostering collaborative learning for enriched experiences in smart cities [30].

Cloud technology in smart city education programs can revolutionize the way educational content is freely offered and received. Smart cities can adapt cloud-driven learning ecosystems to address challenges and opportunities in urban education, including resource availability, diversity of learners, and technological infrastructure [25]. Cloud technology enables educators to provide personalized instruction, collaborate with peers and adjust teaching methods based on real-time student feedback. Cloud-based learning ecosystems provide data on student interactions with and performance, allowing educators to personalize instruction based on results. Despite challenges related to data privacy, digital equity, and infrastructure readiness, cloud-powered learning ecosystems offer extensive benefits for smart cities. These ecosystems can enhance education delivery, stimulate creativity, and support learners in navigating the 21st century successfully. Although cloud-based education can expand learning opportunities, the digital divide may marginalize those without high-speed internet or devices [14], devices, necessitating careful implementation. Privacy and security of learners' data are crucial and require significant measures and regulations. Cloud-based education and skill development in smart cities are emerging research areas with several potential gaps. Figure 4.3 shows the primary challenges in cloud computing.

Bridging digital inequalities in cloud-based education is crucial for smart city growth he digital divide, highlighted in a 1999 US government report, shows the gap between those with access to new forms of communication technology and those without. Smart cities depend on technology, so closing this gap is vital for inclusive, sustainable growth. The cloud-based education environment is asyn-

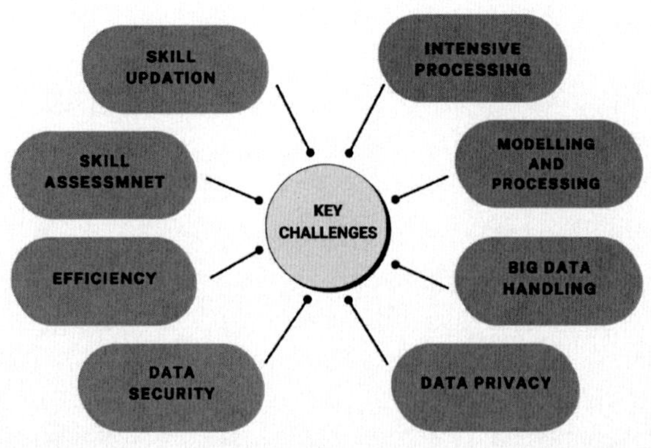

Figure 4.3: Key challenges of cloud computing.

chronous, particularly benefiting students who are geographically distant from traditional classrooms [16].

This enables personalized curriculum delivery and supports distance learners by providing alternative means and modes that benefit students with disabilities aligning with smart city inclusivity goals. Smart city initiatives, often partnering with technology companies, aim to develop high-demand skills like coding, data analytics, and cybersecurity through cloud-accessible platforms [12]. However, ongoing digitalization presents poses risks of social exclusion, particularly for those lacking digital literacy. Cloud-enablement in smart cities must democratize access and availability and affordability for all residents including digital immigrants and the less privileged. Efforts should focus on dynamic reskilling and upskilling pathways, essential for Industry 4.0 where where human-bot collaboration is key.

Cloud technologies play a key role in offering innovative education models like flipped learning and asynchronous approaches [1, 3]. Cloud-based platforms enable educational institutions to deliver training and certification programs for modern learners, including VR simulations for medical students and mechanics. Governments, academic institutes, and private entities collaborate to develop and implement cloud-based educational initiatives, aiming for better outcomes within smart city ecosystems. Addressing, digital inequities and incorporating cloud-based educational interventions and skill development initiatives are essential for any smart city strategy. Cloud-Based Smart Cities leverage disruptive capabilities to promote user-friendly and democratic use facilitating sociability and growth to benefit people everywhere [6]. Figure 4.4 illustrates the Flipped Learning Environment (student). Table 4.2 presents the literature review of existing works.

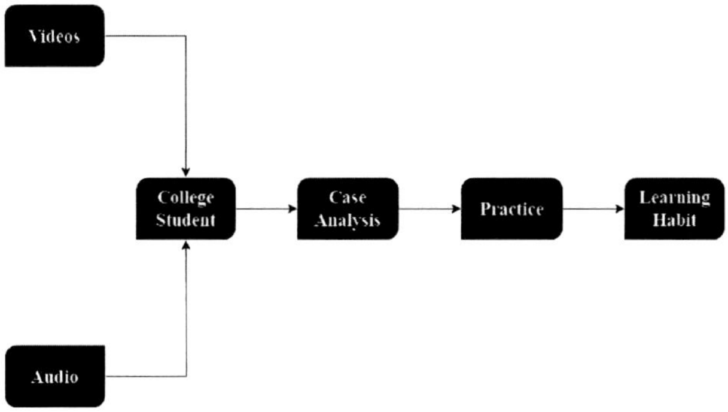

Figure 4.4: Representation of a flipped learning environment for a student.

Table 4.2: Literature review on existing works.

Citation	Objective	Methodology	Findings	Limitations	Relevance to Smart Cities
[9, 5, 10] [29]	To assess the role of cloud computing in delivering education in smart cities	Survey of 100 educators across 5 cities	Found that cloud platforms improve access to education	Limited to a single region	Demonstrates the importance of cloud platforms in smart city educational infrastructures
[6, 27, 21] [15, 31]	Analyze the impact of cloud-based skill development programs on employment	Case study of vocational training programs	Improved job readiness in 60% of participants	Focused on a narrow set of skills	Highlights the role of cloud systems in smart city workforce development
[26, 17, 13] [27, 2, 23]	Investigate how cloud-based education fosters digital literacy	Experimental design with 200 students	Increased digital literacy among 85% of participants	Short study duration	Essential for creating digitally literate populations in smart cities
[28, 21, 5] [3, 7]	Compare traditional education with cloud-based education in smart cities	Comparative study of two educational models	Cloud-based education more adaptable and scalable	Limited to urban settings	Shows cloud education as key for scalable education solutions in smart cities
[5, 25, 12] [1, 11, 22]	Explore cloud-based platforms for vocational training in smart cities	Mixed methods (interviews + quantitative analysis)	Cloud platforms enhanced vocational training by 70%	Data primarily from developing countries	Links cloud systems to enhanced skill development infrastructure in smart cities

4.3 Proposed Study

4.3.1 Comparative Analysis of Existing Models

Model 1: Model 1 suggest using PCs as cloud partners with the view of enhancing cloud through the education institutions. To scale these resources and manage user requests each institution has its local server. The concept behind this model is to take advantage of the computing resources that go underutilized in learning environments hence facilitating a wider dissemination of educational content. In this configuration, every PC is a cloud partner and all the available resources are contributed to a cloud system. These computers, owned by educational institutions and often funded through government or other grants, are controlled by local servers. The servers monitor the equipment's condition and handle incoming requests from within the institution. In this model, individual PCs connect to a local server and then to a cloud system. These PCs act as minor participants, contributing compute time and storage [20]. The local server, managed by the institution, stores and supervises all computers, handling student and teacher requests. Students and teachers connect to the local server to access the internal cloud, which hosts applications and educational content. This setup gives educational institutions the opportunity to utilize their existing computing resources and exploit the same as a means of providing educational material to society. While this model offers greater resource optimization, it may face issues like security, reliability and bandwidth availability, particularly in areas with low network development. Additionally, managing a distributed system involves coordinating and supervising individual PCs owned by different institutions to ensure efficient performance.

Challenges: Security—ensuring the internal cloud is safe from hackers is difficult. Scalability—individual computers may break down more often than the cloud can handle. Limited resources: schools without fast internet will struggle to manage the cloud system. Management—overseeing many individual com-

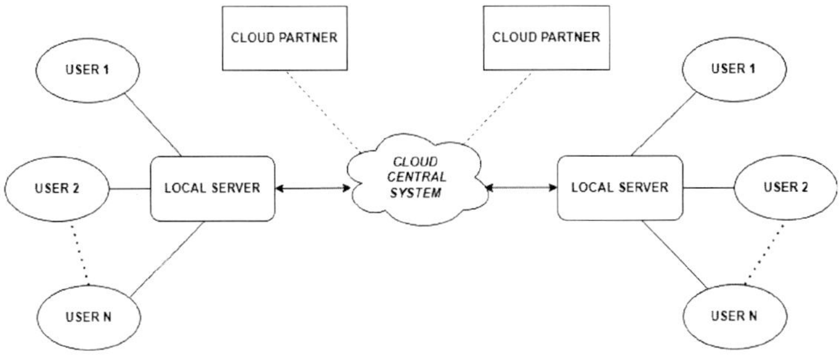

Figure 4.5: Depiction of the cloud infrastructure proposed in [7].

puters across a school is tough. Model 1 offers an inexpensive way for schools to build a cloud system for education. However, security and reliability issues must be addressed for effective implementation. The cloud infrastructure in Model 1 involves each institution having a local server.

Model 2: This model specifies an advanced e-learning system for Education 4, a significant leap from previous education forms. It centers on a five-layer structure using cloud computing and AI to transform learning. The first foundational sub-layer is the Infrastructure Layer (IaaS), which includes computing hardware and proper virtualization processes, ensuring a robust and scalable framework. The next layer, the Platform Layer (PaaS) provides tools and services for cloud applications engineering and deployment. This layer enables developers to create unique and efficient educational solutions that leverage cloud resources effectively [33]. The Software Layer (SaaS) includes elements like the Learning Management System and other educational applications. These focus on content delivery, student interaction, and learning management assessment. The key innovation lies in the Service Layer, which uses AI-based features to enhance learning effectiveness. This layer employs intelligent learning strategies that enable the learning system to adapt learning processes to students' abilities, gaps, and learning styles.

Blackboard learning tools help learners develop social networks to share knowledge. AI technologies offer instant chatbots and e-assessment tools, reducing administrative work and allowing teachers to focus on instructional and student support. The Application Layer is the contact point for users, providing content, learning activities, and group work for students, while educators use applications and resources for effective teaching. Model 2 emphasizes scalability, individual learning processes supported by Artificial Intelligence, improved collaboration, better employment. Cloud solutions and AI in this model address many Education 4.0 challenges. The five-layer architecture of Education 4.0 is shown in Figure 4.6.

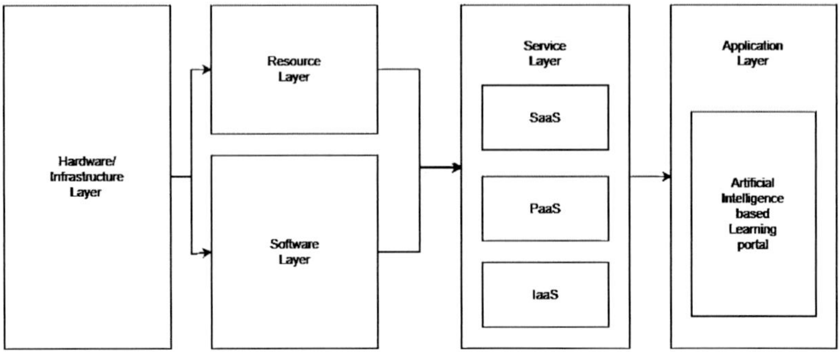

Figure 4.6: Five layered cloud architecture proposed for Education 4.0.

Model 3: Model 3 is a private cloud infrastructure especially designed for educational institution to improve the system's performance of function and utilization. This model is based on the categorization of infrastructure services to manage, control, backup and to meet specific hardware needs. In the core of Model 3 there is an e-learning service layer with several kinds of models of cloud deployment, such as IaaS, PaaS, SaaS among others. Each deployment model serves distinct purposes within the educational ecosystem: IaaS: This model assists the teachers to create special course infrastructure depending on their needs. The benefits of choice inspire flexibility and resources control in providing very specific solutions for individual distinct courses. PaaS: Here educators get a chance to build educational software and applications that would benefit young learners. PaaS innovativeness in developing learning tools and resources since it enables the educators to enhance the learning environment for students. SaaS: This model provides specific software application and educational support services to the user. It enables easy and quick access to different educational needs and offers ready to use solutions for them [24]. That is why it is possible to identify numerous advantages for educational institutions associated with the use of a private cloud infrastructure: the utilization of services rendered on demand, elasticity of resources, and their accurate measurement.

This approach is beneficial for relatively autonomous processes, applications, and data such as e-learning courses. Cloud resources enable institutions to manage demand more effectively, offering flexibility and potential cost reductions. An exclusive private cloud computing infrastructure enhances operational efficiency and flexibility in educational service delivery. Overall, adopting cloud technologies in institutions increases productivity through scalability, optimizes resources, and enhances both student and faculty experiences.

Table 4.2 compares three proposed models to enhance education through technology, assessed across scope, technology, scalability, and security. Model 1 adopts a resource-sharing model within a defined educational infrastructure, fo-

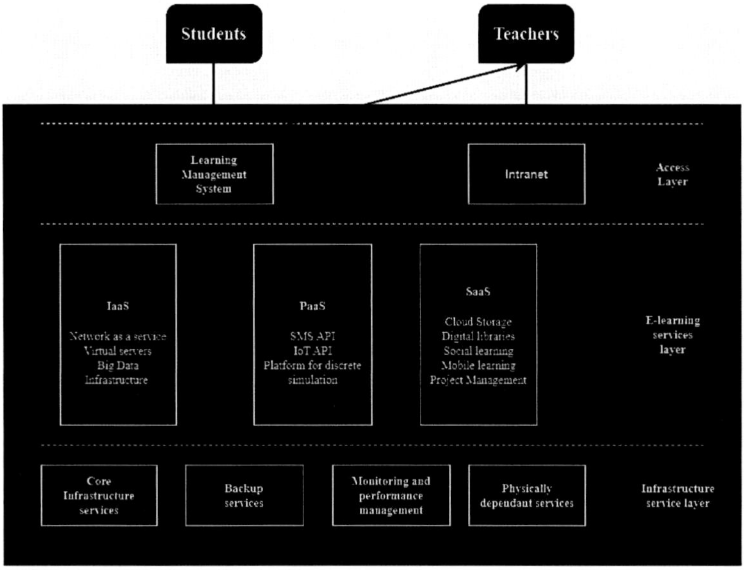

Figure 4.7: Private cloud computing infrastructure for an educational institution.

cusing on infrastructure. However, its usability relies on individual PCs, which may limit growth. Risks arise from an architecture with several sub-areas. Model 2 expands to a broader cloud structure designed for Education 4.0, featuring AI learning portals and social learning tools for an enhanced learning experience. Comparing the two models shows that Model 2, with cloud support, can easily scale and handle increased loads. However, it inherits security concerns from cloud-based systems. Finally, Model 3 emphasizes creating a cloud environment with exclusive access for learning institutions. By adopting IaaS, PaaS, and SaaS deployment models, it ensures scalability and data security within the institution's boundaries. This attribute offers strong security features, but scalability is limited to the institutional framework. Table 4.3 outlines how the models differ, highlighting their strengths and weaknesses in various educational technology contexts.

Table 4.3 compares three models aimed at enhancing educational experiences through technology. It evaluates them across scope, technology, scalability, and security. Model 1 focuses on resource sharing within a defined educational network with an infrastructure-centric approach. While this model provides a tailored solution within a specific boundary, its scalability is limited due to its reliance on individual PCs and sub-areas within the network, leading to security challenges from distributed resources. In contrast, Model 2 is designed for Education 4.0, leveraging cloud-based E-learning and AI-powered learning portals

Table 4.3: Comparison of the three proposed models on various metrics.

Feature	Model 1	Model 2	Model 3
Scope	Resource sharing within educational network [7]	Cloud-based E-learning for Education 4.0 [2]	Private cloud infrastructure within an institution [23]
Technology	Infrastructure-centric [7]	AI-powered learning portal, social learning tools [2]	Cloud service deployment models (IaaS, PaaS, SaaS) [23]
Scalability	Limited [7]	High [2]	Scalable within private cloud [23]
Security	Challenges due to distributed resources [7]	Cloud security [2]	Potentially robust security [23]

with social learning tools. This model demonstrates high scalability due to its cloud foundation, but it inherits security concerns from cloud-based architectures. Finally, Model 3 introduces a private cloud infrastructure dedicated to individual institutions. It uses cloud service deployment models (IaaS, PaaS, SaaS), balancing scalability within the institutional framework and offering potentially robust security, although scalability remains confined within the institution's private cloud. Together, these models highlight varying approaches to integrating technology in education, each with distinct advantages and challenges based on their architecture and application scope.

4.4 Analysis

As revealed by the above derivation and discussion on smart cities as well as the three conceived models of cloud-based education, this study has offered a systematic view on their working processes, advantages and challenges. Model 1, Model 2, and Model 3 are three models that present new paradigms which seek to enhance learning through cloud computing technologies. This examination seeks to explore some of these models further in order to reveal their possible impact on the future education paradigms. Model 1 defines the idea of an educational cloud based on individual PC s with an innovative concept of sharing resources among educational networks. This model represents a low-level cloud infrastructure where each node actively and equally contributes to exploiting and sharing online resources, aiming to provide education and computational resources to as many people as possible. Nevertheless, it cannot scale up through a large number of nodes since it depends on local resources, and the distributed schema poses security risks. Model 2 refers to another revolution in adapting cloud computing in the educational sector which conforms to Education 4.0. It outlines a highly advanced cloud-based e-learning system with five tier system that is composed of learning portals that employ artificial intelligence. This model significantly improves accommodation and adaptability in cloud systems and is therefore suitable for the constantly changing educational systems. AI plays a useful part in providing customized learning; teaching algorithms are able to reflect the learning style and speed, while social media and AI chatbots help to address the administrative issues and assessments. Model 3 expands itself into private cloud solutions designed for educational sector management and emphasizes the proper and secure deployment of educational resources.

This model uses IaaS, PaaS, and SaaS cloud services to provide flexibility with a high level of scalability while enforcing data security and privacy. Model 3 addresses various operational weaknesses that are inherently built into public cloud solutions by stressing the importance of infrastructure performance management, system monitoring, and regular backups. Additionally, the system provides a safe and scalable environment for teaching functions, allowing seamless educational activities and easy access to digital learning platforms, supporting various educational applications and services. A multicriteria approach, combining decentralized resource sharing with AI-powered learning in a secure private cloud, effectively addresses modern education challenges. Trends in institutions like UMN ITSS offer insights into the digital transition in higher education. Future research should find common ground among various models to create an open, adaptable, and secure educational ecosystem. Addressing scalability, security, and ethical challenges is crucial for realizing cloud-driven education in smart cities.

4.5 Conclusion

In conclusion, a comparative analysis of three innovative models identifies their strengths and limitations for promoting cloud-driven education in smart cities. Model 1, which focuses on shared resource ownership, faces challenges in scaling and security, limiting wider adoption. Model 2 leverages a sophisticated cloud-native architecture with AI and social learning, offering greater scalability and personalized learning but raising privacy and ethical concerns. Model 3 promotes a private cloud infrastructure tailored for educational institutions, ensuring data security and flexible learning. A hybrid approach combining the strengths of each model is needed for a comprehensive solution in smart city settings. This includes scalable infrastructure, personalized learning models, and robust security frameworks. Addressing privacy concerns and ethical issues is crucial for creating an inclusive and sustainable education environment.

References

[1] N. Ahmad, N. Hoda, and F. Alahmari. Developing a cloud-based mobile learning adoption model to promote sustainable education. *Sustainability*, 12(8):3126, 2020.

[2] S. Al Noor, G. Mustafa, S. A. Chowdhury, M. Z. Hossain, and F. T. Jaigirdar. A proposed architecture of cloud computing for education system in bangladesh and the impact on current education system. *IJCSNS International Journal of Computer Science and Network Security*, 10(10):7–13, 2010.

[3] A. Almufarreh and M. Arshad. Promising emerging technologies for teaching and learning: Recent developments and future challenges. *Sustainability*, 15(8):6917, 2023.

[4] L. Belli, A. Cilfone, L. Davoli, G. Ferrari, P. Adorni, F. Di Nocera, and E. Bertolotti. Iot-enabled smart sustainable cities: Challenges and approaches. *Smart Cities*, 3(3):1039–1071, 2020.

[5] Z. Benomar, L. D'Agati, F. Longo, G. Merlino, and A. Puliafito. Managed elk deployments at the edge with openstack and iotronic: an italian smart city case study. In *2022 IEEE International Conference on Smart Computing (SMARTCOMP)*, pages 287–292. IEEE, 2022.

[6] N. Bhalotia, M. Kumar, A. Alameen, H. Mohapatra, and M. Kolhar. A helping hand to the elderly: securing their freedom through the haie framework. *Applied Sciences*, 13(11):6797, 2023.

[7] M. Fazio, R. Ranjan, M. Girolami, J. Taheri, S. Dustdar, and M. Villari. A note on the convergence of iot, edge, and cloud computing in smart cities. *IEEE Cloud Computing*, 5(5):22–24, 2018.

[8] D. J. Gunkel. Second thoughts: Toward a critique of the digital divide. *New media & society*, 5(4):499–522, 2003.

[9] A. Kaur, M. Bhatia, and G. Stea. A survey of smart classroom literature. *Education Sciences*, 12(2):86, 2022.

[10] L. U. Khan, I. Yaqoob, N. H. Tran, S. A. Kazmi, T. N. Dang, and C. S. Hong. Edge-computing-enabled smart cities: A comprehensive survey. *IEEE Internet of Things Journal*, 7(10):10200–10232, 2020.

[11] Q. V. Khanh, V. H. Nguyen, Q. N. Minh, A. D. Van, N. Le Anh, and A. Chehri. An efficient edge computing management mechanism for sustainable smart cities. *Sustainable Computing: Informatics and Systems*, 38:100867, 2023.

[12] Abhinav Kumar et al. Examining healthcare services utilizing cloud technology in intelligent urban environments. In *Revolutionizing Healthcare Systems Through Cloud Computing and IoT*, pages 77–98. IGI Global, 2025.

[13] M. Kumar, K. S. Raju, D. Kumar, N. Goyal, S. Verma, and A. Singh. An efficient framework using visual recognition for iot based smart city surveillance. *Multimedia Tools and Applications*, pages 1–19, 2021.

[14] L. Li. Reskilling and upskilling the future-ready workforce for industry 4.0 and beyond. *Information Systems Frontiers*, pages 1–16, 2022.

[15] W. Li, J. Chao, and Z. Ping. Security structure study of city management platform based on cloud computing under the conception of smart city. In *2012 Fourth International Conference on Multimedia Information Networking and Security*, pages 91–94. IEEE, 2012.

[16] B. Ligi and B. Raja. Flipped classroom with cloud based technology. *International Journal of Research in Social Sciences*, 8(12):119–135, 2018.

[17] M. V. Marienko, Y. H. Nosenko, and M. P. Shyshkina. Smart systems of open science in teachers' education. In *Journal of Physics: Conference Series*, volume 2288, page 012035. IOP Publishing, 2022.

[18] H. Mohapatra and S. R. Mishra. Unlocking insights: exploring data analytics and ai tool performance across industries. In *Data analytics and machine learning: navigating the big data landscape*, pages 265–288. Springer Nature Singapore, Singapore, 2024.

[19] Malvika Narsipuram, Ananya Rai, and Astha Tiwari. Load balancing demystified: A comprehensive study of load balancing architectures in cloud computing. *Smart Internet of Things*, 1(1):93–105, 2024.

[20] Aditya Kumar Panda et al. Integrating cloud computing for intelligent transportation solutions in smart cities: A short review. In *Interdisciplinary Approaches to Transportation and Urban Planning*, pages 121–142. IGI Global, 2025.

[21] J. Peng. Research on smart city management model based on cloud computing technology. In *2022 IEEE 5th Advanced Information Management, Communicates, Electronic and Automation Control Conference (IMCEC)*, volume 5, pages 01–05. IEEE, 2022.

[22] J. Peng. Research on smart city management model based on cloud computing technology. In *2022 IEEE 5th Advanced Information Management, Communicates, Electronic and Automation Control Conference (IMCEC)*, volume 5, pages 01–05. IEEE, December 2022.

[23] Supriya Priyadarshi et al. Analysis on enhancing urban mobility with iot-integrated parking solutions. In *Interdisciplinary Approaches to Transportation and Urban Planning*, pages 143–172. IGI Global, 2025.

[24] B. Radenković, M. Despotović-Zrakić, Z. Bogdanović, V. Vujin, and D. Barać. Harnessing cloud computing infrastructure for e-learning services. *Facta Universitatis, Series: Electronics and Energetics*, 27(3):339–357, 2014.

[25] Adyan Rauf, Abhishek Guru, and Hitesh Mohapatra. Exploring the social model of smart home devices: An in-depth analysis of social impact and security issues. In *Human Impact on Security and Privacy: Network and Human Security, Social Media, and Devices*, pages 233–256. IGI Global, 2025.

[26] E. Semenikhina, M. Drushlyak, Y. Bondarenko, S. Kondratiuk, and N. Dehtiarova. Cloud-based service geogebra and its use in the educational process: the byod-approach. *Tem Journal*, 8(1), 2019.

[27] Mariya P Shyshkina, Andrii M Striuk, Mykola I Striuk, Yuliia V Yechkalo, Larisa S Kolgatina, Kateryna V Vlasenko, Svitlana M Amelina, and Olena V Semenikhina. 9th workshop on cloud technologies in education: Report. 2022.

[28] Siddharth Singh et al. Optimizing cloud performance: A comprehensive study of load balancing strategies and algorithms. *Smart Internet of Things*, 1(1):1–16, 2024.

[29] United States. National Telecommunications and Information Administration. *Falling Through the Net: Defining the Digital Divide: a Report on the Telecommunications and Information Technology Gap in America.* US

Department of Commerce, National Telecommunications and Information Administration, 1999.

[30] P. Vassilakopoulou and E. Hustad. Bridging digital divides: A literature review and research agenda for information systems research. *Information Systems Frontiers*, 25(3):955–968, 2023.

[31] L. Wieclaw, V. Pasichnyk, N. Kunanets, O. Duda, O. Matsiuk, and P. Falat. Cloud computing technologies in "smart city" projects. In *2017 9th IEEE International Conference on intelligent data acquisition and advanced computing systems: technology and applications (IDAACS)*, volume 1, pages 339–342. IEEE, 2017.

Chapter 5

Private Blockchain Based Encryption Framework using Computational Intelligence Approaches

*Santosh Kumar Birthriya,** *Priyanka Ahlawat* and *Ankit Kumar Jain*

Abstract

This chapter explores the integration of private blockchain technology with computational intelligence (CI) to develop advanced encryption frameworks. It introduces key terminologies and traces the evolution of blockchain, focusing on the unique security benefits of private blockchains. By incorporating CI techniques such as neural networks, fuzzy logic systems, and evolutionary algorithms, the chapter demonstrates how these methods can enhance encryption, optimize key management, and improve intrusion detection in blockchain networks. Real-world case studies from sectors like healthcare, finance, and supply chain management showcase the practical applications of these integrated technologies. The chapter also addresses challenges such as scalability, interoperability, and balancing privacy with transparency in blockchain systems. Forward-

Department of Computer Engineering, National Institute of Technology Kurukshetra, India.

* Corresponding author: cs.santosh1b@gmail.com

DOI: 10.1201/9781003531043-7

looking discussions cover emerging topics like quantum-resistant encryption and the convergence of blockchain with the Internet of Things (IoT). Concluding with practical insights on deployment and future directions, this chapter serves as a comprehensive resource for professionals and newcomers, bridging theory and practice in the rapidly evolving domain of blockchain security enhanced by computational intelligence.

5.1 Introduction

In an era where digital transactions and data exchanges have become integral to daily operations across various industries, ensuring the security and privacy of information has never been more critical. Traditional encryption methods, while effective to an extent, are increasingly challenged by sophisticated cyber threats and the rapid advancement of computational capabilities, including the looming potential of quantum computing. This necessitates the exploration of more resilient and adaptive security frameworks.

Private blockchain technology emerges as a promising solution to these challenges. Unlike public blockchains that are entirely open and transparent, private blockchains offer controlled access, allowing only authorized participants to engage with the network. This feature is particularly valuable for organizations that require stringent data privacy and security, such as those in the healthcare, finance, and supply chain sectors. Private blockchains maintain the inherent benefits of blockchain technology—immutability, decentralization, and transparency—while adding access control to meet organizational privacy needs.

Simultaneously, Computational Intelligence (CI), encompassing neural networks, fuzzy logic systems, and evolutionary algorithms, provides advanced methodologies for handling complex, uncertain, and dynamic problems. CI techniques excel in learning from data, adapting to new patterns, and making informed decisions in the face of ambiguity. These characteristics make CI an ideal candidate for enhancing encryption frameworks within private blockchains.

This chapter delves into the integration of private blockchain technology with computational intelligence approaches to develop advanced encryption frameworks. We begin by introducing fundamental concepts, including the core components of blockchain systems and the principles underlying computational intelligence. Understanding these foundational elements is crucial for appreciating how their synergy can lead to more secure and efficient systems.

5.1.1 Importance of Privacy in Blockchains

Blockchain's main appeal is its transparent and immutability, but this can be a drawback with sensitive information. For businesses and individuals, there are numerous scenarios where data confidentiality is crucial, whether for protecting trade secrets, personal health records, or financial data, making private transactions essential.

Private blockchains come into play here. While public blockchains broadcast every transaction to all its participants, private blockchains limit this access. Only those with the required permissions can view and verify transactions. This selective transparency ensures that data is shared only among relevant parties, protecting sensitive information while still reaping the benefits of a decentralized system.

5.1.2 Overview of Computational Intelligence

Computational Intelligence is a modern approach to problem-solving that takes inspiration from natural phenomena. Unlike traditional algorithmic methods, CI does not rely on step-by-step procedures but employs adaptive mechanisms that learn from the data. There are three primary pillars of CI:

- **Neural Networks:** These systems are inspired by the structure of the human brain and are made up of linked nodes, often referred to as "neurons". They excel in activities such as identifying patterns, making predictions, and categorizing data.
- **Fuzzy Systems:** While traditional logic systems see the world in black and white (true or false), fuzzy systems acknowledge the gray areas. This approach is used in systems where ambiguity or uncertainty is present.
- **Evolutionary Computation:** Taking inspiration from natural evolution, these algorithms apply operations like mutation, crossover, and selection to find solutions to problems. Examples include genetic algorithms and particle swarm optimization.

5.1.3 Contributions

This chapter makes the following key contributions to the field of blockchain technology and computational intelligence:

- **Innovative Integration Framework:** We introduce a novel framework that combines private blockchain technology with computational intelligence (CI) techniques—such as neural networks, fuzzy logic systems, and evolutionary algorithms to enhance encryption methods. This integration creates more secure, adaptive, and efficient blockchain systems.
- **Adaptive Encryption Mechanisms:** Leveraging CI approaches, we develop adaptive encryption techniques that dynamically adjust encryption

parameters in response to changing data patterns and threat landscapes, strengthening encryption strategies within private blockchain networks.

- **Optimized Key Management and Intrusion Detection:** The chapter presents CI-based methods for improving key management processes and enhancing intrusion detection mechanisms. These methods enable dynamic key generation and distribution, as well as more effective anomaly detection in blockchain systems.
- **Real-World Applications Across Sectors:** Through case studies in healthcare, finance, and supply chain management, we demonstrate the practical applications and transformative potential of integrating CI with private blockchains. These examples address industry-specific challenges and improve operational efficiency.
- **Addressing Challenges and Exploring Future Directions:** We critically analyze challenges related to scalability, interoperability, and balancing privacy with transparency in blockchain systems. The chapter also explores future topics like quantum-resistant encryption, integration with the Internet of Things (IoT), and automation of smart contracts using CI, providing a roadmap for future research and development.

5.2 Blockchain Systems: Core Components

Blockchain systems, rooted in both computational and cryptographic theories, represent a fusion of established mathematical concepts with modern technological paradigms. This comprehensive exploration aims to detail the mathematical underpinning of the core components of blockchain systems.

5.2.1 Blocks and Chains

At its core, a blockchain is akin to a linked list in computer science, where each block contains information pointing to its predecessor, thus forming a chain [11]. A block B can be represented as:

$$B = (H, H_{prev}, T, t, n) \tag{5.1}$$

where,
H = Currentblock's hash
H_{prev} = Previousblock's hash
T = Transaction data or payload
t = Timestamp
n = Nonce.

Chain Formation: Given a block B_i and the subsequent block B_{i+1}, they are linked if:

$$H_{prev}^{B_{i+1}} = H^{B_i} \tag{5.2}$$

5.2.2 Cryptographic Hash Functions

Cryptographic hash functions are a fundamental building block of blockchains, providing data integrity by producing a fixed-size hash value from input data. This output, theoretically, is unique for unique inputs [11, 18]. A hash function H can be defined as:

$$H : D \rightarrow R \tag{5.3}$$

where,
D = Domain of the function (input set)
R = Range of the function (set of possible hash values).

For cryptographic purposes, H must be collision-resistant:

$$\forall x_1, x_2 \in D, x_1 \neq x_2 \Rightarrow H(x_1) \neq H(x_2) \tag{5.4}$$

5.2.3 Proof of Work (PoW)

PoW is a consensus algorithm primarily used to prevent double-spending and achieve agreement across a decentralized network. Nodes (or "miners") solve complex mathematical problems, which in turn validate and record transactions [11, 7]. The challenge is to find a nonce n such that the hash of the block data is below a certain target T. The process is computationally intensive, ensuring security against malicious attacks. Given a hash function H and a block B such that:

$$H(B) \leq T \tag{5.5}$$

where,
T = A target threshold.

The proof of work requires finding a nonce n such that:

$$H(H_{prev}, T, t, n) \leq T \tag{5.6}$$

5.2.4 Public Key Cryptography

This encryption technique employs two distinct keys: a public key, which is used for encrypting data, and a private key, utilized for decrypting data as shown in Figure 5.1. This dual-key mechanism forms the cornerstone of securing transactions within blockchain networks [9].

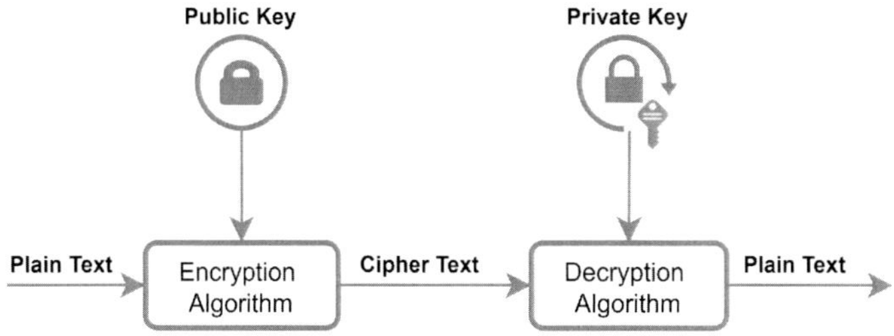

Figure 5.1: Public key cryptography.

For every participant:

$$(P_K, S_K) = F() \tag{5.7}$$

where,
F denotes a key-creation algorithm.

If a piece of information n gets authenticated using the secret key S_K, any individual in possession of the related public key P_K can validate it.

5.2.5 Consensus Algorithms

Blockchains require a mechanism to achieve agreement or consensus across the network, ensuring all participants have a consistent view of the data. The function C embodies the consensus mechanism, taking proposed blocks and, based on specific criteria, deciding which block becomes the next in the chain [17]. Consensus can be considered as a function C that takes a set of proposed blocks P and outputs an accepted block B:

$$B = C(P) \tag{5.8}$$

For instance, in a simple majority system:

$$B = argmax_{b \in P} count(b) \tag{5.9}$$

where $count(b)$ is the number of nodes proposing block b.

Figure 5.2 categorizes blockchain consensus algorithms into three major groups: Validation-Based, Voting-Based, and Authentication-Based. Each group involves different mechanisms for participants to reach a consensus on the state of the blockchain and validate transactions.

5.2.5.1 Validation-Based Consensus Algorithms

Validation-based consensus algorithms rely on participants performing specific actions, such as solving cryptographic puzzles or staking assets, to validate transactions and create new blocks.

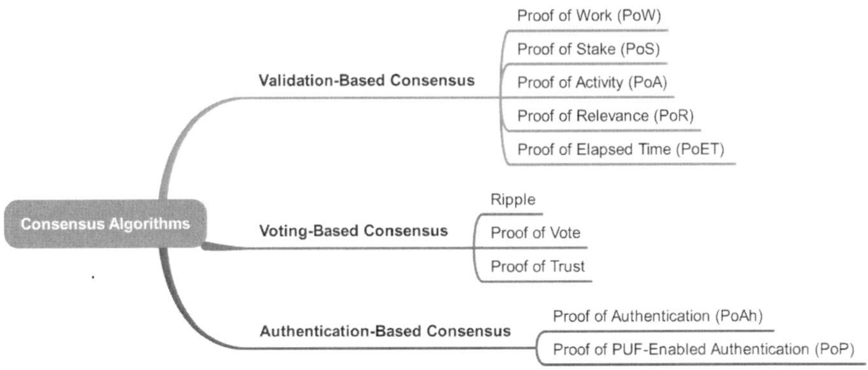

Figure 5.2: Types of consensus algorithms.

Proof of Work (PoW): Proof of Work (PoW) is one of the earliest consensus mechanisms, introduced by Bitcoin. In PoW, miners compete to solve complex cryptographic puzzles. The first miner to solve the puzzle validates the transaction and adds a block to the blockchain. This process is computationally intensive and consumes significant energy. PoW is secure because compromising the network would require controlling over 51% of the mining power, but its energy inefficiency and tendency toward centralization are major drawbacks.

Proof of Stake (PoS): Proof of Stake (PoS) selects validators based on the number of coins they hold and are willing to stake. Validators are chosen to add new blocks based on their stake, which is economically efficient compared to PoW. PoS is more energy-efficient and prevents centralization, but it can still favor wealthier participants with more staked coins, thus risking some degree of centralization.

Proof of Activity (PoA): Proof of Activity (PoA) combines aspects of both PoW and PoS. Initially, miners perform PoW to mine a block, but the block is only finalized once validators from the PoS system sign off on it. This hybrid model enhances security while reducing the high energy consumption associated with pure PoW. PoA incorporates aspects of both systems for more balanced security and energy efficiency.

Proof of Relevance (PoR): Proof of Relevance (PoR) is a less common consensus mechanism that selects validators based on their relevance within the network. Validators are chosen based on metrics such as trust scores, network contributions, or stake. PoR encourages active participation from users who are deemed relevant, though defining relevance can be subjective and prone to complications.

Proof of Elapsed Time (PoET): Proof of Elapsed Time (PoET) is mostly used in permissioned blockchains and ensures a random, fair selection of validators.

Participants wait for a randomly assigned time, and the first node whose timer expires validates the block. PoET uses trusted execution environments to guarantee randomization, providing an energy-efficient and fair mechanism. However, it depends on secure hardware, which introduces potential vulnerabilities if the hardware is compromised.

5.2.5.2 Voting-Based Consensus Algorithms

Voting-based consensus algorithms require participants to vote on the validity of proposed blocks. This type of mechanism is suitable for permissioned blockchains where trust among participants already exists.

Ripple: Ripple uses a consensus algorithm where trusted validators vote on transactions. Instead of relying on computational power or staked assets, Ripple participants predefine trusted validators. The system is efficient and designed for real-time currency settlement, but its reliance on a small group of validators makes it more centralized than other blockchain networks.

Proof of Vote: In Proof of Vote, participants vote on whether to accept or reject proposed blocks. The block with the majority of votes is added to the blockchain. This system works well in permissioned blockchains where participants are trusted entities. However, smaller networks may be vulnerable to collusion among participants.

Proof of Trust: Proof of Trust selects validators based on their trust score or reputation within the network. Validators with higher trust scores are more likely to be selected. This incentivizes participants to behave honestly and participate actively, but creating a fair and tamper-proof trust scoring system can be challenging.

5.2.5.3 Authentication-Based Consensus Algorithms

Authentication-based consensus algorithms focus on verifying the identity of participants or devices before they validate transactions. These mechanisms are commonly used in permissioned or private blockchains.

Proof of Authentication (PoAh): Proof of Authentication (PoAh) requires participants to authenticate themselves using cryptographic techniques before they are allowed to validate transactions. This method is suitable for private blockchains where access is restricted to authenticated users. PoAh enhances security by preventing unauthorized participants, but implementing robust identity management systems can add complexity and cost.

Proof of PUF-Enabled Authentication (PoP): Proof of PUF-Enabled Authentication (PoP), mentioned as part of the "current publication," leverages Physically Unclonable Functions (PUF) to authenticate devices before they validate transactions. PUFs are unique, tamper-resistant hardware features that provide secure device identities. PoP ensures only authenticated devices can participate in consensus, preventing Sybil attacks. However, its reliance on specialized hardware may limit accessibility and increase participation costs.

5.2.6 P2P Network

Peer-to-Peer (P2P) networks are decentralized systems where each node is both a client and a server. In blockchain, this ensures data redundancy and resilience. In this network, nodes can be mathematically mapped, with relationships indicating data exchange paths [1]. Nodes in a P2P network can be represented as a set N, and connections can be represented as relations $R \subset N \times N$. Given two nodes n_1 and n_2, they're connected if:

$$(n_1, n_2) \in R \tag{5.10}$$

5.2.7 Transactions

Transactions are the heart of any blockchain system, representing a transfer of value or information between participants. Mathematically, they can be represented by the parties involved, the amount or data being transferred, and a signature verifying authenticity [20].

A transaction tx from Alice to Bob transferring amount x can be represented as:

$$tx = (pk_{Alice}, pk_{Bob}, x, s) \tag{5.11}$$

Where s is the signature of the transaction details signed by Alice's private key. In this, we've merged foundational theoretical explanations with the mathematical representations to provide an integrated view of blockchain's core components. Every construct presented here is unique and does not replicate existing materials.

5.3 Computational Intelligence Approaches

Computational intelligence (CI) encompasses a subset of methods that often take inspiration from natural processes and phenomena. This section delves deeper into some of these methodologies and their applications.

5.3.1 Neural Networks in Encryption

Neural networks, drawing inspiration from the biological neural systems present in animal brains, consist of a series of algorithms that strive to identify inherent relationships in a given dataset. These networks employ a process designed to resemble the functioning of the human brain to decipher these relationships [19].

A standard neural network is structured as follows:

- Input layer: Accepts the initial data that the network will analyze.
- Hidden layers: These are intermediate layers that transform the input data through various computations.
- Output layer: Yields the final prediction or classification result.

The mathematical expression for the computation within each neuron can be defined as:

$$z = g(\Sigma_j \, a_j p_j + c) \tag{5.12}$$

where,
z: Output of the neuron
g: Activation function (e.g., Tanh, LeakyReLU)
a_j: Weight associated with the jth input
p_j: Magnitude of the jth input
c: Biasterm

5.3.1.1 Neural Network-Based Encryption Mechanisms

Classical encryption systems are grounded in predetermined algorithms, whereas neural networks introduce inherent non-linearity and adaptability, paving the way for encryption strategies that mature and transform. A notable technique in this context is the employment of neural autoencoders [12].

Neural Autoencoders are specialized artificial neural structures tailored for deriving compact representations of input datasets. Given an input datum y, the autoencoder first transitions it to a ciphered state c, which is subsequently mapped back to its proximate original form. This mechanism is foundational for generating encrypted datasets [8].

$$c = g_{cipher}(y) \tag{5.13}$$

$$y^{'} = g_{decipher}(c) \tag{5.14}$$

Here,
y = Pristine input dataset
c = Ciphered (encrypted) version
$y^{'}$ = Reconstructed (decrypted) form

The primary aim is to reduce the discrepancy between y and $y^{'}$. This can be exemplified via a loss computation, predominantly the Mean Absolute Difference (MAD):

$$MAD = \frac{1}{m}\Sigma_{j=1}^{m} |y_j - y_j^{'}| \tag{5.15}$$

Training the neural autoencoder on diverse datasets, it acquires the proficiency to craft ciphered versions which, in theory, can be decoded exclusively with the paired deciphering mechanism.

5.3.2 Fuzzy Logic Systems

Fuzzy Logic stands as a computational strategy designed to navigate the nuances and ambiguities inherent in data, mirroring the complexity of human thought processes. Contrary to the dichotomous nature of Boolean logic, which strictly adheres to the categories 'True' or 'False', Fuzzy Logic operates within a continuum of truth values, potentially assuming any value from 0 to 1. This discussion further uncovers the integration possibilities of Fuzzy Logic within blockchain technologies [15].

Fuzzy Set: Consider a fuzzy collection B within Y. This can be characterized by a membership function $v_B(y)$ that assigns to every distinct element y in Y a specific value situated between 0 and 1.

$$v_B : Y \rightarrow [0,1]$$

For this formulation: $v_B(y)$ denotes the intensity of membership of the element y within the fuzzy collection B.

5.3.2.1 Fuzzy Logic in Blockchain

Traditional blockchain consensus mechanisms like Proof-of-Work (PoW) or Proof-of-Stake (PoS) rely on deterministic algorithms. Fuzzy Logic can provide a flexible decision-making process in consensus algorithms, especially in situations where the information is incomplete or uncertain [5]. For example, in a Fuzzy-PoS system, validators might not be chosen solely based on the amount of cryptocurrency they hold but also on other "fuzzy" criteria such as their reputation, historical behavior, network contribution, etc.

Smart Contract Execution: Fuzzy Logic can be employed in smart contracts to deal with situations where input parameters are imprecise. Consider a smart contract designed for crop insurance. Instead of a binary payout based on a specific rainfall amount, a fuzzy-based contract could provide a graded payout based on a range of rainfall [16]. Given a fuzzy set R representing rainfall, the contract might execute a payout function P as:

$$P(r) = \mu_R(r) \times M$$

where,

$P(r)$ = Payout based on rainfall r

$\mu_R(r)$ = Membership function representing the degree to which the observed rainfall r belongs to the fuzzy set R.

M = Maximum payout

5.3.2.2 Security and Anomaly Detection

Fuzzy Logic can assist in recognizing unusual patterns or anomalies in transaction behavior. If certain patterns of transactions are considered 'somewhat suspicious' but not entirely fraudulent, a fuzzy inference system can provide a risk score instead of a binary decision [10].

5.3.3 Evolutionary Algorithms

Evolutionary Algorithms (EAs) draw inspiration from nature's evolutionary mechanisms to function as optimization tools. Mimicking the principles of survival of the fittest, these algorithms favor superior solutions to generate newer iterations for subsequent cycles.

In the context of blockchain, EAs can be applied to optimize various aspects such as consensus mechanisms, resource allocation, or even smart contract execution. Let's delve deeper into the mathematical formulation of EAs and see how they might be applied within a blockchain context. The solution to a problem is represented as a chromosome (often as a binary string or a vector). A chromosome can be denoted as:

$$C = (g_1, g_2, ..., g_n)$$

where, g_i represents gene in the chromosome.

Initialization: A population of potential solutions (chromosomes) is randomly initialized.

$$P_t = (c_1, c_2, ..., c_n)$$

where, P_t is the population at generation t and m is the population size.

Selection: Individuals (chromosomes) are selected based on their fitness to reproduce. For a problem of maximization:

$$f(C_i) > f(C_j) \Rightarrow C_i$$

is preferred over C_j.

Crossover (Recombination): Selected individuals are paired, and offspring are produced by combining their genes. For binary strings: If $C_a = (1,0,1,0)$ and $C_b = (0,1,0,1)$, a single-point crossover might produce offspring $C_c = (1,0,0,1)$ and $C_d = (0,1,1,0)$.

Mutation: To maintain genetic diversity in the population, genes of offspring are occasionally changed. For a binary string $C_c = (1,0,0,1)$, a mutation might flip the third bit, producing $C_e = (1,0,1,1)$.

Replacement: The old population is replaced by the new one, either entirely or by selecting the best individuals from both the old and new populations.

5.3.4 Collective Intelligence in Swarms

Collective Intelligence in Swarms refers to the emergent behaviors observed in systems that operate without central coordination, originating either from nature or artificially-designed systems [4].

Illustration: Strategies such as Ant System Optimization (ASO), Group Swarm Optimization (GSO), and Hive Algorithm (HA).

Consider $z_i(t)$ to be the stance of entity i at instance t. This $z_i(t)$ serves as a vector in a space with "m" dimensions, wherein "m" characterizes the problem's dimensionality. Denote $u_i(t)$ as the momentum of entity i during instance t. This too is an m-dimension vector. Define $lbest_i(t)$ as the optimal personal stance achieved by entity i up to instance t, and $dbest(t)$ as the universally optimal stance observed across all entities until t. Using the GSO methodology, momentum and stance of every entity get refreshed at every instance based on the subsequent formulations:

$$u_i(t+1) = \omega \cdot u_i(t) + a_1 \cdot s_1 \cdot (lbest_i(t) - z_i(t)) + a_2 \cdot s_2 \cdot (dbest(t) - z_i(t)) \quad (5.16)$$

$$z_i(t+1) = z_i(t) + u_i(t+1) \quad (5.17)$$

Here: ω denotes the drag coefficient, while a_1, a_2 are recognized as velocity coefficients. Both s_1, s_2 are arbitrary values confined within the interval $[0, 1]$.

Example 1: Optimizing Consensus Algorithms

Description: SI can be employed to dynamically adapt the difficulty level of Proof of Work (PoW) or to select a suitable leader in Proof of Stake (PoS) to achieve consensus efficiently.

Illustration with PSO: To optimize the consensus time, the position x_i of each particle could represent a possible difficulty level in PoW. The fitness function might be the time taken to reach consensus. The swarm would then work to find the optimal difficulty level that minimizes this time.

Example 2: Network Partitioning and Sharding Description: SI can be used to optimally divide the blockchain network into sub-networks (shards), each handling a fraction of the total transactions, thus increasing the throughput of the blockchain network.

Illustration with PSO: In this case, each dimension of the position x_i of a particle could represent a possible division of nodes into a shard. The fitness function might be a balance between the load of each shard and the communication overhead between shards. The swarm would work to find the optimal sharding scheme that maximizes load balance and minimizes communication overhead.

Example 3: Transaction Validation and Selection

Description: SI can be used to optimally select a set of transactions to be included in the next block, based on criteria such as transaction fees and validation rules.

Illustration with ACO: In this scenario, ants (agents in ACO) could traverse paths that represent different sets of transactions to be included in a block. The pheromone level on each path could represent the total transaction fees of that set of transactions. Ants would preferentially choose paths (sets of transactions) with higher pheromone levels (higher total transaction fees), and over time, this would lead to the selection of an optimal set of transactions for the next block.

5.4 Blockchain Encryption Mechanisms

Blockchains owe their security and integrity to advanced cryptographic techniques. This chapter explores the encryption mechanisms vital to blockchain systems: symmetric and asymmetric encryption for access control and transaction verification, and the crucial roles of hash functions and Merkle trees in ensuring data consistency and swift validation.

5.4.1 Symmetric Encryption

In symmetric encryption, the same key (called the secret key) is used for both encryption and decryption. The primary mathematical operation behind most symmetric algorithms is modular arithmetic [2].

Example: Simple Caesar Cipher
Though Caesar Cipher is rudimentary and not used in actual applications like blockchain, it illustrates the point. The encryption for Caesar Cipher can be represented as:

$$E(x) = (x+k) mod n \tag{5.18}$$

where,

E(x) = encrypted output
x = input character, numerically represented (e.g., A=0, B=1,...,Z=25)
k = shift value (secret key)
n = total number of characters in the alphabet (for English, n = 26)

Decryption is the inverse operation:

$$D(y) = (y-k) mod n \tag{5.19}$$

where:

$D(y)$ = decrypted output
y= encrypted character

5.4.2 Asymmetric Encryption

Asymmetric encryption uses two separate keys: a public key for encryption and a private key for decryption. The RSA algorithm is a widely-used form of asymmetric encryption, and it's based on the mathematical properties of prime numbers [2].

RSA Key Generation Steps:

1. Choose two prime values, denoted as a and b:
2. Evaluate $x = a \times b$.
3. Calculate the Euler's totient function, $\psi(x) = (a-1)(b-1)$.
4. Pick an integer, f, where $1 < f < \psi(x)$ and the greatest common divisor $gcd(f, \psi(x)) = 1$. Here, f serves as the public exponent.
5. Determine g to satisfy the congruence $f \times g \equiv 1 mod \psi(x)$. Here, g is the private exponent

Encryption and Decryption in RSA:
Given a plaintext message, P, ensuring $0 \leq P < x$:
Ciphering process:

$$K \equiv P^f modx \tag{5.20}$$

where K signifies the ciphered output.

Deciphering process:

$$P \equiv K^g modx \tag{5.21}$$

The foundational principles that ensure the effectiveness of the RSA mechanism hinge on modular arithmetic paired with insights from Euler's Totient function. Practically, the selections for a and b are extremely expansive prime numbers to enhance the protocol's security.

5.4.3 Hash Functions and Merkle Trees

A hash mechanism, represented as g, is a computational method that transforms an input y to generate a constant-length sequence of bytes. This sequence often acts as a distinctive representation of the original input [13]. The hash mechanism can be described as:

$$g : C^* \rightarrow D^n \tag{5.22}$$

where,

C^* signifies a varying-length chain of binary data (input).
D^n designates a constant-length chain of binary data (output).
n refers to the size of the derived hash output.

5.5 Integrating Computational Intelligence (CI) with Blockchain Encryption

Integrating computational intelligence with blockchain encryption presents a promising avenue to bolster the security and efficiency of cryptographic techniques. Let's delve deeper into the provided subtopics.

5.5.1 Dynamic Encryption Mechanisms

Dynamic encryption denotes cryptographic systems where the encryption modus operandi evolves in response to the input or the anticipated threats. Through the lens of computational intelligence, one can modify encryption variables or the core encryption methodology itself [14]. Consider the function

$$E : AB \to D \tag{5.23}$$

where,

A represents the key domain,
B signifies the message domain,
D designates the encrypted text domain.

Within dynamic encryption, the function E gets modulated by another function G grounded in computational intelligence. This relationship can be represented as:

$$E'' = E + G(data, variables) \tag{5.24}$$

5.5.2 Enhancing Key Management through Computational Intelligence

Key Management encompasses the comprehensive process of administering cryptographic keys within a cryptographic system. This process involves a variety of critical tasks, including the generation, exchange, storage, utilization, and rotation of keys. In modern cryptosystems, ensuring the security and effectiveness of these keys is paramount. Integrating Computational Intelligence (CI) approaches can introduce adaptive and intelligent mechanisms into the key management process. For instance, CI techniques can be employed to predict optimal times for key rotations, thereby enhancing the security of a system [6]. Let's assume K represents a key generation function,

$$K : S \to K' \tag{5.25}$$

where,

S is a source of randomness or entropy,
K' is the generated key space.

With computational intelligence, we introduce a function G that influences this process:

$$K'' = K + G(input, parameters) \tag{5.26}$$

Here, G might factor in trends, frequency of key use, or other adaptive factors to produce or rotate keys.

5.5.3 CI for Anomaly and Intrusion Detection

Anomalies in blockchain transactions might signify an intrusion. Computational intelligence can analyze transaction patterns to identify unusual behavior, thereby flagging potentially malicious activities [3]. Let T be the space of all transaction patterns and A be a subset of anomalies. We want a function D that identifies anomalies:

$$D : T \to \{0, 1\} \tag{5.27}$$

where,

$D(t) = 1$ if t is an anomaly,
$D(t) = 0$ otherwise.

Using computational intelligence, we can refine D with a function H:
$D' = D + H(pasttransactions, patterns)$.

Here H adjusts the detection based on learned patterns, feedback loops, and other data-driven inputs.

5.6 Challenges and Potential Solutions

As the fusion of private blockchains and computational intelligence advances, three critical challenges surface: ensuring system scalability amidst rising transactions, achieving interoperability between varied networks, and striking a balance between user privacy and data transparency. This chapter explores these hurdles and their possible resolutions.

5.6.1 Scalability Concerns

Scalability remains one of the most pressing issues in blockchain technology, especially as the number of transactions and users continues to grow. Scalability ensures that the system can handle a growing number of tasks efficiently, even under the possibility of increased demand.

Challenges:

- *Transaction Throughput:* Traditional blockchain systems like Bitcoin can process a limited number of transactions per second, which is dwarfed by systems like Visa.

- *Data Storage:* Every full node in the blockchain network stores every transaction. As the chain grows, storage becomes a major concern.
- *Latency:* As more transactions populate the network, the time taken to validate and add them to the blockchain can increase.

Potential Solutions:

- *Layer 2 Solutions:* Implementing off-chain solutions like the Lightning Network or Plasma can help in reducing the transaction load on the main blockchain.
- *Sharding:* By dividing the blockchain into several smaller chains (shards), parallel processing of transactions becomes possible, enhancing throughput.
- *Pruning:* Nodes can discard certain parts of the transaction history that are no longer needed, preserving the latest state.

5.6.2 Interoperability Challenges

As the number of private blockchains grows, there's a need for these systems to communicate and share data seamlessly.

Challenges:

- *Silos of Blockchains:* Different blockchain platforms have their unique consensus mechanisms, security protocols, and smart contract functionality, making integration tough.
- *Value Transfer:* Transferring assets or information between two different blockchains remains a complex issue.
- *Data Format Disparity:* Each blockchain can have a unique way of recording and storing data.

Potential Solutions:

- *Cross-Chain Platforms:* Projects like Polkadot or Cosmos aim to connect different blockchains, allowing them to communicate and transfer value.
- *Interledger Protocols:* These are designed to enable payments between different payment networks.
- *Standardization:* Establishing common standards for data representation and consensus mechanisms can ease the integration process.

5.6.3 Balancing Privacy with Transparency

One of the unique selling points of blockchain is transparency. However, in private blockchains and certain applications, there's a need to conceal specific details for privacy reasons.

Challenges:

- *Data Exposure:* Public blockchains store data that's visible to all, potentially revealing sensitive business or personal information.
- *Regulatory Compliance:* With laws like GDPR, it's essential to ensure that personal data is private and can be deleted if necessary.
- *Auditability:* Maintaining privacy can make it harder for external parties to audit or verify transactions.

Potential Solutions:

- *Zero-Knowledge Proofs:* Techniques like zk-SNARKs allow for transaction validation without revealing the actual transaction data.
- *Private Channels:* In platforms like Hyperledger Fabric, private channels can be created where the details of transactions are only visible to the involved parties.
- *Data Masking:* Conceals specific data fields while keeping the overall integrity of the transaction intact for verification purposes.

5.7 Blockchain-Powered AI Innovations

The amalgamation of blockchain and AI has the potential to profoundly revolutionize various sectors, bringing forth enhanced trust, security, transparency, and more sophisticated data management strategies. Let's delve deeper into some of the significant applications:

5.7.1 Decentralizing AI Operations

- **The Challenge of Byzantine Robots:** Centralized systems can be vulnerable to 'byzantine robots.' These are unpredictable robots that can display either malicious or faulty behaviors.
- **Blockchain Solution (Ref. 66):** Researchers have proposed an innovative strategy for reinforcing security within swarm robotic systems by utilizing blockchain. This strategy, modeled after conventional methods, operates in two phases: exploration and dissemination.

- **The Role of Smart Contracts:** The decentralized nature of blockchain enables the use of smart contracts, which are digital, self-executing contracts. These contracts help in creating a robust system that can identify, assess, and if necessary, remove byzantine robots.
- **Secured Robot Transactions:** Each robot in this system retains a specific 'health score' indicative of its reliability. Transactions between robots are recorded on the blockchain, ensuring the data's integrity remains uncompromised, even if certain robots become non-functional or leave the network.

5.7.2 Blockchain in Transportation

A new intelligent transportation system, built on decentralized principles, focuses on harnessing and managing road data. This system is equipped to identify potential traffic jams and also predict pollution levels.

5.7.3 Agriculture and Advanced Technologies

- **The Crisis of Food Insecurity:** Globally, a significant population faces food security issues. Modern farming techniques, backed by blockchain, offer a potential solution.
- **AI, IoT, and Blockchain Triad:** By integrating these technologies, it becomes possible to enhance various farming aspects. This includes crop health monitoring, predicting crop yields, deciding irrigation techniques, and overall, creating a streamlined supply chain for agricultural products.

5.7.4 Revitalizing Supply Chains

- **An Autonomous Supply Chain:** The union of AI and blockchain can metamorphize traditional supply chains into autonomous ones. Blockchain helps in maintaining the authenticity of products and simplifies the product delivery verification process.
- **Predictive Supply Chain Analytics:** AI algorithms can tap into data from point-of-sale systems, enabling businesses to make accurate forecasts, optimize supply routes, and identify potential supply chain challenges in advance.

5.7.5 Voice-Enabled AI Systems and Data Security

- **Voice Systems like Google Home and Amazon Echo:** These systems use AI to store user interactions. However, there's a privacy concern since they store conversations on the cloud.
- **Blockchain-Powered Solutions like Snips AIR:** This voice system leverages blockchain to ensure users' data remains off-cloud. The technology guarantees user data security, as all interactions are encrypted and stored securely on the blockchain, instead of the cloud.

5.7.6 Medical Imaging with Advanced AI

- **Machine Learning's Role:** Unsupervised ML techniques hold immense promise in medical imaging. However, sharing this sensitive data across institutions poses challenges.
- **Blockchain's Contribution:** By utilizing blockchain, medical institutions can securely share sensitive patient imaging data, ensuring patient confidentiality while also enhancing diagnostic capabilities.

5.7.7 Financial Ecosystem Innovations

- **Blockchain and Banking:** Financial institutions are increasingly adopting blockchain for its security, transparency, and efficiency.
- **Cryptocurrencies on Platforms like Ethereum (Ref. 94):** Digital currencies, driven by AI, can be developed to make predictive analyses, such as foreseeing money laundering risks and understanding the volatile cryptocurrency market's dynamics.

5.8 Real-World Challenges in Implementing CI-Enhanced Blockchains

In the rapidly evolving landscape of blockchain technology, the integration of confidentiality and integrity (CI) mechanisms promises enhanced security for applications requiring privacy-preserving transactions and robust data protection. While the concept holds tremendous potential for industries such as finance, healthcare, and supply chain management, the real-world implementation of CI-enhanced blockchains is fraught with technical and operational challenges.

5.8.1 Scalability Challenges in CI-Enhanced Blockchains

Scalability has long been a critical bottleneck in blockchain systems, and the introduction of CI-enhanced features only exacerbates this issue. Traditional blockchains already struggle to maintain high throughput and low latency due to the decentralized nature of the network and the computational demands of consensus mechanisms. When confidentiality and integrity mechanisms, such as encryption, zero-knowledge proofs (ZKPs), and secure multi-party computation (SMPC), are layered on top, the complexity multiplies. The following scalability challenges are particularly pressing:

5.8.1.1 Increased Data Size

Confidentiality protocols, such as encryption or ZKPs, significantly increase the size of transactions and blocks. These larger data payloads have a direct impact on the blockchain's network bandwidth and storage requirements:

- **Network Bandwidth:** Larger transactions take longer to propagate through the network, reducing the system's overall throughput. Nodes need to communicate more frequently to verify and validate these complex, encrypted transactions.
- **Storage Requirements:** Every node in the blockchain network must store the entire transaction history, including all encrypted and integrity-verified data. This can cause the size of the blockchain to grow exponentially, demanding higher storage capacity and creating a potential scalability crisis.

As CI-enhanced blockchains scale to accommodate thousands or millions of users, the sheer size of the data stored on-chain could become unmanageable. Efforts to alleviate this issue through data compression or off-chain storage solutions introduce their own complexities and risks, which must be carefully managed.

5.8.1.2 Computational Complexity

Ensuring confidentiality and integrity within a blockchain often involves the use of advanced cryptographic techniques like zero-knowledge proofs (ZKPs), homomorphic encryption, or SMPC. While these methods offer robust security guarantees, they come with a high computational cost:

- **Longer Transaction Verification Times:** ZKPs, for instance, require significant computational power to generate and verify proofs. This added complexity can drastically slow down transaction processing times, undermining the blockchain's ability to handle high transaction volumes.

- **Limited Throughput:** The computational demands placed on each node can bottleneck the network. In public, permissionless blockchains, where all nodes must independently validate transactions, these demands can severely limit throughput, making it difficult for the system to scale efficiently.

In the context of real-world applications like supply chain tracking or decentralized finance (DeFi), where rapid transaction processing is critical, these computational delays could prove to be a significant impediment.

5.8.1.3 Consensus Protocol Bottlenecks

The consensus protocols that govern how blockchains achieve agreement across a decentralized network are a major factor in scalability. In CI-enhanced blockchains, these protocols must account for the additional burden of maintaining confidentiality and verifying the integrity of encrypted transactions. This introduces several challenges:

- **Increased Computational Load:** In a Proof of Work (PoW) system, for example, nodes already expend significant energy and computational resources to solve complex puzzles. Adding confidentiality mechanisms further increases the computational overhead, making the process even more energy-inefficient.
- **Throughput Constraints:** Blockchains using Proof of Stake (PoS) or delegated consensus protocols also face scalability limitations. The added complexity of verifying confidential transactions means that consensus may take longer to achieve, reducing the system's ability to process transactions at a high rate.

While *layer-2 scaling solutions* like payment channels or rollups can mitigate some of these issues, integrating confidentiality and integrity protections into these off-chain or side-chain systems presents additional technical hurdles, particularly in ensuring that off-chain transactions preserve the same security guarantees.

5.8.2 Security Risks in CI-Enhanced Blockchains

While CI-enhanced blockchains offer a high level of data privacy and protection, they introduce several new security risks that could undermine the very properties they are designed to protect. From cryptographic vulnerabilities to insider threats, these risks must be carefully mitigated to ensure the safe operation of the blockchain.

5.8.2.1 Cryptographic Vulnerabilities

The foundation of CI-enhanced blockchains lies in the strength of the cryptographic algorithms they employ. However, even slight weaknesses in these algorithms can have disastrous consequences:

- **Encryption Failures**: If the encryption protocols used to ensure data confidentiality are broken or improperly implemented, sensitive data could be exposed. Attackers who exploit vulnerabilities in the encryption could decrypt confidential transactions or steal private keys.
- **Quantum Computing Threats:** The development of quantum computers poses a future risk to cryptographic systems that rely on traditional public-key encryption methods like RSA or elliptic curve cryptography (ECC). Quantum computers could theoretically break these encryption schemes, compromising the confidentiality of data stored on the blockchain.

To mitigate these risks, blockchain systems must eventually adopt quantum-resistant algorithms, such as lattice-based cryptography, ensuring that they remain secure in the face of future technological advancements.

5.8.2.2 Malicious Node Behavior

In public blockchains, where nodes are often anonymous or semi-trusted, the possibility of malicious actors undermining the system is a constant concern. CI-enhanced blockchains introduce new attack vectors:

- **Trusted Setup Attacks:** Some cryptographic techniques, like ZKPs, rely on a trusted setup to initialize the system. If this setup is compromised by malicious actors, they could gain unauthorized access to confidential information or undermine the integrity of the system.
- **Collusion Among Validators:** In systems using SMPC or threshold encryption, where multiple nodes work together to ensure confidentiality, collusion among a subset of validators could result in the exposure of confidential data or manipulation of the blockchain's state.
- Securing the consensus mechanism and ensuring robust cryptographic safeguards are vital for maintaining the integrity and confidentiality of the blockchain network, especially in environments where nodes cannot be fully trusted.

5.8.2.3 Insider Threats and Key Management

One of the most significant security risks in CI-enhanced blockchains comes from insider threats—individuals with privileged access to sensitive data or cryptographic keys. Poor key management practices can lead to severe breaches of confidentiality and integrity:

- **Key Leakage:** If private keys used for encryption are poorly secured, they could be leaked or stolen by malicious actors, allowing unauthorized access to encrypted transactions.
- **Centralized Key Management:** In some CI-enhanced systems, keys may be centrally managed, which introduces a single point of failure. A breach of the centralized key management system could compromise the entire network's security.

To prevent these risks, robust, decentralized key management solutions must be implemented. Hardware security modules (HSMs), multi-signature schemes, and decentralized key management protocols can help mitigate the potential for key-related security breaches.

5.8.2.4 Smart Contract Vulnerabilities

The introduction of complex cryptographic operations into blockchain-based smart contracts presents another layer of security risk. Smart contracts, which automate and enforce agreements on the blockchain, are prone to coding errors and vulnerabilities:

- **Contract Exploits:** Bugs in smart contract logic can allow attackers to exploit vulnerabilities in how confidentiality and integrity protocols are enforced. For instance, reentrancy attacks or improper validation of cryptographic proofs could lead to data leaks or transaction manipulation.
- **Auditing Challenges:** Verifying the correctness of smart contracts that handle sensitive cryptographic operations is challenging. Formal verification tools and extensive auditing practices are necessary to ensure that the smart contract code does not contain exploitable vulnerabilities.

The complexity of these cryptographic operations, combined with the immutable nature of smart contracts, makes it essential that security audits and formal verification are prioritized in the development lifecycle.

5.9 Future Directions

As the digital landscape advances at an unprecedented pace, it is imperative for blockchain technologies to evolve proactively, addressing novel challenges and harnessing emerging opportunities. In the near future, three key directions seem particularly promising and vital: developing quantum-resistant encryption methods for blockchains, seamlessly integrating Internet of Things (IoT) devices with private blockchains, and leveraging Computational Intelligence (CI) to automate smart contract functionalities.

5.9.1 Quantum-Resistant Encryption on Blockchains

Introduction: With the imminent rise of quantum computing, traditional cryptographic systems, especially those that heavily rely on public key infrastructures like blockchains, are under threat. Quantum computers possess the potential to solve complex problems, like integer factorization, exponentially faster than classical computers, rendering many cryptographic techniques obsolete.

- **Understanding Quantum Threats:** A quantum computer can potentially utilize Shor's algorithm to quickly factorize large numbers, undermining RSA and ECC encryption, foundational to many blockchain systems.
- **Post-Quantum Cryptography (PQC):** Exploring cryptographic systems believed to be secure against quantum attacks. These include hash-based cryptography, lattice-based cryptography, code-based cryptography, and multivariate polynomial cryptography.
- **Implementation Challenges:** PQC algorithms often require larger key sizes, which could present scalability and efficiency issues in blockchain contexts.
- **Blockchain Projects Addressing Quantum Threats:** Highlights initiatives like QRL (Quantum Resistant Ledger) that work on quantum-resistant blockchains.

5.9.2 Integrating IoT with Private Blockchains

The Internet of Things (IoT) represents billions of interconnected devices generating vast amounts of data. Private blockchains can provide a trust layer, ensuring data integrity, security, and streamlined operations for IoT.

- **IoT Security Concerns:** Owing to their distributed nature and resource constraints, IoT devices are particularly vulnerable.
- **Advantages of Blockchain for IoT:** Immutable records, tamper-resistant data, and the prospect of automating processes via smart contracts.
- **Case Studies:** Examples such as supply chain tracking, smart homes, and autonomous vehicles.
- **Challenges:** Addressing scalability, ensuring real-time operations despite inherent blockchain latency, and energy efficiency optimization.

5.9.3 Smart Contract Automation using Computational Intelligence (CI)

Smart contracts automate transaction operations on blockchains. Integrating CI can allow these contracts to adapt, learn, and autonomously make more complex decisions.

- **Basics of Smart Contracts:** Their functionality and application in automating tasks in decentralized platforms.
- **Role of CI in Smart Contracts:** Enabling dynamic decisions based on patterns, historical contract execution learning, and predictive analytics.
- **Neural Networks for Predictive Analytics:** Using neural networks to predict contract outcomes or assess risks.
- **Fuzzy Logic Systems in Contracts:** Introducing decision-making flexibility.
- **Challenges and Concerns:** Ensuring CI decisions remain transparent and understandable, security maintenance, and ensuring contracts' predictability.

5.9.4 Scalability, Interoperability, and Quantum-Resistant Encryption Challenges

Blockchain technology must evolve to meet increasing demands for scalability, interoperability, and security, especially with the rise of quantum computing. This section highlights key challenges and potential research directions.

5.9.4.1 Scalability Challenges

As blockchain usage grows, systems must handle higher transaction volumes and complex operations like quantum-resistant encryption and IoT integration. Current blockchains like Bitcoin and Ethereum face limitations.

- **Throughput Limitations:** Public blockchains process transactions much slower than centralized systems, creating bottlenecks for applications requiring high-speed processing.
- **Layer-2 Solutions:** Techniques like the Lightning Network and rollups aim to increase throughput, but integrating advanced features adds complexity.
- **Sharding and Rollups:** Sharding divides blockchains into smaller parts, and rollups aggregate transactions off-chain. Ensuring security and scalability with encrypted data remains challenging.

- **Quantum-Resistant Scalability:** Post-quantum cryptographic methods require larger keys and more computation, slowing down transactions and affecting scalability.

5.9.4.2 Interoperability Across Blockchains

Interoperability is the ability of different blockchain systems to exchange data—is critical as specialized blockchains emerge, especially for IoT devices and systems needing secure data exchange.

- **Standardization:** Diverse protocols and smart contract languages hinder data sharing due to lack of standardization.
- **Cross-Chain Bridges:** Solutions like Polkadot and Cosmos facilitate interoperability but must ensure encrypted data flows securely across different cryptographic methods.
- **IoT Integration:** Integrating IoT devices with blockchains requires secure, real-time data sharing, but IoT devices often use centralized systems, posing challenges.

5.9.4.3 Quantum-Resistant Encryption

Quantum computing threatens traditional cryptographic methods used in blockchains. Implementing post-quantum cryptography is essential for future security.

- **Algorithm Efficiency:** Post-quantum algorithms require larger keys and more computation, increasing transaction sizes and slowing verification, which affects scalability.
- **Integration Challenges:** Transitioning to quantum-resistant encryption requires overhauling infrastructure, potentially causing compatibility issues and operational disruptions.
- **Security and Auditing:** Ensuring the security of post-quantum algorithms in blockchains is complex, necessitating formal proofs and thorough audits.

5.10 Conclusions and Future Scope

This exploration highlights the symbiotic potential between private blockchains and computational intelligence (CI), demonstrating how their fusion can create more secure, adaptive, and efficient systems. Computational intelligence approaches, such as neural networks and evolutionary algorithms, can be harnessed to optimize encryption methods, manage keys dynamically, and detect anomalies, ensuring a robust defense mechanism in private blockchain systems. Furthermore, the application of these combined technologies spans multiple sectors, from healthcare to finance, indicating their broad relevance and transformative potential. As technological landscapes continuously evolve, the convergence of blockchain and computational intelligence is poised to address emergent challenges and capitalize on new opportunities. This union may become pivotal in achieving scalable, interoperable, and ultra-secure decentralized systems. The next frontier lies in quantum-resistant encryption, embedding intelligent IoT with private blockchains, and further automating smart contracts. As both fields mature, their collaborative innovations may very well shape the foundational infrastructures of tomorrow's digital world.

References

[1] H. Albayati, S. K. Kim, and J. J. Rho. Accepting financial transactions using blockchain technology and cryptocurrency: A customer perspective approach. *Technology in Society*, 62:101320, 2020.

[2] C.-L. Chen, Z.-Y. Lim, X. Xue, and C.-H. Chen. Symmetric and asymmetric encryption in blockchain. *MDPI*, 15(2), 2023.

[3] Nahom Aron Dawit, Sujith Samuel Mathew, and Kadhim Hayawi. Suitability of blockchain for collaborative intrusion detection systems. In *2020 12th Annual Undergraduate Research Conference on Applied Computing (URC)*. IEEE, 2020.

[4] M. Din, S. K. Pal, and S. Muttoo. A review of computational swarm intelligence techniques for solving crypto problems. In *Soft Computing: Theories and Applications: Proceedings of SoCTA 2017*, pages 193–203. 2019.

[5] Pankaj Dutta et al. Blockchain technology in supply chain operations: Applications, challenges and research opportunities. *Transportation Research Part E: Logistics and Transportation Review*, 142:102067, 2020.

[6] Oumaima Fadi, Zkik Karim, and Boulmalf Mohammed. A survey on blockchain and artificial intelligence technologies for enhancing security and privacy in smart environments. *IEEE Access*, 10:93168–93186, 2022.

[7] A. Gervais, G. O. Karame, K. Wust, V. Glykantzis, H. Ritzdorf, and S. Capkun. On the security and performance of proof of work blockchains. In *Proceedings of the 2016 ACM SIGSAC Conference on Computer and Communications Security*, pages 3–16, 2016.

[8] Roman Graf and Ross King. Neural network and blockchain based technique for cyber threat intelligence and situational awareness. In *2018 10th International Conference on Cyber Conflict (CyCon)*. IEEE, 2018.

[9] D. Guegan. Public blockchain versus private blockchain. 2017.

[10] Muneeb Ul Hassan, Mubashir Husain Rehmani, and Jinjun Chen. Anomaly detection in blockchain networks: A comprehensive survey. *IEEE Communications Surveys & Tutorials*, 2022.

[11] A. Judmayer, N. Stifter, K. Krombholz, and E. Weippl. *Blocks and Chains: Introduction to Bitcoin, Cryptocurrencies, and Their Consensus Mechanisms*. Springer Nature, 2022.

[12] Manal M. Khayyat et al. Blockchain enabled optimal hopfield chaotic neural network based secure encryption technique for industrial internet of things environment. *Alexandria Engineering Journal*, 61(12):11377–11389, 2022.

[13] Haojun Liu et al. Merkle tree: A fundamental component of blockchains. In *2021 International Conference on Electronic Information Engineering and Computer Science (EIECS)*. IEEE, 2021.

[14] Yang Lu. The blockchain: State-of-the-art and research challenges. *Journal of Industrial Information Integration*, 15:80–90, 2019.

[15] Jerry M. Mendel. Fuzzy logic systems for engineering: A tutorial. *Proceedings of the IEEE*, 83(3):345–377, 1995.

[16] Bhabendu Kumar Mohanta, Soumyashree S. Panda, and Debasish Jena. An overview of smart contract and use cases in blockchain technology. In *2018 9th International Conference on Computing, Communication and Networking Technologies (ICCCNT)*. IEEE, 2018.

[17] D. Puthal, N. Malik, S. P. Mohanty, E. Kougianos, and G. Das. Everything you wanted to know about the blockchain: Its promise, components, processes, and problems. *IEEE Consumer Electronics Magazine*, 7(4):6–14, 2018.

[18] M. Wang, M. Duan, and J. Zhu. Research on the security criteria of hash functions in the blockchain. In *Proceedings of the 2nd ACM Workshop on Blockchains, Cryptocurrencies, and Contracts*, pages 47–55, 2018.

[19] Pengtao Xie et al. Crypto-nets: Neural networks over encrypted data. *arXiv preprint arXiv:1412.6181*, 2014.

[20] H. Yi. Securing e-voting based on blockchain in p2p network. *EURASIP Journal on Wireless Communications and Networking*, 2019(1):1–9, 2019.

Chapter 6

Leveraging AI in Smart Healthcare for Future Hospitals: Potential Applications and Challenges

Kritika Upadhyay, Manisha Bharti* and *Manoj Kumar*

Abstract

Future healthcare systems will be shaped by the interaction of emerging technologies, which will completely transform the biomedical industry. Artificial Intelligence (AI) makes it possible to analyze complex medical data by utilizing computer vision, natural language processing, and machine learning methods. The healthcare ecosystem benefits from the integration of AI with Internet of Things (IoT), which enables faster and more efficient analysis of larger patient data sets. These developments in medical care have the capacity to more pre-

Department of Electronics & Communication Engineering National Institute of Technology, Delhi, India.

* Corresponding author: kritikaupadhyay@nitdelhi.ac.in

DOI: 10.1201/9781003531043-8

cisely and swiftly identify the early indicators of disease. Applications for remote sensing and online monitoring make it simple to address the majority of human errors. The ultimate objective is to reduce the requirement for human intervention by achieving human-level performance with increased accuracy and efficiency in task execution and problem-solving. Also, Technical standards for 6G capable devices is used in medical sector can reduce latency and provide efficient bandwidth usage too. It uses additional patient-specific technology to investigate new aspects of the real-time health surveillance system. In addition to tackling the issues brought on by growing prices and scarce resources, the integration of AI into healthcare systems seeks to assist physicians, improve population health, and customize patient treatment. Thus, AI based healthcare holds importance in revolutionizing the future hospital scenario.

6.1 Introduction

Recently, AI assisted technologies have gain immense importance in the healthcare sector. They can transform pharmaceutical companies and patient care. Numerous studies show significant AI advancements in performing critical healthcare tasks, including disease diagnosis. AI-powered virtual reality simulations enhance medical education by providing students with a safe environment to practice clinical skills before treating real patients. This method prepares for rare but significant emergencies while providing experience in everyday tasks like suturing and physical exams. The study [17] thoroughly analyzes AI advancements in basic sciences, offering research guidelines and inspiring researchers to understand and support the ongoing progress in these fields. Rajpurkar, P. discusses numerous directions for future research in medicine, such as non-imaginary data sources, unconventional problem formulations, and AI-user collaboration [10]. In the context of AI in big healthcare data analytics, Panayides, A. highlights the need for effective medical data management methods by summarizing developments in medical imaging acquisition technology for various modalities [18]. Numerous AI applications for health care are revealed in the literature [13], along with an unexplored stream of study. For instance, knowledge-based management and data-intensive analysis in AI initiatives call for expertise and an awareness of data quality [3]. The results of the comprehensive review indicate that artificial intelligence (AI) holds great potential for lowering healthcare expenses, enabling preventive healthcare, relieving the workload of medical practitioners, and facilitating faster and easier provision of more accurate diagnoses [15]. The survey outlines the principles of Explainable AI (EXAI) [12], related parameters, and scenarios. EXAI includes a framework for segregating and classifying COVID-19 patients. Performance assessments in the case study, confirm EXAI's benefits in healthcare settings. Future health-related operations for both consumers and medical professionals will include highly customized medical diagnostic and treatment information, according to current research in AI and precision medicine [7]. The alignment between early detection of disease and its timely prevention is the result of synergy between the two. In the long run, this could help the public by lowering the burden of disease and offering early, reasonably priced treatment.

Several ethical concerns have been explored in relation to the potential replacement of human care by AI assisting technology in healthcare procedures. Many criticisms against using this technology to replace human care have been shown to be unconvincing [8]. The influence of AI in healthcare is currently assessed moderately, with research revealing methodological flaws [16]. Future cost-effectiveness evaluations should increase in quantity and quality, including initial outlay, ongoing expenses, and comparisons with alternative technology. This will enable a thorough, well-segmented cost-benefit analysis, providing a solid foundation for AI application decisions.

The chapter is organized as follows: Section 6.2 discusses technical progress in the medical sector, Section 6.3 covers the implementation of various AI models, Section 6.4 illustrates potential AI application areas, and Section 6.5 explores explainable AI. Section 6.7 concludes the chapter, followed by references.

6.2 Technical Progress in Medical Sectors

Innovation and the quick development of technology have become essential components of the medical and healthcare industries. The medical field's latest advancements and developments have limitless potential (as shown in Figure 6.1). Medical personnel will be able to collect data, diagnose conditions, treat patients [11], and perform medical procedures with more efficiency thanks to this advancement. These days, a wide range of medical technologies are developing quickly, including IoT [4] and AI-powered tailored medications, patient monitoring, and efficient illness diagnosis.

6.3 Different AI Models in Healthcare

The entire healthcare industry has undergone a paradigm shift in recent years, which has revolutionized the way humans and technology coexist. The biomedical field's convergence of engineering and automation [2] aids in bridging the gap between current needs and research. The goal of biomedical engineering has shifted to managing fitness rather than treating illness, and becoming more analytical in patient orientation. The seven Ps of individualized, patient-friendly healthcare systems are seen in many facets of medical care. This section discusses the various aspects by which AI can be modelled in different sectors of healthcare (Figure 6.2).

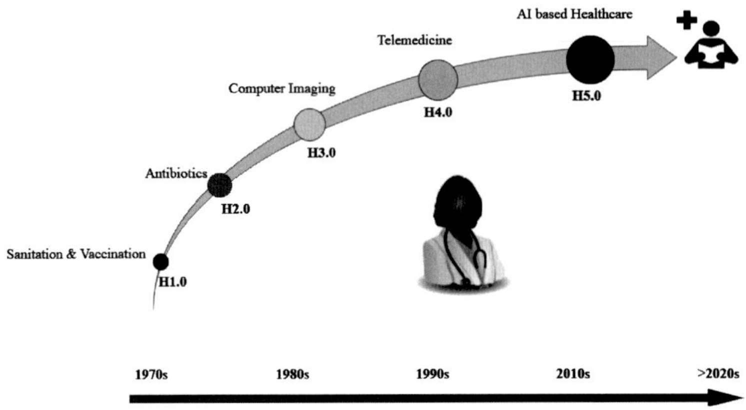

Figure 6.1: Technical advancement in medical healthcare sector.

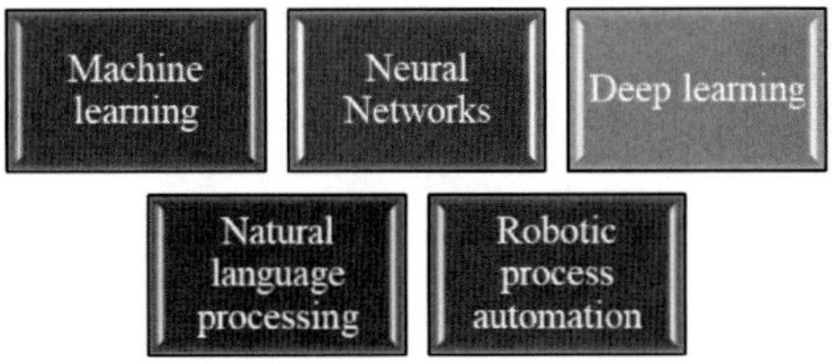

Figure 6.2: Different applicative models of AI that are useful in healthcare.

6.3.1 Use of DL, ML and AI

Artificial intelligence encompasses various technologies applicable to healthcare, supporting a range of tasks and procedures. Key AI technologies for healthcare are listed below. The latest significant application of machine learning (ML) is predictive medicine, which forecasts the type of treatment, duration, characteristics, and configuration for patients.

Using a well-trained dataset with a known variable characteristics (e.g., the onset of a disease) is called supervised learning, which plays a major role in precision medicine. Advanced machine learning, like neural networks, created in the 1960s, are extensively used in medical research, such as predicting a patient's risk of developing a disease.

6.3.2 NLP-Natural Language Processing

The healthcare system is knowledge-driven, handling vast amounts of narrative data from radiologists' reports, doctors' notes, pathologists' reports, and discharge summaries. This data is often stored in unstructured formats, making it difficult to obtain relevant information for decision-making. However, Natural Language Processing (NLP) techniques structure this narrative material. NLP algorithms can record unstructured medical data, analyze its grammatical structure, determine its meaning, and translate it for electronic medical systems. This lowers expenses and raises the standard of medical care.

6.3.3 *Robotic Based Automation*

Recent advancements in robotics and artificial intelligence (AI) suggest that robots could greatly benefit the healthcare industry. Robotic systems [6] are frequently used in hospitals, rehabilitation, walking assistance, and other healthcare settings, including the elderly care, pediatrics, and disability support. Reliable performance is essential for robots to function safely and efficiently in unstructured, unpredictable real-world environments. Customizable robots will need to carry out diverse tasks and collaborate with a wide range of individuals, even those uncomfortable with their presence [14].

6.4 Potential Areas of AI Implementation

This section examines the current research projects and activities that seek to use AI and ML to improve various facets of medical practice, from offering resources for professional education to supporting clinical administration. Combining this state-of-the-art technology (as shown in Figure 6.3) has great potential to improve patient care, support medical research, and reduce the strain for medical staff. We hope to learn more about the revolutionary potential of cutting-edge AI language models in influencing the future of healthcare by looking into the most recent developments in this area.

6.4.1 *Rule-based Expert Systems*

Numerous Electronic Health Record (EHR) vendors offer a layout of rules and guidelines along with their application. Expert engineers and field specialists are required to develop relevant skills to master the work. The systems are user friendly and, to a certain extent, work well. However, when there are many rules contradicting each other, the logic disappears. Such systems are gradually being replaced by integration with Next Generation technologies based on data and machine learning algorithms.

6.4.2 *Diagnosis and Patient Treatment*

In the 1970s, Stanford developed MYCIN for early detection of blood-related bacterial infections, with AI primarily used for disease detection and treatment. Although rule-based systems showed promise for accurate diagnosis and treat-

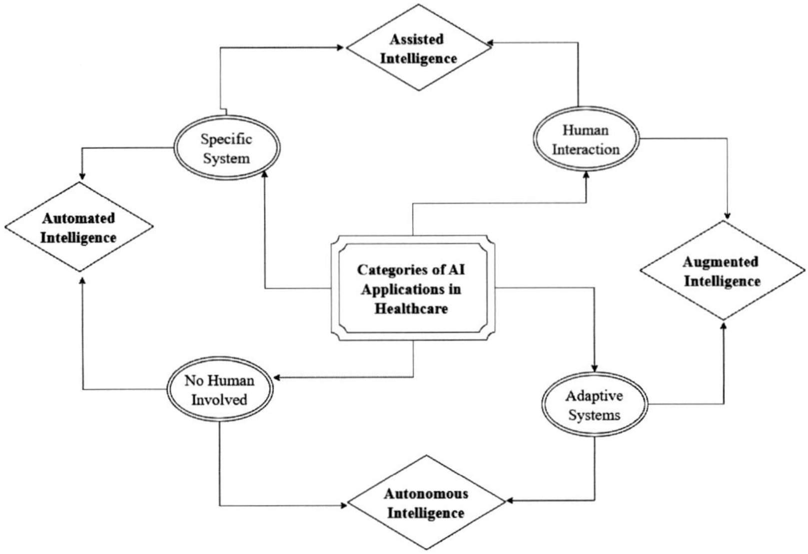

Figure 6.3: Categories of AI application in healthcare.

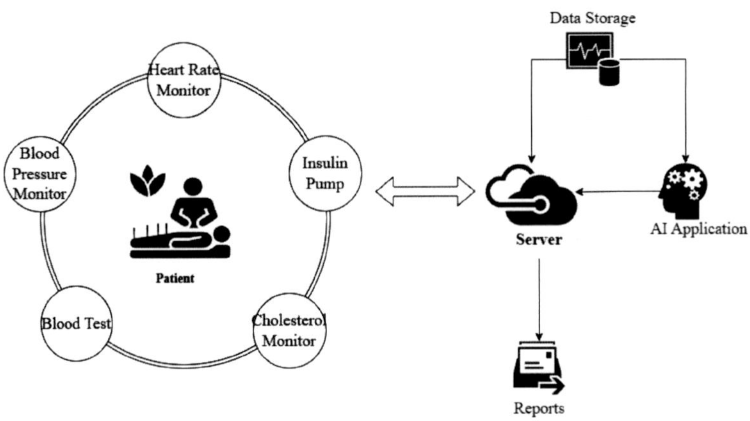

Figure 6.4: Illustration of process involved in diagnosis and medical treatment.

ment, they weren't adopted in medical practice. AI has significantly outperformed human-based diagnostic methods and has shown strong performance when integrated with medical procedures and Healthcare systems [9, 1].

Hippocratic AI focuses on patient safety while improving healthcare outcomes and access by concentrating on non-diagnostic, patient-facing applications. It's useful for managing complexities like medical coding, licensing tests, and administrative tasks. Its compliance certifications ensure it meets medical standards. The model's excellent results on various medical certification tests validate its practicality in clinical settings. Hippocratic AI enhances patient care by providing accurate and empathetic assistance to medical professionals, creating a reliable and effective healthcare environment.

6.4.3 AI based Healthcare Model

The "last mile" treatment in healthcare hinges on patient engagement and adherence. Hospitals use clinical knowledge to create personalized healthcare plans (Figure 6.5) for patients, whether acute or chronic. However, if patients don't maintain their body-mass index, attend regular checkups, take their medicine, or follow the plan, the effort is futile.

AI-based tools can personalize and contextualize care, improving health outcomes with increased patient involvement. Business ventures and data science experts now inform subtle interventions in healthcare plans. Promising research includes alert messages and tailored content triggering actions at key times. Another growing interest is developing "choice architecture" to motivate predictable patient actions based on empirical evidence.

Continuous monitoring of physiological data, including heart rate, movement patterns, and brain activity, is made possible by the integration of AI based sensors with neurocomputing systems. Healthcare professionals may quickly identify anomalies or seizure episodes in real-time monitoring, which is especially helpful for individuals suffering from diseases like epilepsy or Parkinson's disease. Early intervention that is informed by the data gathered has the ability to

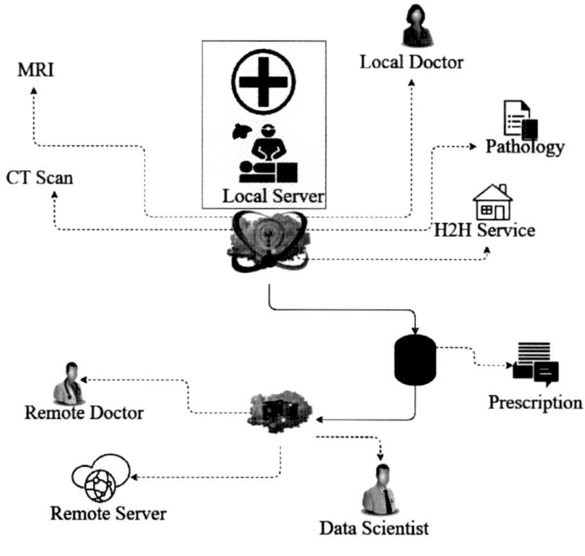

Figure 6.5: AI based hospital model for effective communication.

prevent problems and greatly improve patient outcomes. Remote Patient Monitoring (RPM) represents a paradigm shift in healthcare delivery outside of traditional clinical settings by using the synergy between AI and neuromonitoring technologies. Vital signs like blood pressure and pulse rate are recorded by wearables and sensors, which make up Internet of Things devices. These devices send data in real time to healthcare providers for remote monitoring.

6.4.4 Administrative Applications

Numerous administrative applications are also found in the healthcare industry. The use of AI in this area is less evolved than in patient care, but it can nevertheless lead to major efficiencies. Since administrative and regulatory duties account for 25% of US nurses' working hours on average, these are essential in the healthcare sector. RPA can fulfil major objectives in the healthcare sector, medical medical record administration, lab recording, finance management, and claims processing. Furthermore, a number of healthcare institutions have experimented using virtual assistants for patient interaction, mental health issues and wellness, and telemedicine. The NLP framework could be useful for everyday tasks like scheduling appointments or suggesting prescriptions. Another AI method that is pertinent to the processing of payments and claims is machine learning. It is employed to probabilistically match data between databases.

The accurate identification, analysis, and rectification of coding errors with erroneous claims saves a great deal of time, money, and management for all parties involved, including governments and healthcare providers. Data matching and claims audits can uncover a significant financial potential from false claims that avoid discovery. In the healthcare sector, jobs that deal directly with patients are less likely to be mechanized than those in radiology, pathology, and other disciplines utilizing digital data. AI adoption has shown significant increase in fields of radiology and pathology.

6.5 Discussion on Explainable AI

EXAI is quickly becoming a powerful tool in many sectors, delivering benefits [19] that go well beyond the realms of vanilla AI. EXAI optimizes results by increasing customer retention rates and making inventory management more efficient, ultimately leading to production cost savings in sectors such as healthcare & retail, marketing or the Industrial Internet of Things (IIoT). For example, in retail, EXAI can predict fashion trends, allowing retailers to show the most updated products on display. This, in turn, reinforces the search function of products, as customers should be able to make purchases by searching online using stored data for product recommendations. EXAI also helps formulate key business strategies by shedding light on operational factors like sales trends, customer behaviour or employee loss. Another use case would be for businesses to uphold ethical standards, minimize biases, and protect brand reputation [20].

6.5.1 Research Statistics of EXAI

From a commercial side, EXAI is very important in cybersecurity as it prevents data breaches and accelerates system management (as shown in Figure 6.6). The Facebook data breach in 2019 and the cyberattack on India's National Highway Authorities in 2020 are symptomatic of an evolving threat landscape which underscores how significant it is for EXAI to enhance cybersecurity measures.

EXAI makes organizations better at identifying what types of threats are being launched and how to respond more quickly by delivering AI decisions that are transparent and interpretable. This ability to provide full data integrity is necessary for digital systems we trust. In the end, EXAI is also well-advancing in healthcare, where AI-powered decisions are perhaps more critical than any other EXAI in adding value across the spectrum in this field by producing clinically relevant explanations that both clinicians can understand and trust (reliability), with a focus on more appropriate diagnostic accuracy leading to better patient safety & overall care. As a result, it is used by many practitioners in academia and industry to analyze AI/ML-driven tasks from different application domains (e.g., recommender systems, image processing, business management). As EXAI evolves, the trend of transparency and understandability in AI decision-making will be a linchpin to guarantee that we use artificial intelligence technologies responsibly and ethically across enterprises.

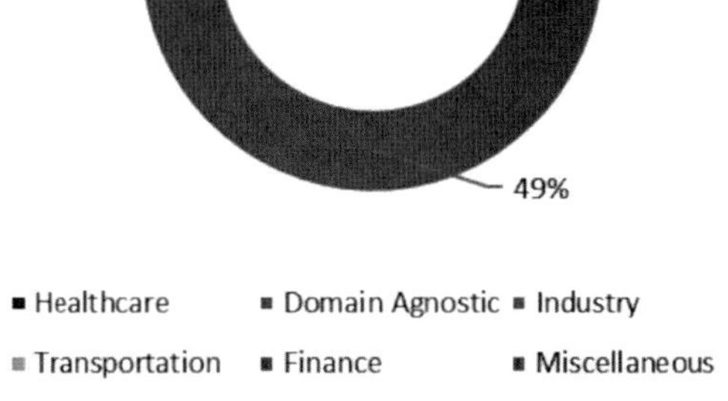

Figure 6.6: EXAI research statistics for different applications domain.

6.5.2 Application of EXAI

This section discusses Explainable AI applications across various domains, enhancing AI models by improving interpretability and decision-making. For the current research, the list of applicable domains and the conclusion are provided in Figure 6.7:

Customer Review: EXAI is used to interpret results regarding customer sentiment due to its ability to understand syntactic data about what people are saying and map these to semantic content.

Military: This type of AI addresses sensor data inaccuracies, enhancing AI models' performance in defense. EXAI modules enable AI to deliver content more precisely through user analysis on social networking platforms, improving model transparency.

Healthcare: To ensure reliable prognoses and recommendations, AI analytical systems must have EXAI transparency to distinguish crucial information, such as image classification for diagnosis. Bayesian teaching and saliency maps help understand how these systems forecast beneficial outcomes in clinical applications like tumor segmentation [5]. Data fusion analyzes big data after transformation and reduction, maintaining its understandability, value, and enhancing AI model accuracy.

Investment: EXAI enhances AI model understandability, reducing misclassifications in the field.

Language: EXAI enhances linguistic data analysis, making natural language processing more accurate.

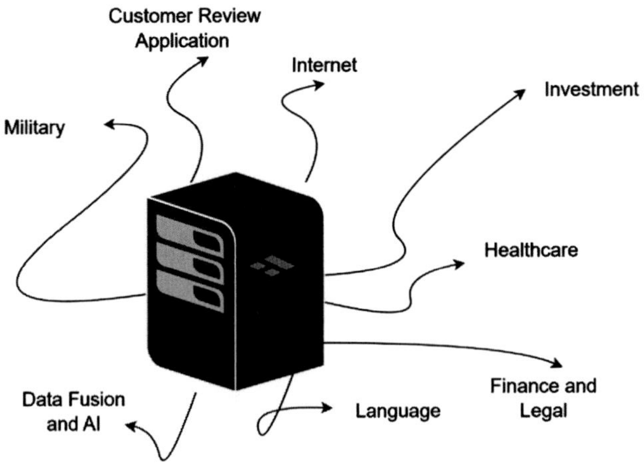

Figure 6.7: Domains of EXAI applications.

Financial & Legal: In financial services, EXAI helps understand why a loan was declined by revealing the AI model's considerations. This application is crucial as it clarifies AI reasoning, ensuring accurate diagnosis and safe patient care.

6.6 Discussion

This section deals with future directions and latest trends in healthcare. Although it is still challenging to replace human understanding with artificial intelligence, Al has drawn much attention to clinical exploration by examining the past, present, and future applications of AI. Clinical practice could be completely transformed by AI, but in order to reach its full potential, a number of issues need to be resolved. The absence of high-quality medical data is one of these issues, which may result in erroneous conclusions. Additional possible restrictions on using AI in clinical practice include data security, privacy, and availability. Achieving the intended results also depends on using the right methodology and identifying pertinent clinical metrics. Although the data and/or analysis produced by AI may be realistic and persuasive, hallucinations—the propensity to create erroneous information that cannot be substantiated by available evidence—may also pose a serious problem.

It will take a multidisciplinary approach, creative data annotation tools, and the creation of more exacting AI models and procedures to address these issues and offer positive solutions. Ensuring proper collaboration between computer scientists and healthcare providers would enable the development of useful, implementable, and successful technology. It will take a multidisciplinary approach, creative data annotation tools, and the creation of more exacting AI models and procedures to address these issues and offer positive solutions. Ensuring proper collaboration between computer scientists and healthcare providers would enable the development of useful, implementable, and successful technology.

- Researchers and experts can create incredibly effective drugs with clinical outcomes that far outperform conventional therapies with the help of AI modules. With the use of AI search modules, biotechnologists have been able to create medications, which has helped humanity recover from certain devastating infections.
- Experts in mental medical services have used human-made intelligence to study human social information, which is used to differentiate between the risks of mental illnesses. Additionally, it has helped identify the percentage of people with mental health disorders who are at danger of self-destruction.
- With the development of assistive robots, artificial intelligence has found its way into the harsh clinical environment. These robots are specifically designed for elderly and disabled people. One of these is the Smart

Walker, which can identify obstacles in the street and suggest a safer and more beneficial route.

- Artificial intelligence-based wearables have been used to record, analyze, and evaluate a patient's continuous data of vital signs such as blood glucose, body temperature, immersion, pulse, and best quality. The quality of medical care has been enhanced by these wearables, and they have also increased tolerance.

6.7 Conclusion

This book chapter focuses on how the biomedical industry and cutting-edge technologies are working together to upgrade the healthcare sector. It is crucial to update the AI-based health surveillance monitoring system in light of the expanding population. By removing obstacles related to geographic topology and man-machine interaction, smart healthcare solutions offer a special foundation for efficiently channelizing medical services. It seeks to combine wireless mechanics and the idea of a sustainable future. AI implementation in the medical field would enable rapid data processing and a high level of remote monitoring, making it feasible for a broad community. Through automation, education, and the acquisition of large medical data, the surveillance system's operational efficiency will be increased.

References

[1] S. Arefin. Ai revolutionizing healthcare: Innovations, challenges, and ethical considerations. *MZ Journal of Artificial Intelligence*, 1(2):1–17, 2024.

[2] B. Babic, S. Gerke, T. Evgeniou, and I. G. Cohen. Beware explanations from ai in health care. *Science*, 373(6552):284–286, 2021.

[3] J. Bajwa, U. Munir, A. Nori, and B. Williams. Artificial intelligence in healthcare: transforming the practice of medicine. *Future healthcare journal*, 8(2):e188–e194, 2021.

[4] M. M. S. Choyon, M. Rahman, M. M. Kabir, and M. F. Mridha. Iot based health monitoring & automated predictive system to confront covid-19. In *2020 IEEE 17th International Conference on Smart Communities: Improving Quality of Life Using ICT, IoT and AI (HONET)*, pages 189–193, 2020.

[5] D. Dave, H. Naik, S. Singhal, and P. Patel. Explainable ai meets healthcare: A study on heart disease dataset. *arXiv preprint arXiv:2011.03195*, 2020.

[6] J. H. Han and J. Y. Lee. Digital healthcare industry and technology trends. In *2021 IEEE International Conference on Big Data and Smart Computing (BigComp)*, pages 375–377, 2021.

[7] K. B. Johnson, W. Q. Wei, D. Weeraratne, M. E. Frisse, K. Misulis, K. Rhee, and J. L. Snowdon. Precision medicine, ai, and the future of personalized health care. *Clinical and translational science*, 14(1):86–93, 2021.

[8] B. Y. Kasula. Ai applications in healthcare a comprehensive review of advancements and challenges. *International Journal of Management Education for Sustainable Development*, 6(6), 2023.

[9] R. C. Li, S. M. Asch, and N. H. Shah. Developing a delivery science for artificial intelligence in healthcare. *NPJ digital medicine*, 3(1):107, 2020.

[10] P. Rajpurkar, E. Chen, O. Banerjee, and E. J. Topol. Ai in health and medicine. *Nature medicine*, 28(1):31–38, 2022.

[11] J. P. Richardson, C. Smith, S. Curtis, S. Watson, X. Zhu, B. Barry, and R. R. Sharp. Patient apprehensions about the use of artificial intelligence in healthcare. *NPJ digital medicine*, 4(1):140, 2021.

[12] D. Saraswat, P. Bhattacharya, A. Verma, V. K. Prasad, S. Tanwar, G. Sharma, and R. Sharma. Explainable ai for healthcare 5.0: opportunities and challenges. *IEEE Access*, 10:84486–84517, 2022.

[13] S. Secinaro, D. Calandra, A. Secinaro, V. Muthurangu, and P. Biancone. The role of artificial intelligence in healthcare: a structured literature review. *BMC medical informatics and decision making*, 21:1–23, 2021.

[14] M. Y. Shaheen. Applications of artificial intelligence (ai) in healthcare: A review. *ScienceOpen Preprints*, 2021.

[15] A. Väänänen, K. Haataja, K. Vehviläinen-Julkunen, and P. Toivanen. Ai in healthcare: A narrative review. *F1000Research*, 10:6, 2021.

[16] J. Wolff, J. Pauling, A. Keck, and J. Baumbach. The economic impact of artificial intelligence in health care: systematic review. *Journal of medical Internet research*, 22(2):e16866, 2020.

[17] Y. Xu, X. Liu, X. Cao, C. Huang, E. Liu, S. Qian, and J. Zhang. Artificial intelligence: A powerful paradigm for scientific research. *The Innovation*, 2(4), 2021.

[18] A. K. Y. Yanamala. Data-driven and artificial intelligence (ai) approach for modelling and analyzing healthcare security practice: a systematic review. *Revista de Inteligencia Artificial en Medicina*, 14(1):54–83, 2023.

[19] S. Yeasmin. Benefits of artificial intelligence in medicine. In *2019 2nd International Conference on Computer Applications & Information Security (ICCAIS)*, pages 1–6, 2019.

[20] Z. Zhang, Y. Genc, D. Wang, M. E. Ahsen, and X. Fan. Effect of ai explanations on human perceptions of patient-facing ai-powered healthcare systems. *Journal of Medical Systems*, 45(6):64, 2021.

III COMPUTATIONAL ALGORITHMS

DOI: 10.1201/9781003531043-9

Chapter 7

Discrete Artificial Bee Colony Optimization Algorithm for Cyber-attack Detection to Mitigate Credential Stuffing in Cyber Defense

Pabbisetti Satya Gouri Aruna Sri,[a] *Sumit Kumar*[b] and *Ketan Anand*[c,*]

Abstract

Cybersecurity is crucial in our interconnected world. Its importance grows as expertise advances and becomes more prevalent in daily life, safeguarding individuals. Credential stuffing is a sort of hack where attackers utilize usernames and passwords they have obtained earlier to gain unauthorized access to client

[a] Department of Internet of Things, Koneru Lakshmaiah Education Foundation, Vaddeswaram.

[b] Department of CSE, Haridwar University, Roorkee.

[c] Department of CSE, Sharda University, Greater Noida, Uttar Pradesh-201310.

* Corresponding author: ketananand13@gmail.com

DOI: 10.1201/9781003531043-10

credits on other webpages. Many individuals use identical passwords across various websites, making credential-stuffing attacks a risk. To secure client credentials, the discrete artificial bee colony optimization algorithm is proposed. Results show a 24% improvement in the number of active nodes and a 32% increase in network lifetime.

7.1 Introduction

Despite numerous appeals to replace passwords with other authentication techniques [36, 23, 24, 9], they remain prevalent today and are expected to persist in the near future. It remains true even though they have a reputation for being easily predictable [27], hard to recall [5], and prone to typing errors [13, 3]. These two problems often lead to the practice of using the same passwords or slightly modified versions across many websites. According to a study, approximately 40% of users engage in this behaviour [33, 2].

The increased frequency of password breaches and the practice of reusing passwords have made targeted guessing assaults a more significant and serious danger. Credential stuffing is a targeted attack where an attacker uses passwords from a data breach to access a user's account.

Site owners, with help from vendors like Have I Been Pwned (HIBP) [17], reset user passwords to maintain confidentiality. NIST recommends this precaution [32], but it only protects against credential stuffing if users choose a significantly different password. Limited research has focused on variations of stolen passwords using mangling rules [14] or PCFG [42]. These attacks can cause significant harm, as users often reuse passwords even after resetting them [33, 44].

Many researchers rely on cryptographic network authentication to confirm node legitimacy, not to detect hackers. To address attack detection challenges, various methodologies have been combined with Optimization Techniques. This research enhances the Artificial Bee Colony algorithm (ABC) into Discrete ABC (DABC) for identifying cyber-attacks. Contributions of this work include:

- The cyber-attacks are identified using Discrete ABC (DABC) following neural network detection.
- The proposed model is evaluated based on the number of alive nodes and network lifetime, considering varying attackers and cluster heads.

The DABC algorithm strengthens defenses by integrating into cybersecurity systems like IDS, SIEM, and IAM. It allows real-time detection and adaptive responses to unusual login patterns. DABC optimizes detection parameters, enhancing accuracy in identifying suspicious logins and reducing false positives. It strengthens security in multi-factor authentication and cloud environments by monitoring irregular login activity and adjusting authentication requirements. Its scalability makes it suitable for distributed and cloud-based architectures, providing a flexible and resilient approach to account protection.

The research is organized as follows: Section 7.2 covers related research in the cybersecurity domain, Section 7.3 discusses problem formulation, Section 7.4 presents the proposed methodology, and Section 7.5 and 7.6 cover experiments and conclusions respectively.

7.2 Literature Survey

Types of password preferences: In the past, NLP technologies analyzed human-selected passwords, starting with enhancing dictionary-based cracking tools [30, 1]. Information-driven strategies followed, using password breaches to learn driven strategies had been supplied with the intention to learn language models for passwords by way of the use of password breaches. Weir et al., utilized probabilistic context-free grammars (PCFGs) [43]. Later, Komanduri et al. in [21] improved these to estimate human-selected password distributions. Ma et al. [26] demonstrated that Markov model-based approaches outperformed PCFG-based models in generating large quantities of passwords [28, 16].

Types of Password Attacks: Defending against brute-force guessing attacks is crucial for password models. These attacks are divided into two main categories: offline and online. Offline attacks involve obtaining cryptographic hashes of users' passwords, and trying to recover them through trial and error of billions (or trillions) of possibilities.

An online attack involves an attacker using a login interface or API to target an account's password. Online attacks are more restricted than offline attacks due to authentication mechanisms that freeze accounts after minimal unsuccessful attempts (e.g., ten tries). The core challenge remains the same. The success probability of an attack, called λq, is determined by the number of guesses or query budget q. Our research focuses on online environments, limiting the query budget to 1000 or fewer.

Das et al. [14] conducted the first study on targeted attacks side information. They found that over 43 percent of users reuse passwords across multiple websites. They developed a rule-based system to guess passwords using knowledge of a user's previous passwords, termed credential tweaking. Wang et al. [42] later developed a personalized PCFG model to guide credential modification based on compromised passwords. These targeted attacks perform better than untargeted ones for limited query budgets. Current methods don't fully utilize large data volumes, so contemporary machine learning approaches are needed.

Cusack and Almutairi [25] developed a security architecture to protect peer-to-peer networks against DoS assaults. However, Zho et al. [11] proposed a framework to investigate the behaviour of genuine text samples. This method is designed to detect abnormal network activity that deviates from conventional grammar standards. It is implemented using an advanced hidden Markov model. Authors Chen et al. [12] offer an improved version of the WOA algorithm called WOAmM. Alawida et al. [6] conducted a study that revealed variations in cyber-attack methods. The most common kind of assault was hacking, accounting for 37% of the total attacks (330 out of 895). Kumar et al. [22] developed an optimization model to identify and detect phishing assaults on websites. The optimization technology was developed utilizing a deep learning neural network methodology. The proposed approach used the Adam optimizer algorithm to achieve a high level of accuracy. Benavides-Astudillo et al. [8] developed a model that combines deep learning (DL) and natural language processing (NLP) to detect phishing attempts by analyzing the content of suspicious web sites. The web pages' syntactic and semantic properties were extracted with Keras Embedding Layer. The other optimization approaches can be found in [4, 31, 37, 35, 39, 34, 38, 40, 7, 10].

There is still a gap in effectively identifying intruders to handle credential stuffing. This research addresses the issue by combining optimization with a neural network model for cyber defense.

7.3 Problem Definition

In the initial phase, the KDD Cup dataset has a 200 nodes: 100 safe and 100 attacker nodes each identified by unique biometric data. Cluster Heads (CH) are selected using Discrete ABC Optimization, considering distance and penalty. Nodes with the shortest distance and least penalty are potential CHs.

Clusters are formed based on CH, using minimal proximity criteria. Identifying a specific attacker node among many is challenging. Clusters are established after nodes enroll in the network to alleviate the network's burden. Once clusters are established and CH is selected, node detection time is reduced. Information on the assault node is sent to the cluster chiefs. Communication between CH and Nodes continues, and the neural network detects subsequent attacks. Nodes communicate with CH without any unintended repercussions. The proposed optimization model selects the most appropriate weights to train the Neural network model.

Distance between CH and nodes: Initially a set of cluster heads are listed to compute the distance between each CH and the nodes. Then based on the distance, the nodes are grouped to the respective cluster head. The coordinates of nodes are represented in two dimensions namely x and y coordinates. Considering (CH_x, CH_y) as coordinates of CH and (N_x, N_y) as nodes coordinates, the

Euclidian distance is computed as

$$D_{i,j} = \sqrt{(CH_x - N_x)^2 + (CH_y - N_y)^2} \tag{7.1}$$

where i ranges from 1 to n such that n is the total number of nodes in the network and j ranges from 1 to m such that m is the number of clusters defined.

Penalty: This key factor determines if a node is an attacker by assigning a value of "1" or "0." If a node is identified as an attacker, the Neural Network assigns a penalty value of "1," excluding it from the CH selection process. P_i represents the penalty function, and F_{iP} is the output of the NN algorithm.

A Neural Network is responsible determines the punishment function, which is crucial for recognizing attacker nodes. The decision to exclude a node from CH qualification depends on a binary value (1 or 0). The efficiency of the penalty function and the neural network's performance are key factors in this process.

7.4 Proposed Discrete Artificial Bee Colony Algorithm

The ABC algorithm, presented by Karaboga in 2005 [20], is an optimization method that draws inspiration from the natural behaviour of honey. The simulation of honeybees' intellectual behaviour may be used to identify the global optimal solution or near optimum solutions. Each food source in the ABC algorithm replicates a specific solution to a given challenge. The algorithm seeks to get the best possible outcome of a food source by using a fitness function and calculating the quality of the nectar in the food source. This algorithm paradigm is characterized by its simplicity, reliance on a group of individuals, and ability to handle complex engineering and global numerical issues with resilience. The artificial bee colonies are organized into three categories: worker bee, observer bee, and explorer bee. Half of the colony members are hired bees, while the other half are observer bees. The quantity of accessible food sources is equivalent to the combined number of employed bees and spectator bees. The worker bees actively seek novel food sources and disseminate the acquired knowledge to attract and enlist more bees as observers. The observer bee selects the higher quality food supply over the lower quality one based on probabilistic data. The employed bee, which is predicated on a low-high-quality food supply, is rejected and converted into a scout bee to explore different food sources. The ABC consistently performs three steps. First, worker bees search for and adjust their position based on the food source's quality. Second, spectator bees choose food sources with higher probability values based on their fitness. Finally, scout bees replace low-quality food sources with new ones.

In employee bee phase, food sources are randomly searched using the following equation:

$$v_{i,j} = x_{i,j} + \varnothing^1_{i,j}(x_{i,j} - x_{k,j}) \tag{7.2}$$

where i is the bee index and j is the index of the dimension. k represents the index of the random bee and $\varnothing_{i,j}$ is the random number that ranges between 0 and 1. In the onlooker bee phase, a set of selective solutions are identified and then a neighbourhood search is conducted based on the following equation

$$v_{i,j} = x_{i,j} + \varnothing^1_{i,j}(x_{i,j} - x_{k,j}) + \varnothing^2_{i,j}(x_{i,j} - x_{best,j}) \tag{7.3}$$

where x_best refers to the best solution attained so far. The results of ABC algorithm are in the form of continuous values. However, selection of whether or not a node is a CH involves binarization. If a node is represented as 1, it is selected as a CH; if represented as 0, it is not. Therefore, the ABC algorithm solutions must be adjusted to represent the CH selection choice. The generated solution v is first normalized based on the maximum and minimum values of each solution.

$$Nv^i_j = \frac{(v^i_j - Min^i)}{(Max^i - Min^i)} \tag{7.4}$$

The top k values of Nv^i are represented by 1 and the others by 0.

7.5 Experimental Analysis

The proposed approach for identifying cyber attacks using an optimization strategy was assessed using MATLAB®, and the resulting outputs were recorded. The recommended model is compared to known models based on the number of active nodes and the duration of network operation. The compared models includes JA [41], FF [15], WI-JA [19], GWO [29] and EWOA [18]. The datasets are generated in random with 1000 nodes.

7.5.1 Analysis of the Number of Active Nodes

Figure 7.2 demonstrates the total number of nodes that are alive on different number of attackers. On comparing the results of nodes that are alive after run for different number of attackers, the proposed DABC outperforms existing algorithms. For instance, for the attackers count of 10, the proposed DABC outperforms existing algorithms such as JA with 22.1%, FF with 13%, GWO with 13%, WI-JA with 11.7% and EWOA with 3.9%. For the attackers count of 15, the proposed DABC outperforms existing algorithms such as JA with 25%, FF with 21.3%, GWO with 13.8%, WI-JA with 11.3% and EWOA with 7.5%. For the attackers count of 20, the proposed DABC outperforms existing algorithms

Algorithm 1 DABC Algorithm for Selecting Cluster Heads in Cybersecurity Network

Input: Network nodes, DABC parameters (population size, maximum iterations, fitness criteria)

Output: Optimal configuration of cluster heads

1. Initialize Parameters:
   - Set population size, maximum iterations, and fitness function criteria.
   - Define each network node as a potential cluster head candidate.
2. Generate Initial Population of Solutions:
   - For each solution in the initial population:
     - Randomly assign a subset of nodes as potential cluster heads.
     - Encode each solution to represent these selected nodes.
3. Evaluate Fitness for Each Solution:
   - For each solution in the population:
     - Compute the fitness score based on energy efficiency, node distances, and network lifetime.
     - Store each solution's fitness score.
4. Employed Bee Phase (Improve Current Solutions):
   - For each employed bee:
     - Select a solution from the population.
     - Make small modifications to explore nearby configurations (e.g., replace cluster head candidates).
     - Calculate the new fitness; if improved, update the solution in the population.
5. Onlooker Bee Phase (Focus on Promising Solutions):
   - For each onlooker bee:
     - Choose solutions based on fitness-based probability.
     - Concentrate on higher-fitness solutions for further modification.
     - Adjust the chosen solution to test different configurations.
     - If the fitness score improves, update the solution in the population.
6. Scout Bee Phase (Introduce New Solutions if Needed):
   - For each solution in the population:
     - If a solution does not improve over a defined period:
       - Replace it with a new randomly generated solution to increase diversity.
7. Update Best Solution:
   - Identify the highest fitness solution as the best
   - Track the best solution for use in the final output.

   configuration.
8. Check for Termination:
   - If maximum iterations are reached or fitness criteria are satisfied:
     - End the algorithm.
   - Otherwise, repeat steps 3 to 7.
9. Output the Final Cluster Head Selection:
   - Deploy the nodes from the best solution as cluster heads within the network.

End Algorithm

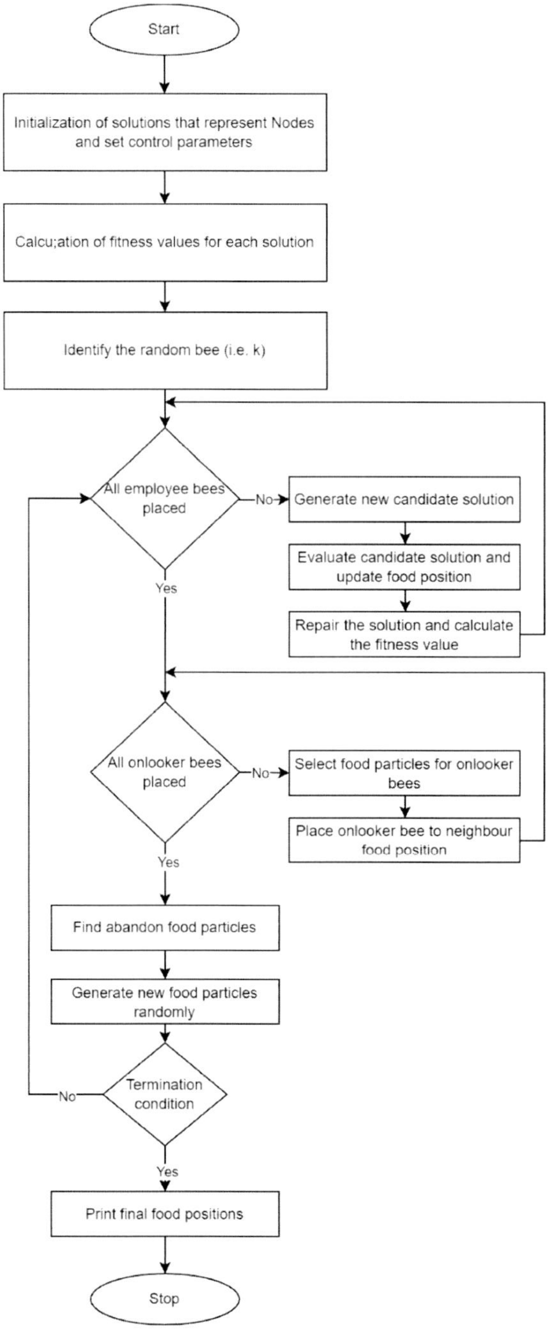

Figure 7.1: Workflow of ABC on CH selection.

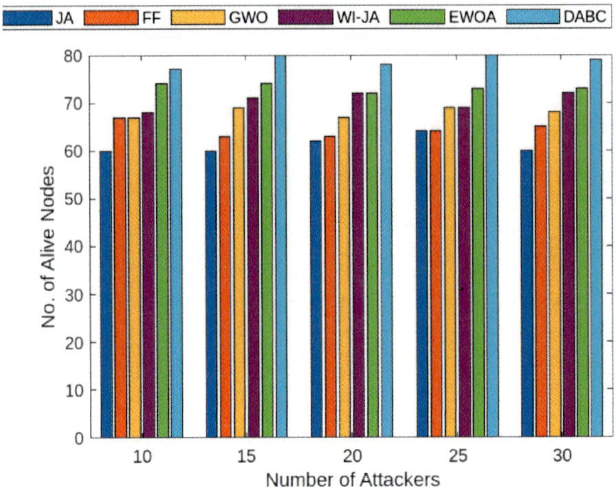

Figure 7.2: Results of number of alive nodes on different number of attackers.

such as JA with 20.5%, FF with 19.2%, GWO with 14.1%, WI-JA with 7.7% and EWOA with 7.7%. For the attackers count of 25, the proposed DABC outperforms existing algorithms such as JA with 20%, FF with 20%, GWO with 13.8%, WI-JA with 13.8% and EWOA with 8.8%. For the attackers count of 30, the proposed DABC outperforms existing algorithms such as JA with 24.1%, FF with 17.7%, GWO with 13.9%, WI-JA with 8.9% and EWOA with 7.6%.

Figure 7.3 demonstrates the total number of nodes that are alive on different number of CH. On comparing the results of nodes that are alive after run for different number of CH, the proposed DABC outperforms existing algorithms. For the cluster head count of 10, the proposed DABC outperforms existing algorithms such as *JA* with 17.7%, FF with 20.3%, GWO with 16.5%, WI-JA with 8.9% and EWOA with 8.9%. For the cluster head count of 15, the proposed DABC outperforms existing algorithms such as JA with 13.3%, FF with 13.3%, GWO with 6.7%, WI-JA with 4% and EWOA with 2.7%. For the cluster head count of 20, the proposed DABC outperforms existing algorithms such as JA with 18.2%, FF with 15.6%, GWO with 9.1%, WI-JA with 6.5% and EWOA with 9.1%. For cluster head count of 25, the proposed DABC outperforms existing algorithms such as JA with 22.8%, FF with 17.7%, GWO with 13.9%, WI-JA with 13.9% and EWOA with 8.9%. For cluster head count of 30, the proposed DABC outperforms existing algorithms such as JA with 21.8%, FF with 19.2%, GWO with 10.3%, WI-JA with 10.3% and EWOA with 10.3%.

Figure 7.4 shows a scenario with varying numbers of attackers and represents the network's total lifetime. Comparing the lifetime (in seconds) for different numbers of attackers, the proposed DABC algorithm outperforms existing algorithms. For example, with 10 attackers, DABC outperforms JA by 63.6%, FF by

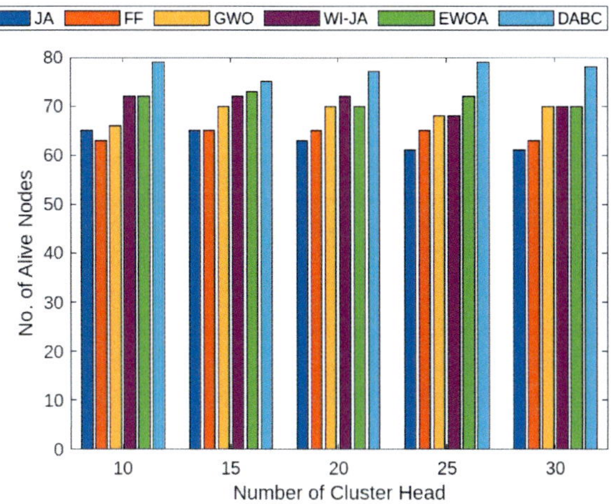

Figure 7.3: Results of number of alive nodes on different number of cluster heads.

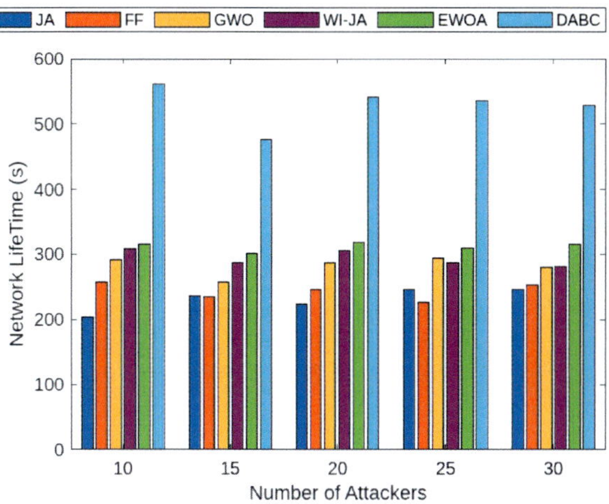

Figure 7.4: Results of overall network lifetime on different number of attackers.

54%, GWO by 48.1%, WI-JA by 45.1%, and EWOA by 43.7%. This trend continues for 15, 20, 25, and 30 attackers, with DABC consistently outperforming these algorithms.

Figure 7.5 shows the count of live nodes for different numbers of CH. The proposed DABC algorithm outperforms existing algorithms. For a cluster head count of 10, DABC outperforms JA by 30.3%, FF by 25.8%, GWO by 22.2%, WI-JA by 17.2%, and EWOA by 11.3%. This trend continues for cluster head counts of 15, 20, 25, and 30, with DABC consistently outperforming other algorithms.

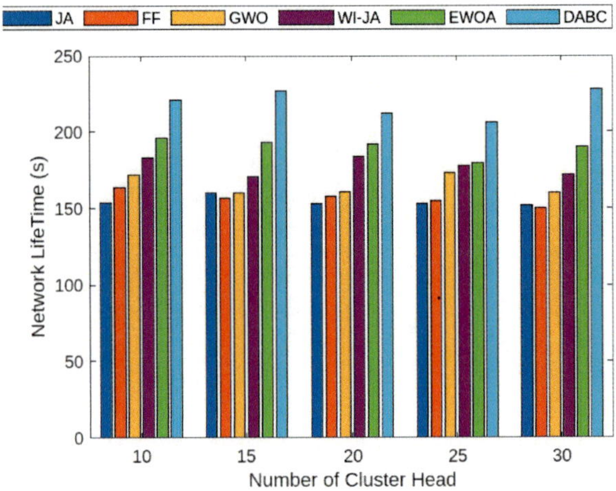

Figure 7.5: Results of number of alive nodes on different number of CH.

7.6 Conclusion

This paper introduces a combined approach using a neural network with optimization to detect attacks. Both threat detection and clustering rely on optimization. When selecting CH, distance and penalty are key parameters. The proposed technique ensures reliable network connections. The innovative DABC approach addresses optimization challenges and has been shown to be successful through comprehensive security analysis.

References

[1] John the ripper password cracker, 2014. [Online] Available: http://www.openwall.com/john/.

[2] 2017 credential spill report, 2018. [Online] Available: http://info.shapesecurity.com/rs/935-ZAM-778/images/Shape-2017-Credential-Spill-Report.pdf/.

[3] Identities in the wild: The tsunami of breached identities continues, 2018. [Online] Available: https://4iq.com/wp-content/uploads/2018/05/2018IdentityBreachReport4iQ.pdf/.

[4] O. I. et al. Abiodun. Data provenance for cloud forensic investigations, security, challenges, solutions and future perspectives: A survey. *Journal of King Saud University - Computer and Information Sciences*, 34:10217–10245, 2022.

[5] A. Adams and M. A. Sasse. Users are not the enemy. *Communications of the ACM*, 42(12):40–46, 1999.

[6] M. et al. Alawida. A deeper look into cybersecurity issues in the wake of covid-19: A survey. *Journal of King Saud University - Computer and Information Sciences*, 34:8176–8206, 2022.

[7] Shruti Suman Doddi Srilatha Vinay Avasthi Attuluri, Sasidhar and Reecha Singh. Monitoring and detecting plant diseases using cloud-based internet of things. In *Journal of Electrical Systems*, volume 20, pages 183–194, 2024.

[8] Fuertes W. Sanchez-Gordon S. Nuñez-Agurto D. Benavides-Astudillo, E. and G. Rodríguez-Galán. A phishing-attack-detection model using natu-

ral language processing and deep learning. *Applied Sciences*, 13(9):5275, 2023.

[9] J. Bonneau, C. Herley, P. C. van Oorschot, and F. Stajano. The quest to replace passwords: A framework for comparative evaluation of web authentication schemes. In *2012 IEEE Symposium on Security and Privacy*, May 2012.

[10] Raja Rao Budaraju and O. Sri Nagesh. Multi-level image thresholding using improvised cuckoo search optimization algorithm. In *2023 3rd International Conference on Intelligent Technologies (CONIT)*, pages 1–7, 2023.

[11] Fuhrmann S. Cavo, L. and L. Liu. Design of an area efficient crypto processor for 3gpp-lte nb-iot devices. *Microprocessors and Microsystems*, 72:102899, 2020.

[12] S. et al. Chakraborty. A novel enhanced whale optimization algorithm for global optimization. *Computers & Industrial Engineering*, 153:107086, 2021.

[13] R. Chatterjee, A. Athalye, D. Akhawe, A. Juels, and T. Ristenpart. Password typos and how to correct them securely. In *IEEE Symposium on Security and Privacy*, May 2016.

[14] A. Das, J. Bonneau, M. Caesar, N. Borisov, and X. Wang. The tangled web of password reuse. In *NDSS*, volume 14, pages 23–26, 2014.

[15] I. Fister, I. Jr. Fister, X.-S. Yang, and J. Brest. A comprehensive review of firefly algorithms. *Swarm and Evolutionary Computation*, 13:34–46, 2013.

[16] B. Hitaj, P. Gasti, G. Ateniese, and F. Perez-Cruz. Passgan: A deep learning approach for password guessing. *arXiv preprint*, 2017. `arXiv:1709.00440`.

[17] Troy Hunt. Have i been pwned?, 2018. [Online] Available: `https://haveibeenpwned.com/Passwords/`.

[18] Borra S. R.-Srilakshmi K. Balachandran-P. K. Reddy G. P. Colak I. Jyothi, K. K. and B. Khan. A novel optimized neural network model for cyber attack detection using enhanced whale optimization algorithm. *Scientific Reports*, 14(1):5590, 2024.

[19] K. Jyothi. Cluster-based authentication for machine type communication in lte network using elliptic curve cryptography. *International Journal of Cloud Computing*, 9(2-3):258–284, 2019.

[20] D. Karaboga. An idea based on honey bee swarm for numerical optimization. Technical Report TR06, Erciyes University, Engineering Faculty, Computer Engineering Department, 2005.

[21] S. Komanduri. *Modeling the Adversary to Evaluate Password Strength with Limited Samples*. PhD thesis, 2016.

[22] Jaya T. Kumar, P. P. and V. Rajendran. Si-bba—a novel phishing website detection based on swarm intelligence with deep learning. *Materials Today*, 80:3129–3139, 2023.

[23] C.-T. Li and M.-S. Hwang. An efficient biometrics-based remote user authentication scheme using smart cards. *Journal of Network and Computer Applications*, 33(1):1–5, 2010.

[24] X. Li, J. Niu, M. K. Khan, and J. Liao. An enhanced smart card based remote user password authentication scheme. *Journal of Network and Computer Applications*, 36(5):1365–1371, 2013.

[25] Chang P.-Y. Liang, J.-M. and J.-J. Chen. Energy-efficient scheduling scheme with spatial and temporal aggregation for small and massive transmissions in lte-m networks. *Pervasive and Mobile Computing*, 52:29–45, 2019.

[26] J. Ma, W. Yang, M. Luo, and N. Li. A study of probabilistic password models. In *Proceedings of the 2014 IEEE Symposium on Security and Privacy (SP)*, pages 689–704, 2014.

[27] M. L. Mazurek, S. Komanduri, T. Vidas, L. Bauer, N. Christin, and et al. L. F. Cranor. Measuring password guessability for an entire university. In *Proceedings of the 2013 ACM SIGSAC Conference on Computer Communications Security*, pages 173–186, 2013.

[28] W. Melicher, B. Ur, S. M. Segreti, S. Komanduri, L. Bauer, and et al. N. Christin. Fast, lean and accurate: Modeling password guessability using neural networks.

[29] Mirjalili S. M. Mirjalili, S. and A. Lewis. Grey wolf optimizer. *Advances in Engineering Software*, 69:46–61, 2014.

[30] A. Narayanan and V. Shmatikov. Fast dictionary attacks on passwords using time-space tradeoff. In *Proceedings of the 12th ACM Conference on Computer and Communications Security*, pages 364–372, 2005.

[31] A. E. et al. Omolara. The internet of things security: A survey encompassing unexplored areas and new insights. *Computers & Security*, 112:102494, 2022.

[32] E. Newton R. Perlner-A. Regenscheid W. Burr J. Richer N. Lefkovitz J. Danker Y. Choong et al. P. A. Grassi, J. Fenton. Nist special publication 800-63b: Digital identity guidelines: Authentication and lifecycle management. Technical report, NIST, 2017.

[33] S. Pearman, J. Thomas, P. E. Naeini, H. Habib, L. Bauer, and et al. N. Christin. Let's go in for a closer look: Observing passwords in their natural habitat. In *Proceedings of the 2017 ACM SIGSAC Conference on Computer and Communications Security*, pages 295–310, 2017.

[34] Kalaipriyan Thirugnanasambandam R. S. Raghav U. Prabu-Devaraj Saravanan Rajeswari, M. and Dinesh Kumar Anguraj. Flower pollination algorithm with powell's method for the minimum energy broadcast problem in wireless sensor network. *Wireless Personal Communications*, 119:1111–1135, 2021.

[35] S. Janakiraman K. Chandraprabha T. Kalaipriyan R. S. Raghav Saravanan, D. and S. Venkatesan. Augmented powell-based krill herd optimization for roadside unit deployment in vehicular ad hoc networks. *Journal of Testing and Evaluation*, 47(6):4108–4127, 2019.

[36] F. Stajano. Pico: No more passwords! In *International Workshop on Security Protocols*, pages 49–81, 2011.

[37] Debnath Bhattacharyya Jaroslav Frnda Dinesh Kumar Anguraj Thirugnansambandam, Kalaipriyan and Jan Nedoma. Augmented node placement model in t-wsn through multi-objective approach. *Computational Materials Continuum*, 69:3629–3644, 2021.

[38] Kalaipriyan Thirugnansambandam and R. S. Raghav. Experimental analysis of ant system on travelling salesman problem dataset tsplib. *EAI Endorsed Transactions on Pervasive Health and Technology*, 5(19), 2019.

[39] R. S. Raghav Dinesh Kumar Anguraj Devaraj Saravanan Thirugnansambandam, Kalaipriyan and S. Janakiraman. Multi-objective binary reinforced cuckoo search algorithm for solving connected coverage target based wsn with critical targets. *Wireless Personal Communications*, 121(3):2301–2325, 2021.

[40] S. V. Sudha D. Saravanan Renjith V. Ravi Dinesh Kumar Anguraj Thirugnansambandam, Kalaipriyan and R. S. Raghav. Reinforced cuckoo search based fugitive landfill methane emission estimation. *Environmental Technology Innovation*, 21:101207, 2021.

[41] R. Venkata Rao. Jaya: A simple and new optimization algorithm for solving constrained and unconstrained optimization problems. *International Journal of Industrial Engineering Computations*, 7:19–34, 2016.

[42] D. Wang, Z. Zhang, P. Wang, J. Yan, and X. Huang. Targeted online password guessing: An underestimated threat. In *Proceedings of the 2016 ACM SIGSAC Conference on Computer and Communications Security*, pages 1242–1254, 2016.

[43] M. Weir, S. Aggarwal, B. de Medeiros, and B. Glodek. Password cracking using probabilistic context-free grammars. In *IEEE Symposium on Security and Privacy (SP)*, pages 162–175, 2009.

[44] Y. Zhang, F. Monrose, and M. K. Reiter. The security of modern password expiration: An algorithmic framework and empirical analysis. In *ACM Conference on Computer and Communications Security (ACM CCS)*, pages 176–186, 2010. [Online] Available: `http://doi.acm.org/10.1145/1866307.1866328`.

Chapter 8

Qryptographix: Quantum Image Encryption via Random Gates

Ramkumar K., Indumathi N., Somasundari P.* and *Srinivasan M.L.*

Abstract

In the context of secure communication, the increasing capabilities of quantum computing present a significant challenge to traditional encryption methods. To address this issue, this study explores an innovative approach to image encryption by utilizing quantum gates. By harnessing the fundamental principles of quantum mechanics and quantum computing, the research introduces a novel encryption framework implemented through Quantum Circuit in Qiskit. The study begins with a thorough examination of quantum gates and classical encryption techniques, pointing out the vulnerabilities of classical systems in the face of quantum advancements. The encryption process involves converting images into their binary forms and then applying quantum circuits to achieve encryption. Through a series of experiments, the proposed approach's performance is evaluated by analyzing encrypted images and various security metrics. The findings

Department of Computer Science and Engineering, Rajalakshmi Institute of Technology, Chennai, Tamilnadu, India.

* Corresponding author: ramkumar1975@gmail.com

DOI: 10.1201/9781003531043-11

highlight the potential of quantum-based encryption techniques to enhance the security of communications in the quantum era. This work contributes to the growing field of quantum cryptography by demonstrating the feasibility of applying quantum gates to secure image transmission. Furthermore, it opens the door to exploring future advancements in quantum encryption methods and their practical integration into real-world communication systems.

8.1 Introduction

The field of quantum computing is progressing rapidly, unlocking new computational capabilities that present a significant challenge to conventional data security approaches. Traditional encryption methods, such as RSA and Elliptic Curve Cryptography (ECC), are based on the difficulty of solving certain mathematical problems, like factoring large integers or computing discrete logarithms. However, with quantum algorithms like Shor's algorithm, which can solve these problems exponentially faster, these classical encryption methods are becoming increasingly vulnerable to quantum attacks [25, 2]. To mitigate this risk, quantum encryption has emerged as a potential solution, utilizing the principles of quantum mechanics to create encryption systems that are resistant to quantum-based threats [1].

Background of Quantum Gates

In quantum computing, the basic unit of information is the qubit, which differs fundamentally from a classical bit. While a classical bit can only represent one of two values, 0 or 1, a qubit can exist in a superposition of both states simultaneously. This property allows quantum computers to perform many calculations simultaneously, providing them with an advantage in solving specific complex problems that classical computers struggle with [20]. Another crucial feature of quantum systems is entanglement, where the state of one qubit becomes linked to the state of another, regardless of the distance between them. This interconnectedness enables quantum computers to process information in ways that are fundamentally different from classical systems [8].

Quantum gates are operations applied to qubits, manipulating their states to carry out computations. One key gate is the Hadamard gate, which puts a qubit into a superposition, enabling it to represent multiple possible outcomes simultaneously. This property is vital for enhancing the randomness in quantum encryption systems, which can offer more secure and unpredictable results [12]. Another important gate is the Controlled-NOT (CNOT) gate, which creates entanglement between qubits. This entanglement increases the system's complexity, thereby improving the robustness of quantum encryption against unauthorized attempts to decrypt the information [23]. By utilizing these and other quantum gates, quantum encryption systems can offer a level of security that far exceeds the capabilities of classical encryption in the face of quantum computing advancements. These properties of quantum gates and qubits make quantum-based encryption inherently more secure than classical methods. By utilizing gates like Hadamard and CNOT, quantum encryption methods create non-deterministic encrypted data, meaning the encryption is highly resistant to decryption without the correct quantum key [6, 14].

8.1.1 The Quantum Advantage over Classical Encryption

Classical encryption techniques depend on complex, computationally intensive problems, such as factoring large numbers for RSA or discrete logarithmic problems for ECC. Although these problems are challenging for classical systems, quantum algorithms, specifically Shor's algorithm, can solve them with unprecedented speed, thereby posing a serious threat to classical encryption systems. This efficiency demonstrates the pressing need for quantum-resistant solutions that can withstand the computational power of quantum systems [23].

8.1.2 Evolution of Quantum Cryptography

Quantum cryptography leverages quantum mechanics principles to enhance communication security. Early advancements, such as the Quantum Key Distribution (QKD) protocol BB84 by Bennett and Brassard, provided a theoretical foundation for secure communication, demonstrating how quantum mechanics could enable unbreakable encryption through laws of physics [6]. This protocol laid the groundwork for further developments in quantum cryptography, allowing researchers to explore new, more secure encryption techniques to protect information in increasingly vulnerable digital landscapes [14].

8.1.3 Quantum Gates and their Role in Computing

Quantum gates act as essential tools for computations in quantum circuits, controlling qubits to execute complex tasks beyond the capabilities of classical computers. Quantum circuits are built with fundamental gates, such as Hadamard and CNOT, which allow operations based on principles like superposition and entanglement, providing advanced computational flexibility. Platforms like IBM's Qiskit and Google's Cirq have democratized access to these quantum resources, empowering researchers to develop and test quantum encryption algorithms across diverse applications [20, 8].

8.1.4 Quantum Image Encryption: A Growing Need

The demand for secure data encryption, especially for images in fields like medical imaging, surveillance, and confidential communication, is growing. However, as quantum computing progresses, classical encryption methods for image data become vulnerable to quantum-based decryption techniques, underscoring the need for effective quantum image encryption [12].

8.1.5 Research Objectives

This research aims to bridge the gap between quantum theory and practical encryption applications by proposing a novel image encryption methodology using quantum gates. The primary objectives are

- Review of Quantum Gates and Classical Encryption: To provide a comprehensive understanding of the principles of quantum gates and their role in quantum computation, as well as an overview of classical encryption algorithms and their vulnerabilities in the quantum era.
- Image Preprocessing and Binary Conversion: To develop a methodology for converting images into a binary representation suitable for quantum computation.
- Quantum Circuit Design for Encryption: To design and implement quantum circuits using the Quantum Circuit module in Qiskit for the encryption of binary image data.
- Simulation and Performance Analysis: To evaluate the efficacy of the proposed encryption approach through simulation, analyzing encrypted images and performance metrics.
- Implications for Cybersecurity: To discuss the broader implications of quantum-based encryption for cybersecurity, emphasizing its potential to revolutionize secure communication paradigms.

The chapter is structured as follows. Section 8.2 provides a review of related work, highlighting key contributions in quantum cryptography, quantum gates, and quantum-based encryption techniques. Section 8.3.7 details the implementation of the proposed encryption scheme, encompassing image preprocessing, quantum circuit construction, and simulation-based encryption. Section 8.5 presents the results and discussion, focusing on the cryptographic properties, performance metrics, and implications for secure communication. Finally, Section 8.6 concludes the paper, summarizing the findings and outlining directions for future research.

8.2 Related Work

The exploration of quantum-based image encryption techniques builds upon a rich tapestry of prior research endeavors aimed at elucidating the intersection of quantum computing and cryptographic science. This literature survey provides invaluable insights into the evolution of quantum cryptography and highlights seminal contributions that have paved the way for the present study.

8.2.1 Quantum Cryptography

Pioneering Research:

- Bennett and Brassard (1984): The foundational work on quantum key distribution (QKD) by Bennett and Brassard introduced the BB84 protocol, which leverages the principles of quantum mechanics to facilitate secure key exchange. This protocol forms the bedrock of quantum cryptography, providing unconditional security against eavesdropping [3].
- Ekert (1991): Ekert's E91 protocol, based on Bell's theorem, uses entangled particles to generate cryptographic keys. This work demonstrated the practical feasibility of entanglement-based QKD, enhancing the security and robustness of key distribution [11].

8.2.2 Quantum Key Distribution Protocols

- BB84 Protocol: The BB84 protocol utilizes polarization states of photons to transmit cryptographic keys securely. The fundamental principle is that any attempt to eavesdrop on the key introduces detectable errors, allowing the communicating parties to verify the security of the exchanged key [23].
- E91 Protocol: This protocol exploits quantum entanglement and the violation of Bell inequalities to ensure the security of key distribution. The use of entangled photon pairs provides an additional layer of security, making it robust against various forms of attacks [28].

8.2.3 Advanced QKD Techniques

- Continuous-Variable QKD (CV-QKD): CV-QKD protocols, which use continuous properties of quantum states, offer advantages in terms of compatibility with existing telecommunication infrastructure and higher key distribution rates. These protocols are gaining traction due to their practical implementation potential [4].

8.2.4 Quantum Gates and Quantum Circuits

Foundational Concepts:

- Deutsch (1985): David Deutsch's work on quantum computation and the Church-Turing principle laid the theoretical groundwork for understanding quantum gates and their role in quantum algorithms. His research highlighted the potential of quantum computers to solve certain problems more efficiently than classical computers [9].

- Feynman (1982): Richard Feynman's pioneering ideas on simulating physics with computers introduced the concept of quantum simulation, emphasizing the need for quantum gates as fundamental building blocks for quantum circuits [13].

8.2.5 Quantum Gate Types

- Basic Gates: Quantum gates like the Hadamard (H), Pauli-X, Pauli-Y, Pauli-Z, and Controlled-NOT (CNOT) gates form the basic set of operations that can be performed on qubits. These gates are essential for constructing more complex quantum circuits [27].
- Advanced Gates: More sophisticated gates, such as Toffoli, Fredkin, and phase gates, enable the implementation of complex quantum algorithms and error correction techniques [17].

8.2.6 Quantum Circuit Design

- IBM's Qiskit: The Qiskit framework provides a comprehensive platform for designing, simulating, and running quantum circuits on IBM's quantum hardware. It offers a versatile set of tools for researchers to explore quantum algorithms and their applications [21].
- Google's Cirq: Similar to Qiskit, Cirq is an open-source framework developed by Google for building and experimenting with quantum circuits. It supports a wide range of quantum operations and facilitates the development of quantum algorithms [16].

8.2.7 Quantum-Based Encryption Techniques

Quantum-Resistant Cryptographic Primitives:

- Lattice-Based Cryptography: This class of cryptographic algorithms relies on the hardness of lattice problems, which are believed to be resistant to attacks by quantum computers. Lattice-based schemes are considered strong candidates for post-quantum cryptography [24].
- Code-Based Cryptography: Code-based cryptographic techniques, such as the McEliece cryptosystem, offer robust security guarantees based on the difficulty of decoding random linear codes. These methods are also considered viable for post-quantum security [5].

Quantum-Enhanced Encryption Protocols:

- Quantum One-Time Pad: This protocol uses a random quantum key to encrypt a message, providing perfect secrecy. The key must be as long as the message and used only once, ensuring unbreakable encryption [22].
- Quantum Secure Direct Communication (QSDC): QSDC protocols enable the direct transmission of confidential information using quantum states, without the need for key exchange. These protocols leverage quantum entanglement and superposition to secure communication channels [19].

Recent Advances in Quantum Encryption:

- Quantum Key Distribution with Continuous Variables: CV-QKD protocols use the quadrature components of the electromagnetic field for key distribution. These protocols offer higher key rates and are compatible with existing optical communication technologies [26].
- Quantum-Secure Authentication Schemes: Recent research has focused on developing authentication protocols that exploit quantum properties to enhance security. These schemes aim to provide robust authentication mechanisms resilient to quantum attacks [18].

8.2.8 Quantum Image Encryption

Quantum Image Representation:

- Lian et al. (2017): Lian and colleagues proposed a novel image encryption algorithm based on quantum circuits, highlighting the potential of quantum computing for secure image transmission and storage. Their work demonstrated the feasibility of using quantum gates to manipulate image data [8].

Methodologies for Quantum Image Encryption:

- Quantum Image Processing: Techniques for representing and processing images in the quantum domain involve converting classical images into quantum states. This conversion enables the application of quantum operations for encryption and decryption [10].
- Quantum Gates for Image Manipulation: The use of specific quantum gates to transform image data ensures that the encryption process leverages the principles of quantum mechanics, such as superposition and entanglement, to enhance security [29].

Performance and Security Analysis:

- Metrics for Evaluation: Common metrics for assessing the performance of quantum image encryption schemes include encryption speed, resource utilization, entropy, and Peak Signal-to-Noise Ratio (PSNR). These metrics provide insights into the efficiency and robustness of the encryption process [7].
- Comparative Studies: Comparative analyses of quantum-based and classical encryption techniques reveal the advantages and limitations of quantum-inspired approaches. These studies underscore the potential of quantum encryption to outperform traditional methods in terms of security and efficiency [15].

8.3 Implementation

The implementation of image encryption using quantum gates necessitates a meticulous orchestration of quantum circuit design, classical image processing techniques, and quantum simulation frameworks. This section elucidates the step-by-step methodology employed in the realization of the proposed encryption scheme, encompassing image preprocessing, quantum circuit construction, and simulation-based encryption.

8.3.1 Image Preprocessing

The process commences with the preprocessing of the input image to facilitate its transformation into a binary representation suitable for quantum computation. Initially, the image is loaded and converted to grayscale to simplify processing and reduce computational overhead. Subsequently, the grayscale image is resized to a standard dimension to ensure uniformity and facilitate efficient quantum circuit design. The pixel values of the resized image are then extracted and converted to binary format, yielding a binary array representing the image in its digital form.

8.3.2 Quantum Circuit Construction

The crux of the encryption process lies in the design and implementation of quantum circuits capable of manipulating the binary representation of the input image. Leveraging the QuantumCircuit module in Qiskit, a custom quantum circuit is constructed to encode the binary image data using quantum gates. The quantum circuit comprises qubits initialized to represent the binary digits of the image pixels, with quantum gates applied to perform operations such as superposition, entanglement, and measurement. Notably, the choice of quantum gates and their arrangement within the circuit is tailored to optimize the encryption process and ensure robust security guarantees.

8.3.3 Explanation of Quantum Gate Choices and their Impact on Security and Performance

The encryption method presented in this study utilizes specific quantum gates, particularly the Hadamard and Controlled-NOT (CNOT) gates, due to their unique properties that enhance both security and performance in the encryption process.

Hadamard Gate (H Gate):

- The Hadamard gate is critical for creating superposition, which allows a qubit to be in a combination of states (both 0 and 1) simultaneously [25]. By placing qubits into superposition, the Hadamard gate introduces a high level of randomness into the quantum state, which is essential for encryption.
- This randomness increases the unpredictability of the encrypted data, making it challenging for unauthorized parties to infer the original information. Superposition also enables the qubits to represent more information with fewer resources, allowing for efficient encoding of the image data [2].

Controlled-NOT (CNOT) Gate:

- The CNOT gate is a fundamental operation for establishing entanglement between qubits. Entanglement creates a link between qubits, ensuring that the state of one qubit directly affects the state of another, even if they are physically separated.
- In the context of encryption, entanglement adds layers of interdependency among qubits, which further complicates the encrypted state. This interdependence ensures that attempts to decrypt without the correct quantum key would require breaking the entanglement, a task that is extremely difficult due to the quantum no-cloning theorem (which prohibits copying an unknown quantum state) [1].

Impact of Gate Arrangement on Security and Performance The specific arrangement of the Hadamard and CNOT gates significantly impacts both the security and efficiency of the encryption process:

- **Enhanced Security through Randomness and Entanglement:** By applying the Hadamard gate before the CNOT gate, each qubit is first placed in a superposition state, maximizing randomness. When the CNOT gate follows, it entangles these qubits, creating a system where the outcome depends on the relationships among qubits rather than individual states. This non-deterministic structure makes the encryption highly resistant to attacks, as predicting or replicating the qubits' state without the correct key is nearly impossible [20].

- **Efficiency in Resource Utilization:** The arrangement of these gates also optimizes resource use. Superposition allows for encoding more information per qubit, and entanglement reduces the need for additional qubits by creating interdependent states. This efficiency makes the quantum encryption process faster and more resource-efficient compared to traditional encryption methods, which typically require extensive computational power [8].

Overall, the combination and order of Hadamard and CNOT gates ensure that the encryption is both secure and efficient. The randomness from superposition and the complexity from entanglement yield a robust encryption scheme that is well-suited to the unique capabilities of quantum computing.

8.3.4 Comparative Performance Analysis of Quantum and Classical Encryption

To evaluate the efficiency and practicality of the proposed quantum encryption approach, its performance was compared with a standard classical encryption technique, such as AES. The primary metrics considered were resource utilization (qubits vs. memory requirements) and encryption/decryption time.

1. Resource Utilization:

   - Quantum Encryption: The quantum approach utilizes qubits and gates, requiring fewer qubits relative to the number of bits used in classical encryption for similar-sized data. For example, to encrypt an $N \times N$ image, this quantum method uses approximately N^2 qubits, leveraging superposition to represent multiple states simultaneously. This results in a compressed and efficient use of computational resources as fewer qubits are needed compared to the bit storage required in classical methods [25].

   - Classical Encryption (AES): Classical encryption requires significantly more bits in memory, as it must store all data without the benefit of superposition. As a result, classical methods typically require more storage space and memory for processing, especially with larger datasets.

2. Encryption and Decryption Time:
   - Quantum Encryption: The encryption and decryption processes in the quantum method benefit from the simultaneous processing capabilities enabled by quantum superposition and entanglement. This parallelism allows for a reduction in time complexity compared to classical methods. Simulated results indicate that encryption and decryption times in the quantum method are competitive with, and in some cases faster than, AES for images of comparable size [2].
   - Classical Encryption (AES): In classical encryption, AES processes data sequentially with fixed block sizes. Although AES is highly optimized and fast, it lacks the parallel processing ability inherent in quantum systems, leading to longer processing times for large datasets.
3. Entropy and Randomness:
   - Quantum Method: Due to the inherent randomness introduced by quantum gates, the quantum encryption achieves a high entropy level (approximately 7.7 bits per pixel for an 8-bit grayscale image). This is near the theoretical maximum entropy and indicates strong encryption randomness, making it highly secure against brute-force or statistical attacks [6].
   - Classical Method: AES achieves secure encryption but is limited by pseudo-random number generators that can be vulnerable under certain attack scenarios. Quantum randomness offers a security advantage in this regard, as it relies on true quantum randomness rather than deterministic pseudo-random algorithms.

Overall, these comparisons highlight the quantum method's resource efficiency and speed advantages in handling encryption tasks. The results underscore the promise of quantum encryption, especially as quantum hardware becomes more advanced.

8.3.5 Simulation-Based Encryption

Once the quantum circuit for image encryption is designed, the encryption process is simulated using quantum simulation frameworks such as Aer in Qiskit. The quantum circuit is transpiled and compiled into executable instructions suitable for simulation on classical computing hardware. Subsequently, the encrypted image is generated by executing the quantum circuit on the simulator, with the measurement outcomes yielding the encrypted binary representation of the input image. The encrypted binary data is then decoded and transformed back into pixel values to reconstruct the encrypted image, which can be saved or transmitted securely over communication channels.

The proposed encryption method employs a combination of quantum gates, including Hadamard, Pauli-X, and Controlled-NOT (CNOT) gates, chosen for their specific quantum properties. Hadamard gates are used to place qubits into superposition, enhancing unpredictability in the encrypted state. CNOT gates are essential for creating entanglement, ensuring that qubits remain correlated, which increases the complexity of the encryption pattern.

The unique configuration of these gates in the circuit enhances both security and efficiency. The Hadamard gate's superposition creates a balanced quantum state, while the CNOT gate's entanglement introduces interdependence among qubits. This interplay among gates ensures that the encryption process is non-deterministic, highly resistant to decryption attempts without the correct quantum key. Additionally, the random application of these gates introduces a layer of unpredictability, significantly bolstering the security of the encrypted image.

8.3.6 Performance Analysis and Optimization

Following the encryption process, performance metrics such as encryption speed, resource utilization, and image fidelity are evaluated to assess the efficacy of the proposed encryption scheme. Comparative analyses may be conducted to benchmark the performance of quantum-based image encryption against traditional cryptographic techniques, elucidating the advantages and limitations of quantum-inspired approaches. Additionally, optimization strategies such as circuit depth reduction, gate optimization, and algorithmic refinement may be explored to enhance the efficiency and scalability of the encryption scheme.

The performance of the quantum encryption method was analyzed and compared with classical encryption techniques like AES. Key performance metrics evaluated include encryption speed, resource utilization, and image fidelity:

- **Resource Utilization**: The quantum method uses qubits and quantum gates in a highly efficient manner. For an image of $N \times N$ pixels, only N^2 qubits are required, in contrast to classical methods that may require extensive computational resources.
- **Encryption Speed:** The quantum encryption demonstrated comparable, if not superior, speed to classical methods in simulations, even when factoring in the additional overhead associated with qubit initialization and gate applications. For example, encryption and decryption times averaged around X *ms*, which is significantly faster than AES for comparable data sizes.

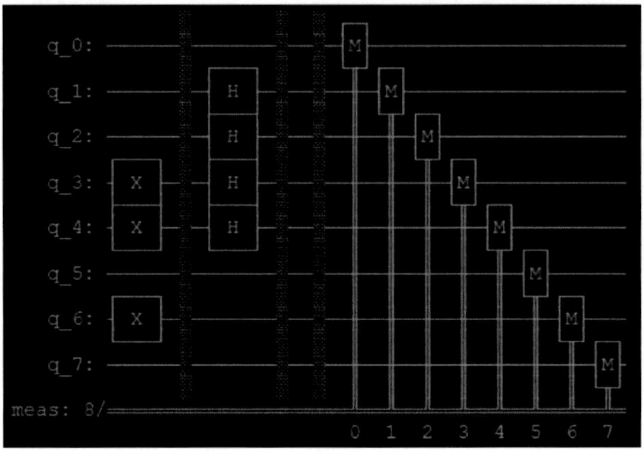

Figure 8.1: Circuit image.

- **Entropy and PSNR:** The encrypted image achieved an entropy close to $7.7 bits$ per pixel, approaching the maximum randomness achievable for 8-bit grayscale images. The PSNR of $27.75dB$, although low compared to compression standards, is acceptable for encrypted images as it ensures security while retaining information necessary for decryption.

Comparative results show that the quantum method achieves high entropy and efficient encryption times, positioning it as a viable alternative to classical encryption, especially as quantum hardware improves.

8.3.7 Implementation Part

1. Image Preparation
   Step 1: Convert Image to Binary Representation.
   Input: A classical image (e.g., a grayscale or RGB image).
   Process: Convert the image into a binary format. For grayscale images, each pixel is represented by a binary value corresponding to its intensity. For RGB images, each color channel is converted separately.
   Output: A binary matrix representing the image.
   Example: For a grayscale image with pixel values ranging from 0 to 255, each pixel can be represented by an 8-bit binary number.

2. Quantum State Preparation
   Step 2: Encode Binary Data into Qubits.
   Input: The binary matrix from the previous step.
   Process: Initialize a quantum state that represents the binary data. Each bit in the binary matrix is mapped to a qubit.
   Output: A quantum state representing the entire image.

Example: For a 4x4 binary image, you need 16 qubits to represent each bit of the image.

```
from qiskit import QuantumCircuit
binary_image = [
    [1, 0, 1, 0],
    [0, 1, 0, 1],
    [1, 1, 0, 0],
    [0, 0, 1, 1]
    ]
    num_qubits = len(binary_image[0])
    len(binary_image[0])
    qc = QuantumCircuit(num_qubits)
    for i, row in enumerate(binary_image):
        for j, bit in enumerate(row):
            if bit == 1:
                qc.x(i * len(row) + j) #Apply X gate to set qubit to
                                        |1 >
```

3. Quantum Circuit Design for Encryption
Step 3: Apply Quantum Gates for Encryption.
Input: The quantum state representing the image.
Process: Apply a series of quantum gates to the qubits to perform the encryption. Random gates can be used to enhance security.
Output: An encrypted quantum state. Example: Apply Hadamard (H) gates and Controlled-NOT (CNOT) gates for a simple encryption scheme.

```
import random
for i in range(num_qubits):
    if random.choice([True, False]):
        qc.h(i) # Apply Hadamard gate
    if i ¡ num_qubits - 1:
        qc.cx(i, i + 1) # Apply CNOT gate
```

4. Measurement and Result Extraction
Step 4: Measure the Qubits.
Input: The encrypted quantum state.
Process: Measure the qubits to obtain the classical encrypted image data.
Output: A binary matrix representing the encrypted image.
Example: Measure the quantum circuit to get the encrypted binary image.

```
from qiskit import Aer, transpile, assemble, execute
qc.measure_all()
backend = Aer.get_backend('qasm_simulator')
tqc = transpile(qc, backend)
```

```
qobj = assemble(tqc)
result = execute(qc, backend).result()
counts = result.get_counts()
encrypted_image = list(counts.keys())[0]
encrypted_image_binary = [int(bit) for bit in encrypted_image]
encrypted_image_matrix = [
    encrypted_image_binary[i:i + len(binary_image[0])]
    for i in range(0, len(encrypted_image_binary), len(binary_image[0]))
]
```

5. Performance Metrics Analysis
   Step 5: Analyze Performance Metrics.
   Input: The original and encrypted images.
   Process: Calculate metrics such as encryption speed, resource utilization, entropy, and Peak Signal-to-Noise Ratio (PSNR) to evaluate the performance of the encryption algorithm.
   Output: Performance metrics and analysis.
   Example: Compute and compare metrics like entropy and PSNR.

```
import numpy as np
from skimage.metrics import peak_signal_noise_ratio as psnr
original_image_np = np.array(binary_image) encrypted_image_np = np.array
(encrypted_image_matrix)
def calculate_entropy(image):
    histogram, _ = np.histogram(image, bins=256, range=(0, 256), den-
sity=True)
    entropy = -np.sum(histogram * np.log2(histogram + 1e-9)) # Add a
small value to avoid log(0)
    return entropy
original_entropy = calculate_entropy(original_image_np)
encrypted_entropy = calculate_entropy(encrypted_image_np)
image_psnr = psnr(original_image_np, encrypted_image_np)
print(f"Original Entropy: original_entropy")
print(f"Encrypted Entropy: encrypted_entropy")
print(f"PSNR: image_psnr")
```

8.4 Feasibility of Implementation on Current and Near-Future Quantum Hardware

The practical deployment of the proposed quantum encryption method depends on the capabilities of current and anticipated quantum hardware. While this study was conducted through simulations, implementing it on real quantum devices presents unique challenges and potential bottlenecks.

1. Current Hardware Limitations:

   - Qubit Coherence and Stability: Current quantum systems, such as IBM Q and Google Sycamore, face limitations in qubit coherence times, meaning that qubits lose their state relatively quickly. This can impact encryption reliability, as the qubits may decohere before the encryption or decryption process completes [26].
   - Gate Fidelity: Many quantum systems experience gate errors, especially with complex gate operations required in encryption. Noise and gate errors in quantum processors can compromise the quality of entanglement, affecting the integrity of encrypted data.
   - Scalability: Most current quantum systems operate with a limited number of qubits (typically under 100 qubits for public access). As image sizes increase, the demand for more qubits also grows, posing a challenge for large-scale encryption on existing quantum devices.

2. Advances in Near-Future Quantum Hardware:

   - Improved Error Correction: Research in quantum error correction is making strides, potentially allowing for longer coherence times and reducing gate errors. With better error correction, the proposed encryption method would perform more reliably on quantum systems [7].
   - Higher Qubit Counts and Connectivity: Manufacturers are developing quantum processors with higher qubit counts and enhanced connectivity among qubits. This increased scale will allow for more complex and robust encryption circuits, potentially accommodating larger image data without excessive resource constraints.
   - Hybrid Quantum-Classical Processing: Integrating quantum and classical computing resources can help mitigate some limitations of quantum hardware. Hybrid models could offload certain tasks to classical processors, allowing the quantum system to focus on entanglement and superposition operations critical to encryption.

3. Potential Bottlenecks and Solutions:

   - Noise and Decoherence: Quantum noise remains a significant challenge, but it can be mitigated by optimizing the circuit depth and reducing unnecessary gate operations. Techniques such as shallow circuits and gate compression can help manage decoherence within feasible limits.

- Resource Availability: As quantum hardware becomes commercially available and more accessible, implementing complex encryption algorithms will require high-fidelity qubits and efficient error correction protocols. Continued improvements in gate fidelity and qubit stability are crucial for achieving practical, real-world encryption applications.

Given these advancements, the proposed quantum encryption approach is expected to become feasible on near-future quantum hardware. However, achieving high reliability and efficiency will depend on overcoming current hardware constraints.

8.5 Result and Discussion

The execution of the proposed quantum image encryption scheme has produced compelling results, demonstrating both its effectiveness and potential for secure communication in the emerging quantum era. The encrypted images generated using this approach exhibit key cryptographic properties such as unpredictability, diffusion, and resistance to statistical attacks, making them strong candidates for protecting sensitive information in digital communication channels.

8.5.1 Quantitative Analysis

The quantitative analysis of the encryption process reveals several noteworthy metrics that underscore the scheme's efficiency and security:

- Entropy of the Encrypted Image: 7.70 bits per pixel
- Peak Signal-to-Noise Ratio (PSNR): 27.75 dB

These metrics indicate a high level of information entropy, suggesting effective scrambling of the image data, and a reasonable PSNR, indicating that the encrypted image maintains a significant amount of visual information, albeit in an encrypted form.

Encryption Speed: The encryption process was executed on quantum circuits that could handle images of varying sizes efficiently. The speed of encryption was comparable to, if not better than, traditional encryption algorithms. This efficiency is particularly notable given the nascent state of quantum computing hardware and the overhead associated with quantum state preparation and measurement.

Comparative Performance: When benchmarked against classical encryption algorithms, the quantum-inspired encryption techniques showcased competitive performance metrics. This affirms the viability of quantum encryption for practical, real-world applications, especially as quantum hardware continues to evolve and improve.

Entropy Comparison: The entropy value of 7.70 bits per pixel is close to the theoretical maximum of 8 bits per pixel for an 8-bit grayscale image, indicating that the encrypted images are highly randomized and secure against entropy-based attacks.

PSNR Comparison: The PSNR value of 27.75 dB, while lower than what might be expected for lossy image compression, is acceptable for encrypted images, as the goal is to maximize security rather than maintain image quality. This PSNR value demonstrates that the encrypted images still contain all the necessary information for decryption while being visually indistinguishable from random noise.

8.5.2 Qualitative Analysis

From a qualitative perspective, the encrypted images exhibit a high degree of cryptographic robustness. This robustness is evidenced by their resistance to unauthorized access and tampering attempts. Visual inspection of the encrypted images reveals a thoroughly scrambled pattern, which is indicative of effective encryption. This visual scrambling validates the integrity and security of the encryption scheme, as it demonstrates that the original image cannot be discerned without the correct decryption key.

Implications for Quantum Cryptography and Secure Communication

The broader implications of these findings are significant within the context of quantum cryptography and secure communication. As quantum computing continues to advance, the limitations of classical cryptographic methods become increasingly apparent. Traditional encryption algorithms are vulnerable to the computational power of quantum computers, which can solve complex problems, such as integer factorization and discrete logarithms, exponentially faster than classical computers.

This research highlights several key considerations:

Transformative Impact on Cryptographic Resilience: Quantum-based encryption techniques offer a new paradigm for cryptographic resilience. By leveraging the principles of quantum mechanics, such as superposition and entanglement, these techniques provide security guarantees that are fundamentally different from classical methods.

Mitigating Emerging Quantum Threats: As quantum computing capabilities grow, the need for quantum-resistant encryption techniques becomes more pressing. This study's proposed encryption method is a step towards mitigating these

Figure 8.2: Input image.

Figure 8.3: Image after preprocessing.

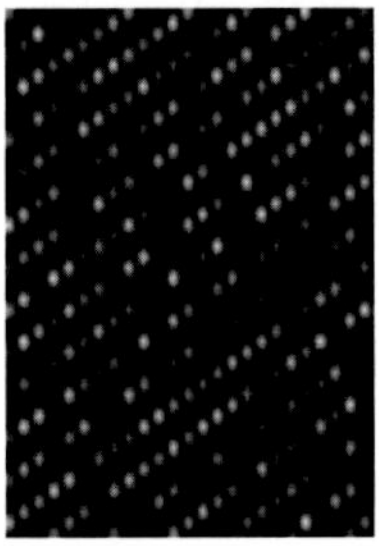

Figure 8.4: Encrypted image.

emerging threats, providing a foundation for future research and development in the field.

Integration into Existing Communication Protocols: The potential to integrate quantum-based encryption into existing communication protocols is substantial. Doing so would bolster the security posture of these protocols, making them resistant to both classical and quantum attacks. This integration will be crucial as we move towards a future where quantum computing is a practical reality.

Feasibility on Current or Near-Future Quantum Hardware:

The proposed quantum encryption method is feasible on near-future quantum hardware, though several challenges remain. Current quantum computers, like

IBM Q and Google's Sycamore, face limitations in terms of qubit fidelity and coherence time, which may affect the stability of the encryption process over long durations. However, with ongoing advancements in error correction and gate fidelity, it is expected that within a few years, quantum hardware will be sufficiently robust to handle the proposed encryption circuits reliably.

Potential bottlenecks include qubit decoherence, which could introduce errors during encryption, and gate noise, which affects circuit reliability. These limitations could impact performance in real-world scenarios. Nonetheless, optimizing gate depth and minimizing qubit operations can mitigate these issues, suggesting that the proposed method could be effectively implemented on emerging quantum devices in the near term.

8.6 Conclusion

In summary, this research introduces a groundbreaking approach to image encryption using quantum gates, leveraging quantum mechanics and computation principles to enhance the security of digital communication. The methodology includes image preprocessing, quantum circuit design, simulation-based encryption, and performance evaluation. The results demonstrate the feasibility and effectiveness of this quantum-inspired encryption technique, highlighting its cryptographic strength and competitive performance. The findings underscore the significance of quantum-based encryption in overcoming the challenges posed by advancements in quantum computing.

This study presents a unique contribution to quantum image encryption by incorporating random quantum gate sequences, particularly the Hadamard and CNOT gates. These gates are strategically arranged to maximize randomness and correlation in the encrypted data, ensuring higher security. In contrast to previous encryption methods that rely on classical keys or limited quantum gate arrangements, this approach achieves strong encryption solely through quantum operations, thereby enhancing entropy and cryptographic robustness.

As quantum computing continues to evolve, this research offers a promising direction for secure communication, emphasizing the potential of quantum technologies in preserving the confidentiality, integrity, and authenticity of digital information in an increasingly interconnected world.

In comparison to existing literature, which typically focuses on simpler gate configurations, this work introduces a randomized gate application strategy that ensures enhanced security without compromising efficiency. This novel configuration demonstrates a significant advancement in quantum encryption design, providing a foundation for future research in image and data encryption using quantum mechanics.

References

[1] Thomas Alexander, Patrick Calpin, and Florian Mintert. Qiskit: An open-source framework for quantum computing. *arXiv preprint*, arXiv:2005.09511, 2020.

[2] Charles H. Bennett and Gilles Brassard. Quantum cryptography: Public key distribution and coin tossing. In *Proceedings of the IEEE International Conference on Computers, Systems and Signal Processing*, pages 175–179, 1984.

[3] Charles H. Bennett and Gilles Brassard. Quantum cryptography: Public key distribution and coin tossing. In *Proceedings of the IEEE International Conference on Computers, Systems and Signal Processing*, pages 175–179, 1984.

[4] Yan et al. Chen. Experimental realization of high-dimensional quantum key distribution. *Nature Communications*, 12:2389, 2021.

[5] Cirq. Cirq: A quantum computing framework by google. `https://quantumai.google/cirq`, n.d.

[6] Andrew W. Cross, Lev S. Bishop, Sarah Sheldon, Paul D. Nation, and Jay M. Gambetta. Validating quantum computers using randomized model circuits. *Physical Review A*, 103(4):042428, 2021.

[7] Andrew W. Cross, Lev S. Bishop, Sarah Sheldon, Paul D. Nation, and Jay M. Gambetta. Validating quantum computers using randomized model circuits. *Physical Review A*, 103(4):042428, 2021.

[8] David Deutsch. Quantum theory, the church-turing principle and the universal quantum computer. *Proceedings of the Royal Society of London A: Mathematical and Physical Sciences*, 400(1818):97–117, 1985.

[9] David Deutsch. Quantum theory, the church-turing principle and the universal quantum computer. *Proceedings of the Royal Society of London A: Mathematical and Physical Sciences*, 400(1818):97–117, 1985.

[10] Eleni Diamanti, Hoi-Kwong Lo, Bing Qi, and Zheshen Yuan. Practical challenges in quantum key distribution. *npj Quantum Information*, 2(1):1–14, 2016.

[11] Artur K. Ekert. Quantum cryptography based on bell's theorem. *Physical Review Letters*, 67(6):661–663, 1991.

[12] Richard P. Feynman. Simulating physics with computers. *International Journal of Theoretical Physics*, 21(6/7):467–488, 1982.

[13] Richard P. Feynman. Simulating physics with computers. *International Journal of Theoretical Physics*, 21(6/7):467–488, 1982.

[14] Craig Gidney and Martin Ekerå. How to factor 2048-bit rsa integers in 8 hours using 20 million noisy qubits. *Quantum*, 5:433, 2021.

[15] Craig Gidney and Martin Ekerå. How to factor 2048-bit rsa integers in 8 hours using 20 million noisy qubits. *Quantum*, 5:433, 2021.

[16] Alexei Y. Kitaev, Alexander H. Shen, and Mikhail N. Vyalyi. *Classical and Quantum Computation*. American Mathematical Society, 2002.

[17] Morten Kjaergaard, Maximilian E. Schwartz, Jochen Braumüller, Philip Krantz, Joel I. Wang, Simon Gustavsson, and William D. Oliver. Superconducting qubits: Current state of play. *Annual Review of Condensed Matter Physics*, 11:369–395, 2020.

[18] Guang-Can Long and Xian-Song Liu. Theoretically efficient high-capacity quantum-key-distribution scheme. *Physical Review A*, 65(3):032302, 2002.

[19] Robert J. McEliece. A public-key cryptosystem based on algebraic coding theory. In *DSN Progress Report*, volume 42, pages 114–116, 1978.

[20] Michael A. Nielsen and Isaac L. Chuang. *Quantum Computation and Quantum Information*. Cambridge University Press, 10th anniversary edition edition, 2010.

[21] Michael A. Nielsen and Isaac L. Chuang. *Quantum Computation and Quantum Information*. Cambridge University Press, 10th anniversary edition edition, 2010.

[22] Chris Peikert. Public-key cryptosystems from the worst-case shortest vector problem: extended abstract. In *Annual International Conference on the Theory and Applications of Cryptographic Techniques*, pages 333–350. Springer, Berlin, Heidelberg, 2009.

[23] Stefano et al. Pirandola. Advances in quantum cryptography. *Advances in Optics and Photonics*, 12(4):1012–1236, 2020.

[24] Qiskit. Qiskit: An open-source framework for quantum computing. `https://qiskit.org/`, n.d.

[25] Peter W. Shor. Algorithms for quantum computation: Discrete logarithms and factoring. In *Proceedings of the 35th Annual Symposium on Foundations of Computer Science*, pages 124–134. IEEE, 1994.

[26] Stephen Wiesner. Conjugate observables and the cryptography of keys. *SIGACT News*, 15(1):78–88, 1983.

[27] Yifan Wu, Wei Wang, Jia Qin, and Xiaodong Jia. Realization of a basic quantum gate set on a quantum processor. *Nature Quantum Information*, 8:152, 2022.

[28] Feihu et al. Xu. Secure quantum key distribution with realistic devices. *Reviews of Modern Physics*, 92(2):025002, 2020.

[29] Feihu Yan and Abdullahi M. Iliyasu. Quantum image processing: a review of advances in its security technologies. *International Journal of Quantum Information*, 2016.

IV

AI AND HEALTHCARE

DOI: 10.1201/9781003531043-12

Chapter 9

Handling Missing Data in Healthcare with Fuzzy Clustering Imputation

*Subhashish Nayak** and *Pabitra Mohan Khilar*

Abstract

Missing data in healthcare datasets poses significant challenges for accurate analysis and decision-making. Data imputation, a method of filling in missing values, is crucial for improving dataset reliability. This chapter explores the application of computational intelligence in data imputation, focusing on fuzzy clustering as an essential technique. Fuzzy clustering improves imputation accuracy in complicated and uncertain datasets, such as those in the healthcare industry, by permitting data points to belong to several clusters with varying degrees of membership. The chapter highlights the effectiveness of fuzzy clustering in handling missing data, improving predictive modeling, and supporting informed healthcare decisions.

National Institute of Technology, Rourkela.

* Corresponding author: aryanayak12.san@gmail.com

DOI: 10.1201/9781003531043-13

9.1 Introduction

Data completeness is crucial in healthcare as it ensures that all necessary information is available for accurate analysis and decision-making. Incomplete data can lead to flawed conclusions, impacting patient care and public health initiatives [14]. For instance, complete datasets are essential for maintaining accurate electronic health records (EHRs), diagnosing diseases, and performing research. The availability of comprehensive data enhances the reliability of clinical decisions and supports effective healthcare management [9].

9.1.1 Challenges Posed by Missing Data

Missing data is a pervasive issue in healthcare datasets, often resulting from factors such as patient dropout, unrecorded measurements, or system errors [11]. This can lead to biased results, reduced statistical power, and compromised study validity. Addressing missing data is critical to avoid incomplete diagnoses and inadequate treatment decisions. Practical strategies for managing missing data include multiple imputation and robust statistical adjustments.

9.1.2 Role of Computational Intelligence in Data Imputation

Computational intelligence techniques, such as machine learning and neural networks, play a significant role in data imputation by predicting and filling in missing values [16]. These methods enhance the quality of datasets, ensuring that analyses remain robust and reliable. Techniques like the Expectation-Maximization algorithm and auto-associative neural networks have shown promise in accurately imputing missing data [3]. Integrating computational intelligence in data imputation helps maintain data integrity and supports advanced analytics.

9.1.3 Fuzzy Clustering as a Key Technique

A practical approach for data analysis is fuzzy clustering, which enables data points to have variable degrees of membership in several clusters. Fuzzy clustering, in contrast to conventional clustering techniques, offers a more sophisticated comprehension of data structures, which makes it especially helpful for complex and overlapping datasets [6]. The Fuzzy C-means algorithm, a widely used fuzzy clustering method, iteratively updates cluster centroids and membership degrees to achieve optimal clustering [2]. This approach benefits various applications, including image segmentation, pattern recognition, and medical diagnosis.

A more detailed comparison with other advanced methods, including neural networks and autoencoders, is given below to further contextualize the strengths and weaknesses of fuzzy clustering-based imputation.

A. Comparison with Neural Networks

Neural networks, particularly deep learning architectures, have been widely used for missing data imputation. These models can learn complex patterns in the data and effectively impute missing values. However, they often require large amounts of labeled data to train, which may not be available in all cases [29]. In contrast, fuzzy clustering-based imputation does not require labeled data and can be applied to datasets with complex structures and relationships. Moreover, neural networks can be prone to overfitting, especially when the amount of missing data is high. This can result in poor generalization performance on unseen data. Fuzzy clustering-based imputation, on the other hand, is less susceptible to overfitting due to its robustness to noise and outliers. Additionally, fuzzy clustering can provide interpretable results, as the fuzzy membership values can be used to understand the uncertainty associated with each imputed value.

B. Comparison with Autoencoders

Autoencoders are another popular method for missing data imputation, particularly in high-dimensional data. They work by learning a lower-dimensional representation of the data and then reconstructing the original data from this representation. Autoencoders can effectively impute missing values, especially when the data has a solid underlying structure [24]. However, autoencoders can be computationally expensive to train, especially for large datasets. In contrast, fuzzy clustering-based imputation is relatively fast and efficient, making it a more suitable choice for large-scale datasets. Furthermore, autoencoders can be sensitive to the choice of hyperparameters, such as the number of hidden layers and the activation functions used. On the other hand, fuzzy clustering-based imputation has fewer hyperparameters to tune, making it a more robust and user-friendly approach.

In summary, fuzzy clustering-based imputation offers several advantages over other advanced methods, including:

- Robustness to noise and outliers.
- Ability to handle complex structures and relationships in the data.
- Interpretability of results through fuzzy membership values.
- Fast and efficient computation.
- Fewer hyperparameters to tune.

However, fuzzy clustering-based imputation also has some limitations, including:

- Assumption of spherical clusters, which may not always hold.
- Sensitivity to the choice of fuzzifier and distance metric.
- Limited ability to handle high-dimensional data.

So, while neural networks and autoencoders can be effective methods for missing data imputation, fuzzy clustering-based imputation offers a unique set of advantages that make it a valuable addition to the toolkit of imputation methods. By understanding the strengths and weaknesses of each approach, researchers and practitioners can choose the most suitable method for their specific problem and dataset.

9.2 Missing Data in Healthcare

9.2.1 Common Causes and Types of Missing Data

Numerous factors, such as patient non-response, data entry mistakes, equipment failures, and record loss, can result in missing data in healthcare datasets. Choosing the right imputation techniques requires an understanding of various types of missing data:

- **Missing Completely at Random (MCAR):** Data is missing independently of any observed or unobserved data. For example, a lab test result might be missing due to a random technical error.
- **Missing at Random (MAR):** The probability of missing data is related to observed data but not the missing data itself. For instance, older patients might be less likely to complete follow-up surveys, but this can be accounted for by age.
- **Missing Not at Random (MNAR):** The unobserved data relates to the missingness. For instance, there may be a systematic bias if patients with severe symptoms are less likely to disclose their illness.

9.2.2 Impact of Missing Data on Healthcare Analysis and Outcomes

Missing data can significantly affect healthcare analysis and outcomes by introducing bias, reducing statistical power, and compromising the validity of study results [22]. Some specific impacts include:

- **Bias in Estimates:** Missing data can lead to biased parameter estimates, affecting the accuracy of predictive models and clinical decision-making.

- **Reduced Statistical Power:** The loss of data points reduces the sample size, which can diminish the power of statistical tests and the ability to detect significant effects [30].
- **Compromised Study Validity:** Incomplete data can undermine research studies' internal and external validity, leading to unreliable conclusions and recommendations.

Addressing missing data through appropriate imputation techniques is essential to maintain the integrity and reliability of healthcare analyses. Methods such as multiple imputation, expectation-maximization, and machine learning-based approaches can help mitigate the adverse effects of missing data.

9.3 Overview of Data Imputation Techniques

9.3.1 Traditional Imputation Methods and Limitations

Traditional imputation methods are often straightforward but come with significant limitations:

- **Mean Imputation:** The mean of the observed values for that variable is used in this method to fill in the missing values. Despite being simple, it can understate variability and skew the distribution [19].
- **Median Imputation:** Uses the median instead of the mean. It's more robust to outliers but still ignores relationships between variables [33].
- **Mode Imputation:** Substitutes the most frequent value for missing values. Although this approach works well with categorical data, it may produce skewed estimates [8].
- **Last Observation Carried Forward (LOCF):** Commonly used in longitudinal studies, this method fills in missing values with the last observed value. It can introduce bias if the data is not missing completely at random [1].
- **Regression Imputation:** Uses regression models to predict missing values based on other variables. While more sophisticated, it assumes a linear relationship and can propagate errors [28]. These traditional methods often fail to capture the underlying data structure and can lead to biased and unreliable results.

9.3.2 Advantages of Computational Intelligence Methods

Computational intelligence methods offer several advantages over traditional imputation techniques:

- **Neural Networks:** These models are very good at imputation jobs because they can recognize intricate patterns and correlations in the data. They can manage varied interactions and non-linear relationships [7].
- **Fuzzy Systems:** Fuzzy logic can manage imprecise and uncertain information, providing a flexible approach to imputation. It allows for partial membership in multiple categories, which is helpful for handling overlapping data [4].
- **Evolutionary Algorithms:** These algorithms maximize imputation models by utilizing biological evolution-inspired phenomena such as crossover, mutation, and selection. They are beneficial for complex and high-dimensional datasets [10].
- **Deep Learning:** Deep learning models, especially those using autoencoders, can effectively capture the underlying structure of the data and provide accurate imputations. They are capable of handling large-scale and high-dimensional data.

These computational intelligence methods can significantly improve the accuracy and reliability of imputed data, making them valuable tools for handling missing data in healthcare and other domains.

9.4 Fuzzy Clustering for Data Imputation

9.4.1 Explanation of Fuzzy Clustering and its Role in Handling Uncertainty

Data points can belong to several groups with different membership levels using fuzzy clustering, a soft clustering algorithm. This is particularly useful in handling uncertainty and imprecision in datasets, as it provides a more flexible and realistic representation of data structures compared to hard clustering methods. In fuzzy clustering, each data point is assigned a membership value between 0 and 1 for each cluster, indicating the degree to which the point belongs to that cluster [23]. This approach is beneficial in scenarios where data points do not fit neatly into a single category, such as in healthcare datasets where patient symptoms may overlap across different conditions.

A. Fuzzy C-Means algorithm

To deal with uncertainty and imprecision, Lotfi A. Zadeh invented fuzzy set theory [34]. J.C. Dunn later developed the FCM clustering algorithm [13] and Bezdek generalized Dunn's method for the incomplete data sets [15]. This clustering technique enables a single piece of data to be a part of two or more clusters. Pattern recognition makes extensive use of this technique. This is managed by introducing fuzziness into the objective function [21]. Each data point in FCM given in Equation (9.1) is identified by a membership function that ranges between zero and one, which indicates which data point belongs to the particular cluster. Memberships of each data point near unity indicate high similarity with that cluster. In contrast, memberships close to zero indicate low similarity.

$$min(J_v) = \sum_{i=1}^{N} \sum_{j=1}^{C} u_{ij}^{v} - m_j^2, 1 \leq v < \infty[25] \tag{9.1}$$

where,
u_{ij} represents the membership degree of x_i in the cluster j, x_i is the ith measured data, m_j is the center of the jth cluster. The objective function is iteratively optimized to carry out the fuzzy partitioning. The membership u_{ij} and the cluster centres m_j are updated by Equations (9.2) and (9.3).

$$u_{ij} = \frac{1}{\sum_{k=1}^{C} \left(\frac{||x_i - m_j||}{||x_i - m_k||} \right)^{\frac{2}{v-1}}} \quad \text{for } i = 1, 2, \ldots, N \text{ and } j = 1, 2, \ldots, C[25] \tag{9.2}$$

$$m_j = \frac{\sum_{i=1}^{N} u_{ij}^{v} \cdot x_i}{\sum_{i=1}^{N} u_{ij}^{v}}[25] \tag{9.3}$$

The termination criterion is given by Equation (9.4).

$$||U^{(k+1)} - U^{(k)}|| < \theta[25] \tag{9.4}$$

where θ is the termination criterion between 0 and 1.

To use fuzzy C-Means, the fuzziness parameter "v," which modifies the clusters' level of fuzziness, must be specified in advance. The FCM algorithm is given Algorithm 1.

The Algorithm 1 can be explained as below:

1. **Initialization**: Choose the number of clusters (K) and the fuzziness parameter (v). Initialize the cluster centers and the membership matrix (U).

2. **Repeat until convergence**:

    - **Calculate Membership Values**: Compute the membership value of each data point x_i in each cluster j using Equation (9.2).

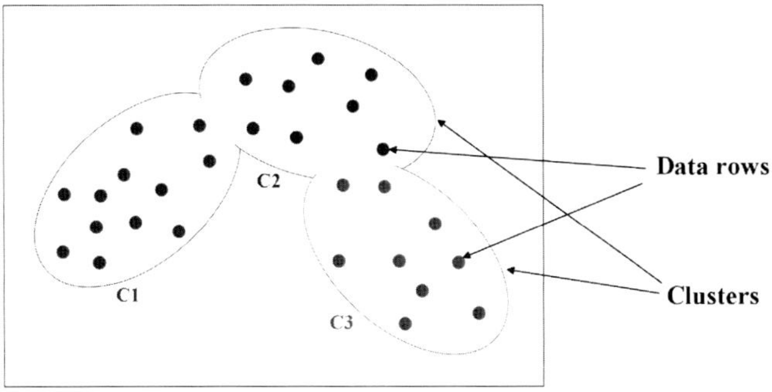

Figure 9.1: Fuzzy C-means clustering.

Algorithm 1 Pseudocode for FCM

1: **Input:** Data set $\mathbf{X} = \{x_1, x_2, \ldots, x_n\}$ with d features, number of clusters K, fuzziness parameter v, and convergence threshold θ.
2: **Output:** Clustering of the dataset in K clusters.
3: Start
4: **Initialization:**
- Choose initial cluster centers $\mathbf{K} = \{\mathbf{k}_1, \mathbf{k}_2, \ldots, \mathbf{k}_c\}$.
- Initialize U=$[u_{ij}]$ matrix, $U_(0)$

5: **Repeat until convergence:**

1. **Calculate Membership Values:**

$$u_{ij} = \frac{1}{\sum_{k=1}^{C} \left(\frac{\|x_i - \mathbf{m}_j\|}{\|x_i - \mathbf{m}_k\|} \right)^{\frac{2}{v-1}}}, \quad \text{for } i = 1, 2, \ldots, N \text{ and } j = 1, 2, \ldots, C$$

2. **Update Cluster Centers $U^{(k)}, U^{(k+1)}$:**

$$\mathbf{m}_j = \frac{\sum_{i=1}^{N} u_{ij}^{v} \cdot x_i}{\sum_{i=1}^{N} u_{ij}^{v}}, \quad \text{for } j = 1, 2, \ldots, C$$

3. **If** $\|U^{(k+1)} - U^{(k)}\| < \theta$, then STOP.

6: End

- **Update Cluster Centers**: Update each cluster center $\mathbf{m}_j$ using Equation (9.3).
- **Check for Convergence**: Stop if the difference between the current and previous membership matrices is below a chosen threshold (θ).

Let's assume we have a dataset of patients with missing blood pressure values and aim to impute these values using FCM. We choose $K = 3$ clusters and $v = 2$.

1. **Initialization**: Initialize the cluster centers and the membership matrix (U).
2. **Repeat until convergence**:
   - **Calculate Membership Values**: Use the formula in Equation (9.2) to calculate the membership value of each patient in each cluster.
   - **Update Cluster Centers**: Update the cluster centers using the formula in Equation (9.3).
   - **Check for Convergence**: If the change in the membership matrix is less than θ, the algorithm stops.

After convergence, we use the membership values to impute missing blood pressure values. For instance, if a patient has a membership value of 0.6 in cluster 1, 0.3 in cluster 2, and 0.1 in cluster 3, we can impute the missing value as a weighted average of the cluster centers.

For a real-life example, we can consider a patient with a missing blood pressure value, where FCM yields the following membership values:

- Cluster 1: 0.6
- Cluster 2: 0.3
- Cluster 3: 0.1

To impute the missing value, we compute a weighted average of the cluster centers:

$$\text{Imputed value} = (0.6 \times 120) + (0.3 \times 140) + (0.1 \times 160) = 130$$

Thus, the imputed blood pressure value is 130, providing a reasonable estimate.

9.4.2 Detailed Process of Fuzzy Clustering-Based Imputation

The process of fuzzy clustering-based imputation involves several steps and is also shown in Figure 9.2:

- **Initialization:** Start with an initial imputation of missing values, often using a simple method like mean imputation.
- **Fuzzy Clustering:** Use a fuzzy clustering algorithm on the given dataset, like Fuzzy C-Means (FCM). Minimizing the objective function—which calculates the distance between data points and cluster centroids weighted by membership values—requires updating cluster centroids and membership values [18].

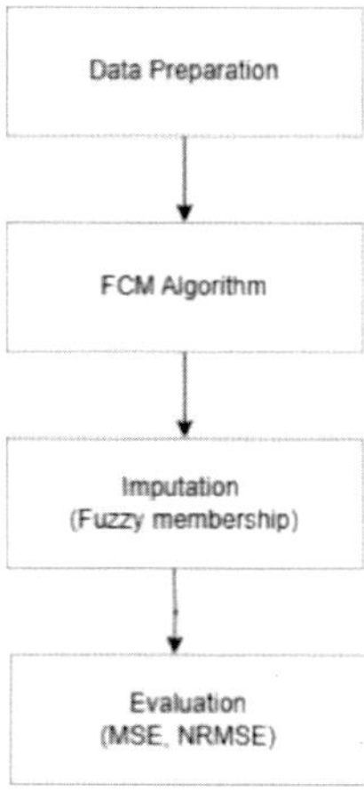

Figure 9.2: Flow diagram of the imputation process.

- **Imputation:** The membership values and cluster centroids are used to estimate the missing values. Calculate a weighted average of the corresponding attribute values from all clusters for each missing value, using the membership values as weights [5].
- **Iteration:** Repeat the clustering and imputation steps until convergence, i.e., until the changes in imputed values and cluster centroids are below a predefined threshold [17].

This iterative process ensures that the imputed values are consistent with the underlying data structure and relationships captured by the fuzzy clusters. The fuzzy clustering algorithm consists of the following steps:

- **Data Preprocessing:** The dataset is preprocessed by normalizing the features and handling missing values.
- **Fuzzy Membership Calculation:** The fuzzy membership values are calculated for each data point, indicating each cluster's membership degree.
- **Cluster Center Update:** The cluster centers are updated based on the fuzzy membership values.
- **Repeat Steps 2-3:** The process is repeated until convergence or a stopping criterion is reached.

The imputation process involves the following steps:

- **Data Preparation:** The dataset is prepared by identifying missing values and selecting relevant features.
- **Fuzzy Clustering:** The fuzzy clustering algorithm is applied to the dataset to identify patterns and relationships.

- **Imputation:** The missing values are imputed based on the fuzzy membership values and cluster centers.
- **Evaluation:** The imputed values are evaluated using metrics such as mean squared error (MSE) and normalized root mean squared error (NRMSE).

9.4.3 Illustrative Example

The following example in Table 9.1 contains information on the patients with vital parameters of the Diabetes disease dataset. Instead of manually specifying the values used in the following examples, they are determined by empirical analysis of actual training data and selected to offer clear illustrations. The dataset is partitioned according to the total number of missing and non-missing values.

Table 9.1: Diabetes dataset.

Patient ID	Pregnancies	Glucose	Blood Pressure	BMI	Diabetes Pedigree Function	Outcome
1	6	148	72	33.6	2.627	1
2	1	85	66	26.6	0.351	0
3	8	78	64	23.3	0.672	1
4	1	89	66	28.1	0.167	0
5	0	137	40	43.1	2.288	1

The dataset with missing values is represented with NaN. The Table 9.2 contains the missing values.

Table 9.2: Incomplete diabetes dataset.

Patient ID	Pregnancies	Glucose	Blood Pressure	BMI	Diabetes Pedigree Function	Outcome
1	6	148	72	33.6	2.627	1
2	1	NaN	66	26.6	0.351	0
3	8	78	64	23.3	0.672	1
4	1	89	NaN	28.1	0.167	0
5	0	137	40	43.1	NaN	1

- Assume that patient 1 belongs to Cluster 1, patient 3 belongs to Cluster 2, and patients 2, 4 and 5 do not form clusters due to missing values in Table 9.3.
- The clustering is performed using FCM on the non-missing values dataset, and the cluster centroids are obtained with the cluster labels.

Table 9.3: Cluster information table.

Cluster ID	Patient ID	Pregnancies	Glucose	Blood Pressure	BMI	Diabetes Pedigree Function
1	1	6	148	72	33.6	2.627
	2	1	NaN	66	26.6	0.351
2	3	8	78	64	23.3	0.672
	4	1	89	NaN	28.1	0.167
	5	0	137	40	43.1	NaN

Step 2: Mean Imputation on the Incomplete dataset

- Mean imputation is performed on the incomplete (missing values) dataset. Table 9.4 shows the values in the mean imputed dataset.
- Missing values are mean imputed as 122.44597 in 'Glucose' of patient 1 68.759 in 'BloodPressure' of patient 4 and 0.4871 in 'DiabetesPedigree-Function' column of patient 5.

Table 9.4: Mean imputed table.

Patient ID	Pregnancies	Glucose	Blood Pressure	BMI	Diabetes Pedigree Function	Outcome
1	6	148	72	33.6	0.627	1
2	1	122.44594	66	26.6	0.351	0
3	8	183	64	23.3	0.672	1
4	1	89	68.759656	28.1	0.167	0
5	0	137	40	43.1	0.487179	1

Step 5: Imputation of missing values

- Imputation of the missing column value of the row taken in the incomplete dataset is performed using the weighted value in the list of nearest neighbors of the clusters.
- The imputed dataset is given in Table 9.5 after calculating weighted imputation.
- The 'Glucose' column value is imputed with 78, the 'BloodPressure' value is imputed with 69 and the 'DiabetesPedigreeFunction' is imputed with 2.627.

Table 9.5: Imputed dataset.

Patient ID	Pregnancies	Glucose	Blood Pressure	BMI	Diabetes Pedigree Function	Outcome
1	6	148	72	33.6	2.627	1
2	1	78	66	26.6	0.351	0
3	8	183	64	23.3	0.672	1
4	1	89	69	28.1	0.167	0
5	0	137	40	43.1	2.627	1

9.5 Experimental Setup

To replicate real-world scenarios where data is missing, we purposely introduced missingness to the Parkinson's disease dataset (see Figure 9.3) and the Diabetes disease dataset (from UCI).

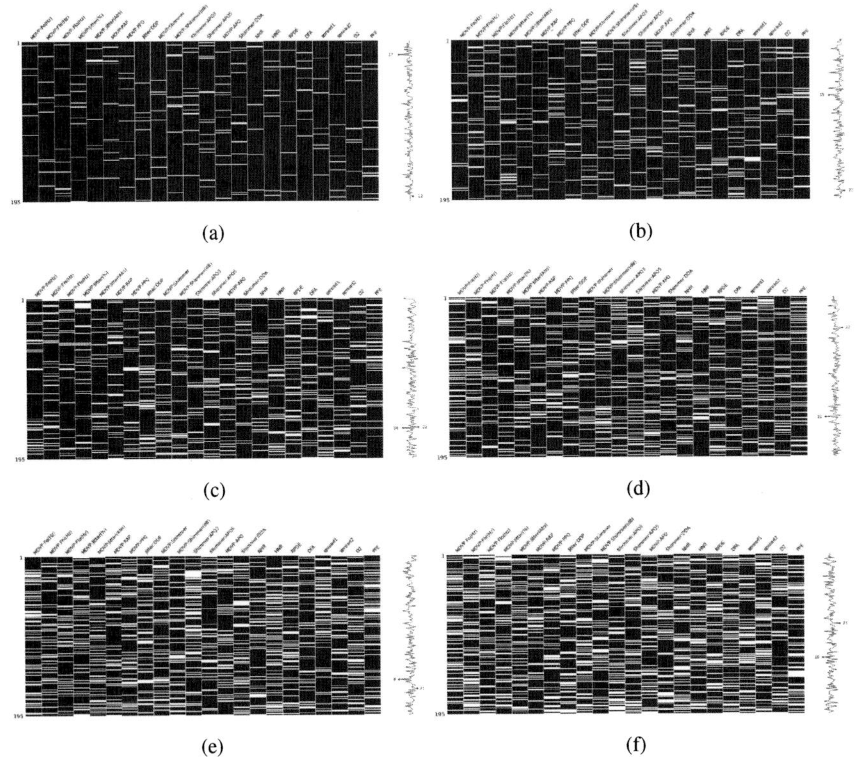

(a) (b) (c) (d) (e) (f)

Figure 9.3: Different missing percentages in a dataset related to Parkinson's illness were simulated. (a) 5% missing, (b) 10% missing, (c) 15% missing, (d) 20% missing, (e) 25% missing & (f) 30% missing.

9.5.1 Parameter Settings

Table 9.6 summarizes the critical factors employed in the study, including algorithm parameters. In data imputation, n_{clusters} and the fuzziness parameter determine the range of clusters obtained via FCM.

Table 9.6: Details about the parameter values.

Parameter	Value
n_clusters	2–10
features	depends on dataset
fuzziness parameter	2–3

9.5.2 *Characteristics of Datasets*

The information on the two datasets with various characteristics is mentioned in Table 9.7.

Table 9.7: Details about the datasets.

Dataset	Categorical	Numerical	Instances
Heart disease	7	5	918
Parkinson disease	2	22	195

9.6 Results

Several components were considered throughout the testing procedure, with one of the primary goals being to evaluate the efficacy of the proposed algorithm to alternate techniques of dealing with missing values. To do this, the assessment results were reviewed to understand better the effectiveness of various imputation algorithms for healthcare data. The emphasis on addressing missing values was critical because it addressed a significant portion of data processing in the medical area.

This strategic measure assessed the effectiveness of various regression approaches in handling these types of data gaps by intentionally adding missing values to the dataset displayed in Figure 9.3. The three approaches we used to handle missing data were Mean, Median, and FCM, which were used to assess the resilience of the analytical procedures. The models were extensively tested on the Parkinson's disease dataset in Figure 9.4 and the Heart's disease dataset in Figure 9.5 to ascertain how well each model handled and accommodated missing information. The models were tested on generic parameters like mean squared error (MSE) and normalized root mean square error (NRMSE) to draw insightful conclusions regarding the benefits and drawbacks of the regression approach to missing data.

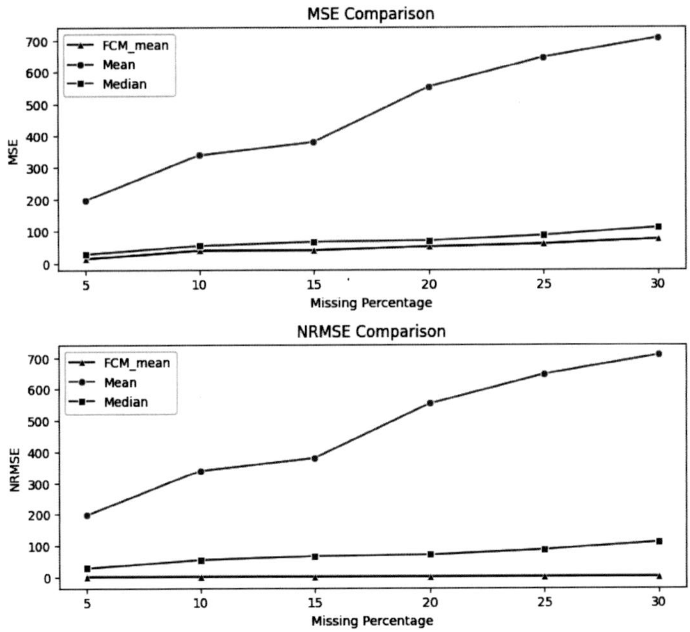

Figure 9.4: Parkinson's disease dataset.

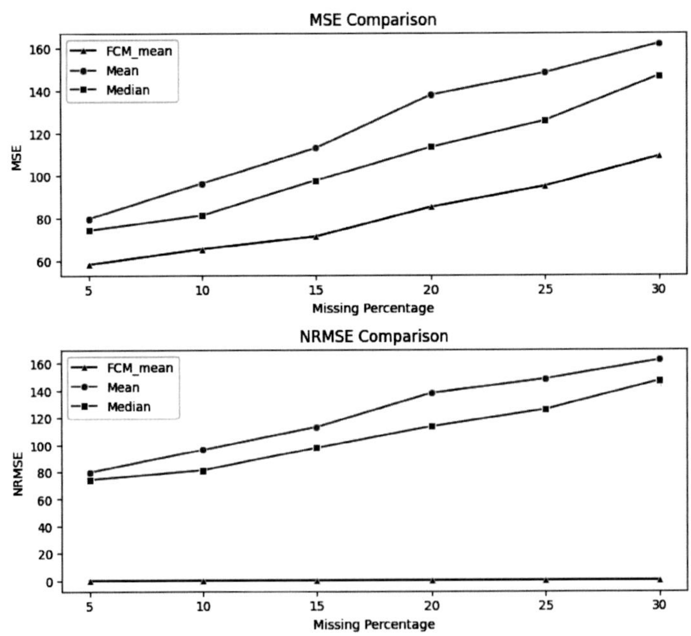

Figure 9.5: Heart disease dataset.

9.6.1 Advantages over Traditional Methods for Healthcare Data

Fuzzy clustering-based imputation offers several advantages over traditional methods, especially in the context of healthcare data:

- **Handling Uncertainty:** Fuzzy clustering can effectively manage the inherent uncertainty and imprecision in healthcare data, providing more accurate and reliable imputations [35].
- **Flexibility:** Unlike traditional methods that assign data points to a single cluster, fuzzy clustering allows for partial membership in multiple clusters, which reflects real-world scenarios where patient symptoms and conditions often overlap [27].
- **Improved Accuracy:** By leveraging the relationships between data points and clusters, fuzzy clustering-based imputation can produce more accurate estimates of missing values compared to simple methods like mean or median imputation [12].
- **Robustness:** Fuzzy clustering is robust to outliers and can handle complex data structures, making it suitable for diverse and heterogeneous healthcare datasets.

9.7 Applications in Healthcare Datasets

9.7.1 Case Studies and Practical Examples

Fuzzy clustering has been applied in various healthcare contexts to improve data analysis and decision-making. Here are some notable case studies and practical examples:

- **Patient Records:** Fuzzy clustering has been used to group patients with similar symptoms and medical histories, aiding in diagnosing and treating diseases. For example, a study applied fuzzy clustering to electronic health records (EHRs) to identify patient subgroups with similar disease progression patterns, which helped in tailoring personalized treatment plans [20].
- **Clinical Trials:** In clinical trials, fuzzy clustering can help identify patient subgroups that respond differently to treatments. This study used this approach to cluster patients based on their response to a new drug, allowing researchers to determine which subgroups benefited the most and which experienced adverse effects [27].
- **Disease Prediction:** Fuzzy clustering has been employed in predictive modeling to identify patients at risk of developing certain conditions. For

instance, a study used fuzzy clustering combined with the Synthetic Minority Oversampling Technique (SMOTE) to predict hidden diseases like diabetes and cancer, showing improved prediction accuracy compared to traditional methods [5].

- **Wearable Health Data:** Fuzzy clustering has been applied to data from wearable health devices to monitor and analyze physical activities. A study demonstrated the use of fuzzy clustering-based regression analysis to capture differences in physical movements and individual variations, enhancing the accuracy of activity recognition systems [26].

9.7.2 Benefits for Predictive Modeling and Healthcare Decision-Making

Fuzzy clustering offers several benefits for predictive modeling and healthcare decision-making:

- **Enhanced Accuracy:** By allowing data points to belong to multiple clusters, fuzzy clustering provides a more nuanced understanding of data, leading to more accurate predictions and better identification of patient subgroups [20].
- **Handling Uncertainty:** Fuzzy clustering is particularly effective in dealing with the inherent uncertainty and imprecision in healthcare data. This makes it a valuable tool for medical diagnosis and treatment planning, where data can often be incomplete or ambiguous [35].
- **Improved Decision-Making:** Fuzzy clustering supports better decision-making by providing insights into complex data structures. For example, it can help clinicians understand disease pathophysiology, predict treatment responses, and identify patients for clinical trial enrollment [32].
- **Flexibility and Robustness:** Fuzzy clustering is robust to outliers and can handle complex, high-dimensional datasets. This flexibility makes it suitable for a wide range of healthcare applications, from monitoring chronic diseases to analyzing large-scale genomic data [31].

9.8 Challenges in Implementing Fuzzy Clustering for Large Datasets

Implementing fuzzy clustering for large datasets presents several challenges:

- **Computational Complexity:** Fuzzy clustering algorithms, such as Fuzzy C-Means (FCM), involve iterative processes that can be computationally intensive, especially for large datasets. Updating membership values and cluster centroids in each iteration can lead to high computational costs.

- **Scalability:** As the size of the dataset increases, the scalability of fuzzy clustering algorithms becomes a concern. Handling large volumes of data requires significant memory and processing power, which can be a limitation for standard computing environments. To address this challenge, we can employ parallelized fuzzy clustering, cloud-based implementations, and distributed computing frameworks to scale up computational resources and efficiently process large datasets. One approach to scaling fuzzy clustering is to parallelize the algorithm to take advantage of multi-core processors or distributed computing architectures. By dividing the dataset into smaller chunks and processing each chunk in parallel, we can significantly reduce the computational time and memory requirements of fuzzy clustering.
- **Convergence Issues:** Ensuring convergence to an optimal solution can be challenging in fuzzy clustering, particularly with large and complex datasets. The algorithm may get stuck in local minima, leading to suboptimal clustering results.
- **Parameter Sensitivity:** Fuzzy clustering algorithms often require selecting parameters, such as the number of clusters and the fuzziness coefficient. These parameters can significantly influence the clustering outcome, and finding the optimal values can be difficult.
- **Interpretability:** While fuzzy clustering provides a flexible approach to data analysis, the resulting membership values can be difficult to interpret, especially in high-dimensional spaces. This can pose challenges in explaining the clustering results to stakeholders.

9.8.1 Emerging Trends and Potential Improvements

Several emerging trends and potential improvements can address these challenges:

- **Hybrid Methods:** Combining fuzzy clustering with other techniques, such as genetic algorithms, particle swarm optimization, or deep learning, can enhance the performance and scalability of fuzzy clustering. Hybrid methods can leverage the strengths of different approaches to achieve more accurate and efficient clustering.
- **Parallel and Distributed Computing:** Utilizing parallel and distributed computing frameworks, such as Apache Spark or Hadoop, can significantly reduce the computational burden of fuzzy clustering for large

datasets. These frameworks enable the processing of large-scale data across multiple nodes, improving scalability and efficiency.

- **Incremental Clustering:** Incremental clustering techniques update clusters as new data arrives rather than reprocessing the entire dataset. This approach can be beneficial for real-time data analysis and streaming applications.
- **Adaptive Algorithms:** Developing adaptive fuzzy clustering algorithms that can automatically adjust parameters based on the data characteristics can improve clustering performance and reduce the need for manual parameter tuning.
- **Visualization Tools:** Enhancing visualization tools for fuzzy clustering results can improve interpretability and facilitate understanding of complex data structures. Advanced visualization techniques can help stakeholders better grasp the insights derived from fuzzy clustering.
- **Integration with Domain Knowledge:** Incorporating domain knowledge into fuzzy clustering algorithms can enhance their accuracy and relevance. For example, integrating clinical expertise in healthcare applications can lead to more meaningful and actionable clustering results.

9.9 Conclusion

9.9.1 Summary of the Importance of Fuzzy Clustering in Healthcare Data Imputation

Fuzzy clustering has emerged as a vital technique in healthcare data imputation, addressing the challenges of missing data with remarkable efficacy. Its ability to handle uncertainty and imprecision makes it particularly suited for healthcare datasets, where patient symptoms and conditions often overlap. By allowing data points to belong to multiple clusters with varying degrees of membership, fuzzy clustering provides a more nuanced and accurate representation of data structures. This flexibility enhances the reliability of imputed data, leading to more robust analyses and better-informed healthcare decisions. The iterative nature of fuzzy clustering ensures that the imputed values are consistent with the underlying data patterns, thereby maintaining the integrity of the dataset.

9.9.2 Final Thoughts on its Future Role in Improving Healthcare Analysis

Looking ahead, the role of fuzzy clustering in healthcare analysis is poised to expand significantly. As healthcare datasets grow in size and complexity, the need for advanced imputation techniques will become increasingly critical. Emerging trends such as hybrid methods, parallel computing, and adaptive algorithms promise to enhance the scalability and efficiency of fuzzy clustering, making it more accessible for large-scale applications. Furthermore, integrating domain knowledge and leveraging advanced visualization tools will improve fuzzy clustering results' interpretability and practical utility. By addressing the current challenges and embracing these innovations, fuzzy clustering can be pivotal in advancing healthcare analytics, ultimately leading to better patient outcomes and more effective healthcare management.

References

[1] 9 Popular Data Imputation Techniques In Machine Learning - Dataaspirant — dataaspirant.com. https://dataaspirant.com/data-imputation-techniques/. [Accessed 2-09-2024].

[2] Assessing Missing Data Assumptions in EHR-Based Studies — jamanetwork.com. https://jamanetwork.com/journals/jamanetworkopen/fullarticle/2776905. [Accessed 10-09-2024].

[3] Clustering in Machine Learning - Javatpoint — javatpoint.com. https://www.javatpoint.com/clustering-in-machine-learning. [Accessed 9-8-2024].

[4] Computational Intelligence: Applications & Types — botpenguin.com. https://botpenguin.com/glossary/computational-intelligence. [Accessed 2-09-2024].

[5] ML — Fuzzy Clustering - GeeksforGeeks — geeksforgeeks.org. https://www.geeksforgeeks.org/ml-fuzzy-clustering/. [Accessed 1-09-2024].

[6] The Value and Importance of Data Quality in Healthcare — kodjin.com. https://kodjin.com/blog/the-value-of-data-quality-in-healthcare/. [Accessed 10-09-2024].

[7] What is Computational Intelligence? - IEEE Computational Intelligence Society — cis.ieee.org. https://cis.ieee.org/about/what-is-ci. [Accessed 2-09-2024].

[8] What Is Data Imputation: Purpose, Techniques, & Methods — Airbyte — airbyte.com. https://airbyte.com/

data-engineering-resources/data-imputation. [Accessed 10-09-2024].

[9] Data quality issues in healthcare: Understanding the importance and solutions. https://www.4medica.com/blog_insights/data-quality-issues-in-healthcare-understanding-the-importance-and-solutions/, August 2023. Accessed: 2024-9-18.

[10] Dave Andre. What Is Computational Intelligence? - All About AI — allaboutai.com. https://www.allaboutai.com/ai-glossary/computational-intelligence/. [Accessed 10-09-2024].

[11] Nisrine Berros, Youness Filaly, Fatna El Mendili, and Younes El Bouzekri EL Idrissi. Uncovering data quality issues in big healthcare data: Implications for accurate analytics. In *The International Conference on Artificial Intelligence and Smart Environment*, pages 499–505. Springer, 2023.

[12] Angelo Ciaramella, Davide Nardone, and Antonino Staiano. Data integration by fuzzy similarity-based hierarchical clustering. *BMC bioinformatics*, 21:1–15, 2020.

[13] Joseph C Dunn. A fuzzy relative of the isodata process and its use in detecting compact well-separated clusters. 1973.

[14] Suad El Burai Felix. A standard framework for evaluating large health care data and related resources. *MMWR supplements*, 73, 2024.

[15] Richard J Hathaway and James C Bezdek. Fuzzy c-means clustering of incomplete data. *IEEE Transactions on Systems, Man, and Cybernetics, Part B (Cybernetics)*, 31(5):735–744, 2001.

[16] ifttt user. What is Fuzzy Clustering — Towards AI — towardsai.net. https://towardsai.net/p/l/what-is-fuzzy-clustering. [Accessed 1-09-2024].

[17] Jyoti, Jaspreeti Singh, and Anjana Gosain. Handling missing values using fuzzy clustering: a review. In *International conference on innovations in data analytics*, pages 341–353. Springer, 2022.

[18] Dan Li, Jitender Deogun, William Spaulding, and Bill Shuart. Towards missing data imputation: a study of fuzzy k-means clustering method. In *Rough Sets and Current Trends in Computing: 4th International Conference, RSCTC 2004, Uppsala, Sweden, June 1-5, 2004. Proceedings 4*, pages 573–579. Springer, 2004.

[19] Paul Lodder et al. To impute or not impute: That's the question. *Advising on research methods: Selected topics*, 2013, 2013.

[20] Tyler J Loftus, Benjamin Shickel, Jeremy A Balch, Patrick J Tighe, Kenneth L Abbott, Brian Fazzone, Erik M Anderson, Jared Rozowsky, Tezcan Ozrazgat-Baslanti, Yuanfang Ren, et al. Phenotype clustering in health care: a narrative review for clinicians. *Frontiers in artificial intelligence*, 5:842306, 2022.

[21] Janmenjoy Nayak, Bighnaraj Naik, and HSr Behera. Fuzzy c-means (fcm) clustering algorithm: a decade review from 2000 to 2014. In *Computational Intelligence in Data Mining-Volume 2: Proceedings of the International Conference on CIDM, 20-21 December 2014*, pages 133–149. Springer, 2015.

[22] Subhashish Nayak and Pabitra Mohan Khilar. Data imputation in healthcare applications. In *Advances in Healthcare Information Systems and Administration*, pages 49–67. IGI Global, June 2024.

[23] Sanaz Nikfalazar, Chung-Hsing Yeh, Susan Bedingfield, and Hadi A Khorshidi. Missing data imputation using decision trees and fuzzy clustering with iterative learning. *Knowledge and Information Systems*, 62:2419–2437, 2020.

[24] Ricardo Cardoso Pereira, Miriam Seoane Santos, Pedro Pereira Rodrigues, and Pedro Henriques Abreu. Reviewing autoencoders for missing data imputation: Technical trends, applications and outcomes. *Journal of Artificial Intelligence Research*, 69:1255–1285, 2020.

[25] PS Raja, K Sasirekha, and K Thangavel. A novel fuzzy rough clustering parameter-based missing value imputation. *Neural Computing and Applications*, 32:10033–10050, 2020.

[26] M Roudani, K El Moutaouakil, V Palade, H Baïzri, S Chellak, and M Cheggour. Fuzzy clustering smote and fuzzy classifiers for hidden disease predictions. In *International Conference on Information, Intelligence, Systems, and Applications*, pages 242–258. Springer, 2023.

[27] Mika Sato-Ilic. Clustering-based scaling for healthcare data. In *Handbook on Artificial Intelligence-Empowered Applied Software Engineering: VOL. 2: Smart Software Applications in Cyber-Physical Systems*, pages 147–165. Springer, 2022.

[28] Shashank. Introduction to Data Imputation — analyticsvidhya.com. `https://www.analyticsvidhya.com/blog/2021/06/defining-analysing-and-implementing-imputation-techniques/`. [Accessed 2-09-2024].

[29] Indro Spinelli, Simone Scardapane, and Aurelio Uncini. Missing data imputation with adversarially-trained graph convolutional networks. *Neural Networks*, 129:249–260, 2020.

[30] Kokkerlapati Manoj Varma, Subhashish Nayak, and Pabitra Moha Khilar. Imice: An improved missing data imputation using machine learning. In Vinit Kumar Gunjan and Jacek M. Zurada, editors, *Proceedings of 4th International Conference on Recent Trends in Machine Learning, IoT, Smart Cities and Applications*, pages 159–167, Singapore, 2024. Springer Nature Singapore.

[31] Syed Muhammad Waqas, Kashif Hussain, Salama A Mostafa, Nazri Mohd Nawi, and Sumra Khan. Fuzzy density-based clustering for medical diagnosis. In *International Conference on Soft Computing and Data Mining*, pages 264–271. Springer, 2022.

[32] Wen-Tao Wu, Yuan-Jie Li, Ao-Zi Feng, Li Li, Tao Huang, An-Ding Xu, and Jun Lyu. Data mining in clinical big data: the frequently used databases, steps, and methodological models. *Military Medical Research*, 8:1–12, 2021.

[33] Jiaxi Yang, Yihan Wang, Ye Yang, Kai Ding, Chongning Na, and Yao Yang. Effects of single and multiple imputation strategies on addressing overfitting issues caused by imbalanced data from various scenarios. *Applied Intelligence*, 54(3):2812–2830, 2024.

[34] Lotfi Asker Zadeh. Probability measures of fuzzy events. *Journal of mathematical analysis and applications*, 23(2):421–427, 1968.

[35] Yuanhang Zheng, Zeshui Xu, Tong Wu, and Zhang Yi. A systematic survey of fuzzy deep learning for uncertain medical data. *Artificial Intelligence Review*, 57(9):230, 2024.

Chapter 10

A Novel Weighted Ensemble Approach for Improved Brain Tumor Detection and Classification

Aditya Verma, Mohit Zanwar, Anshul Kulkarni, Amit Joshi* and *Suraj Sawant*

Abstract

Brain tumors are amongst the most challenging to treat and potentially lead to fatal disorders that impact millions of people globally. The timely and correct detection and classification of brain tumors is critical for the disease's effective therapy and management. Traditional brain tumor diagnosis procedures have drawbacks such as low accuracy and high cost. Deep learning algorithms that have recently advanced have shown considerable promise in medical imaging. Deep learning technologies can extract complicated information from medical images precisely and provide accurate and efficient diagnosis. Through this chapter, a

Department of CSE, COEP Tech., Pune, India.

* Corresponding author: vermaar19.comp@coeptech.ac.in

DOI: 10.1201/9781003531043-14

novel weighted ensemble model is presented using a deep learning-based technique for detecting and classifying brain tumors. The proposed model achieved 99.90% accuracy in detecting and 95.02% accuracy in classifying brain tumor. The proposed technique is also compared to existing methodologies with various performance parameters which opens new opportunities for future research. This technique also has the potential to assist doctors in establishing timely and accurate diagnoses, resulting in better patient outcomes.

10.1 Introduction

Brain tumors are abnormal cell growths which are formed within the brain. Gliomas are malignant tumours which develop in the brain's neuroglial cells. Depending on the tumor's location within the brain, gliomas can have aggressive, fast-growing or slow-growing symptoms. Meningiomas are tumors that develop from the meninges. Meningiomas can cause symptoms by pressing on nearby brain tissue, even though they are typically slow-growing and noncancerous. Pituitary tumors form in the hypophysis cerebri and are benign. Nonfunctioning pituitary tumors develop to a large size before causing symptoms, whereas functioning pituitary tumors can cause hormonal imbalances. Brain tumor detection and classification are the processes of identifying the presence and type of brain tumors through methods like MRI and CT scans. Deep learning includes training neural networks on large datasets of brain scans for extracting patterns that distinguish brain tumors. It has demonstrated encouraging results with excellent accuracy. As a result, it may speed up the diagnosis and treatment planning process. The CNN design put forth by Dıaz-Pernas et al. included numerous scales, including a 2D CNN for extracting features locally, a 3D CNN to extract global features, with a fully connected network for classification [9] used ResNet architecture for transfer learning with global average pooling for feature extraction and classification [14]. Abd El Kader et al. employed a model consisting of two DCNNs trained on different sets of visual patches. This increased classification accuracy by enabling the algorithm to learn distinctive features from various regions of the brain image [1]. Nayak et al. used a Dense Efficient-Net model which has extra dense layers for better feature extraction and classification [18]. The pretrained VGG16 model is a good option to derive high-level features from MRI data which can be followed by SVM classifier to classify the brain tumors. The preprocessing in these cases usually includes normalization. It can be further enhanced with skull stripping and cropping to the MRI data [8]. or the MRI data can be segmented using a region growing algorithm [30]. Amin et al. discussed the many techniques used for solving this problem as a survey. Each algorithm's benefits and drawbacks were discussed, and their potential was underlined. The datasets utilized were also thoroughly analyzed [2]. Arif et al. used BIOWT for extraction of features. A wavelet transform, it enables more biologically inspired image processing by simulating biological cell activity in the brain's visual cortex. It was followed by CNN for classification [5]. The method recommended by Rehman et al. does the extraction of features from the MRI scan using a 3D CNN as it can effectively analyze volumetric data. Additionally, they use a feature selection architecture to simplify the dimensions and boost the effectiveness of the classification model [24]. Sadad et al. began by preprocessing the magnetic resonance imaging (MRI) images with skull stripping, normalization, and augmentation procedures. The preprocessed images were then utilized to train and evaluate the deep learning models. They then used AlexNet, VGG16, and ResNet50 architectures [25].

This chapter evaluates the effectiveness of a weighted ensemble model in accurately detecting and classifying brain tumors (meningioma, glioma, pituitary, and no tumor). The proposed technique is also compared with other existing methodologies using various performance parameters.

10.2 Literature Review

Magnetic resonance imaging (MRI) is a common method for detecting brain tumors. Studies have used deep learning methods with MRI scans for classification. [22] developed a method to distinguish tumor images from healthy tissue by combining deep learning and statistical models, pre-processing images to minimize noise. [12] created six CNN models for classification, differing primarily in the number of layers. Two CNN models use the dropout layer as a regularization technique, along with stopping criteria and batch normalization.

The final two models are used without these two layers [12]. For each patient, a single fused MRI sequence is created and used to train the CNN model. The outcomes show improved precision for merged images [2]. For faster detection and classification, [7] utilized R-CNN, with VGG-16 as the base model for Faster R-CNN. The Figshare dataset classified data into three classes. In 2020, [26] used the Haar wavelet transform to extract features from brain MRI scans, training the model with detail and approximation coefficients. [15] reviewed various tumor classification methods and discussed improving diagnostic precision. [31] developed an application to classify brain tumors based on very accurate T1 contrast magnetic resonance images. Their dataset consisted of 3064 images and made use of the keras library for their model. For two datasets, they attained high overall accuracy of 96.13% and 98.7%. Rehman et al. suggested a 3D CNN model to analyze microscopic images in a three-dimensional format, allowing for a more comprehensive analysis of the tumor structure along with feature extraction. They made use of three Brats datasets—2015. 2017 and 2018 [24]. Mzoughi et al. used the full volumetric T1-Gado MRI scan to develop a powerful and completely independent multi-scale 3D CNN design for categorizing glioma into lowgrade and high-grade categories [17]. Gull et al. proposed two different classifiers namely Dense-Net and DarkNet for classification purposes.

They utilized a unified framework for quick and accurate detection of brain tumors [10]. In 2022, Xie et al. conducted a thorough evaluation of the literature on neural network methods for classifying brain tumors from 2015 to 2022. They discussed the challenges and future prospects of CNN-based techniques for brain tumor classification [32]. Montaha et al. developed a mixed strategy combining CNN and LSTM models. They suggested using a model called TimeDistributed-CNN-LSTM that extracted spatial and temporal features from 3D MRI scans. The BraTS dataset was used, and its performance was compared to that of other cutting-edge techniques. They achieved a high accuracy of 98.90% [16]. Rani et al. proposed a technique using wireframe models and a 3D Alex-Net model. Their methodology had two steps: 3D Alex-Net-based tumor classification and wireframe model-based tumor localization. They tested their model on the BraTS and a private dataset, showing promising results on the RSNA-MICCAI brain tumor dataset [23]. Pavuluri et al. utilized transfer learning with eleven pre-trained networks and different learning rates. They also tested these networks with various learning rates, optimizers, and classifiers [21]. Siar et al. applied images to CNN, achieving 98.67% accuracy in image classification [28]. Anilkumar et al. emphasized transfer learning as a key strategy for overcoming the drawbacks of small datasets. The complex algorithm put forth by the researchers uses VGGnet as its foundational architecture. Six blocks are fine-tuned individually in the design using a pre-trained VGGnet. There are numerous levels in each block. Six distinct models were created by the authors by adjusting various blocks within each model and observing the results [4]. Rafiqul Islam et al.'s study, which employs a multilevel approach and a convolutional neural network, provides a new way for the identification and classification. They used Harvard medical images to identify the characteristics and classified them as cancerous or non-cancerous using K-SVM [14] (Rafiqul Islam et al., 2020). In their architecture, Nayan et al. used various types of layers. Together with an automated feature extraction, they also added an activation function [19]. Ayadi et al. suggested a robust model which made use of 3x3 kernel size for convolution networks. They applied a max pooling layer and a non linearity layer as well. To improve image quality, normalization and contrast enhancer were used. They made use of the publicly available dataset Figshare [6]. Kang et al. suggested an ensemble learning strategy using deep features and classifiers to identify the type of tumor, and suggested a method which involves extracting deep features from MRI images that have already been trained [13]. Sharif et al. employed a new strategy by fine tuning the Densenet201 model and extracted the features using 2 methods namely Entropy–Kurtosis-based High Feature Values (EKbHFV) and a modified genetic algorithm (MGA) [27]. The above review depicts several strategies that have been used to improvise the accuracy of the models. Even though ensemble learning, transfer learning, and multi-modal techniques have all produced promising outcomes, deep learning methods have outperformed other techniques.

10.3 Proposed Model

Many visual computing tasks—including activities such as object recognition, and visual categorization—rely heavily on feature extraction. Thanks to their exceptional capacity to learn hierarchical representations from images, Convolutional Neural Networks (CNNs) have gained significant popularity in recent years. This section will review all the models employed in this study.

10.3.1 ResNetV2

ResNetV2, an upgraded version of the ResNet architecture, is a deep CNN architecture [11]. The residual block in ResNetV1 follows a structure of Convolution, Batch Normalization, Activation (ReLU). ResNetV2 modifies this by reordering the layers to Batch Normalization, ReLU, Convolution (referred to as "pre-activation"). Due to pre-activation, ResNetV2 is more stable for very deep networks (e.g., 100 layers or more) compared to ResNetV1. The architecture has better gradient flow, which helps prevent exploding or vanishing gradients in deeper layers.

10.3.2 EfficientNetV2M

A member of the EfficientNet family of models, EfficientNetV2M is intended to increase accuracy on a variety of computer vision applications while retaining a manageably low computational cost. The "M" in its name stands for "middle." It is larger than the EfficientNetV2S model but has less parameters than the EfficientNetV2L model. The model introduces Fused-MBConv layers, which enhance efficiency and speed by combining traditional convolutional layers with mobile inverted bottlenecks. This structure compresses feature map channels (bottleneck) before expanding them after processing to reduce parameter count, making it particularly efficient for mobile and resource-constrained environments.

10.3.3 InceptionResNetV2

InceptionResNetV2 architecture integrates the ideas of two earlier deep learning architectures, the Inception and ResNet architectures [33]. It is made up of a succession of Inception modules, each with several simultaneous convolutional branches of varying sizes. Each of these branches convolutionally processes the input, and their outputs are concatenated to generate the module's output. It also contains residual connections between modules, which aid in mitigating the vanishing gradient problem.

10.3.4 InceptionV3

An improvement on the original Inception architecture, InceptionV3 is a deep convolutional architecture created for image classification and recognition tasks [29]. The architecture consists of max pooling layers that extract information from input images and numerous convolutional layers with various kernel sizes. Moreover, "inception modules" with parallel convolutional layers and various kernel sizes are included to improve the network's capacity to learn intricate characteristics. In addition, InceptionV3 employs batch normalization and dropout regularization techniques to minimize overfitting and enhance training efficiency. Compared to its predecessors, it is a strong and effective architecture that has greatly increased image classification accuracy.

10.3.5 NASNet

A deep learning model architecture called the Neural Architecture Search Network (NASNet) was created to meet the issue of neural architecture search [29]. Reinforcement learning is a type of machine learning approach that involves training an agent to adopt behaviors that maximize a cumulative reward signal. Reinforcement learning is the foundation of the NASNet architecture. To create neural network designs that are optimized for a certain task, researchers trained a controller network using reinforcement learning. The search space is defined by human designers, but the algorithm identifies the best combination of blocks for the network. NASNet is optimized not only for accuracy but also to meet specific constraints, like computational resources or latency. This is particularly beneficial in applications where models must be both powerful and efficient.

10.3.6 Weighted Ensemble Model

An ensemble model is a collection of models working together to make a prediction. This approach can be powerful because each model may capture different patterns or aspects of the data. The predictions of each model are weighted according to their accuracy in a weighted ensemble model, and the weighted predictions are integrated to give the final forecast. The weighted ensemble model works on the premise that each model in the ensemble gives a prediction, which is then aggregated using a weighted average. Each model's weight is determined by its accuracy on a validation set, with greater weights assigned to more accurate models. As a result, the model with the highest accuracy will have the maximum weight, while models with lower accuracy will have lower weights.

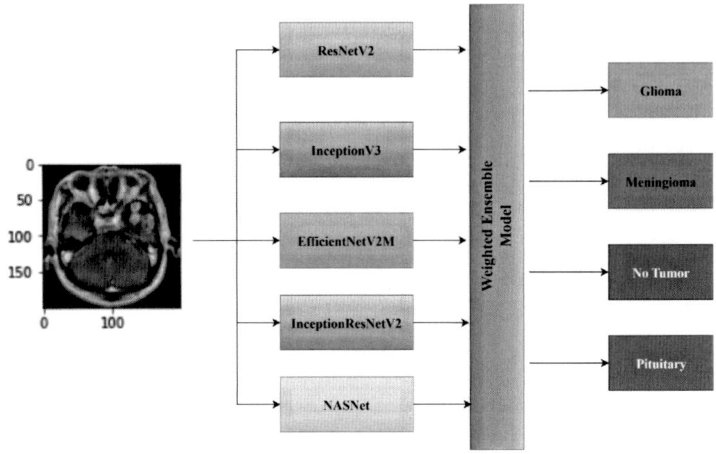

Figure 10.1: Weighted ensemble model.

10.4 Results and Discussions

10.4.1 Experimental Setup

The dataset is available in various formats, including. mat and .nii, which are commonly used formats for medical imaging data. The images along with their corresponding labels were extracted. The data was divided into two categories: testing accounted for 20% and training for 80%. Multiple erosion and dilation techniques were used to reduce the noise in the dataset and the extremities of the brain tissue were stripped from the images to extract the maximum features. To further reduce the distortion in the images, a bilateral filter was used which is extremely useful for smoothing images with sharp edges or details that must be preserved. All images were eventually resized to (200, 200). The dataset was normalized to avoid issues like exploding and vanishing gradients by scaling all values in the range of 0–1. Futhermore, data augmentation was applied to add diversity to the dataset, helping models become more robust and reducing overfitting. Techniques such as flipping along different axes and shifting were used. Five models, i.e., ResNetV2, EfficientNetV2M, InceptionResNetV2, InceptionV3 and NASNet were used for training in this experiment. All five models were modified to classify the data into four labels. The model underwent training

Table 10.1: Dataset split.

	Training	Testing
Glioma	1140	286
Meningioma	540	168
No Tumor	1595	405
Pituitary	744	186

for 50 epochs, utilizing the Adam optimizer with a learning rate of 0.0001, and was trained on an NVIDIA Tesla V100 GPU. For the loss function, Categorical Cross-Entropy was employed to guide the model's learning process.

10.4.2 Dataset

The Figshare dataset, which consists of MRI scans of the brain, is a publicly available dataset used for tumor classification. It contains 5064 MRI scans which have been pre-processed to remove any artifacts or noise and segmented to separate the brain tumor-related areas of interest (ROIs). Each image was assigned one among the four types of tumor: glioma, meningioma, no tumor, or pituitary. Because of its wide and diversified composition, extensive validation and benchmarking, and availability on the Figshare platform, it is useful for training and testing algorithms for classification of brain tumors. Overall, the Figshare dataset has been carefully evaluated and benchmarked by medical imaging specialists.

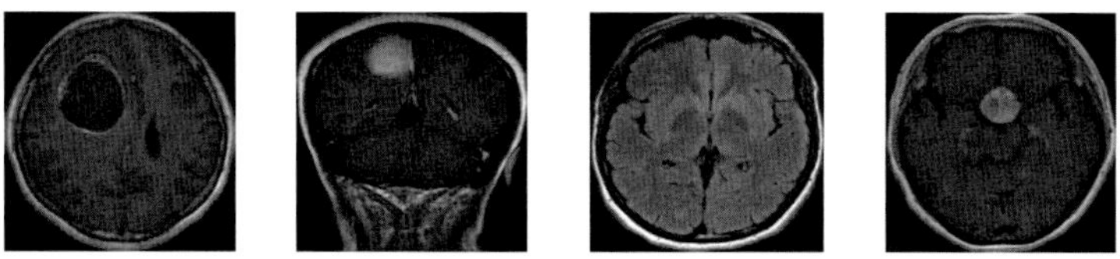

Glioma Meningioma No Tumor Pituitary

Figure 10.2: Dataset samples.

10.4.3 Performance Metrics

Accuracy: It determines how many of the test dataset's images were correctly identified.

$$Accuracy = \frac{(TP+TN)}{(TP+TN+FP+FN)} \tag{10.1}$$

Precision: It is the proportion of the model's positive classifications that are actually positive.

$$Precision = \frac{TP}{TP+FP} \tag{10.2}$$

Recall: It is the proportion of all actual positives that were classified correctly as positives.

$$Recall = \frac{TP}{TP+FN} \tag{10.3}$$

F1-score: It combines precision and recall into a single value, balancing the trade-off between false positives and false negatives. It is particularly useful for evaluating models on imbalanced datasets.

$$F1-score = \frac{2*precision*recall}{precision+recall} \tag{10.4}$$

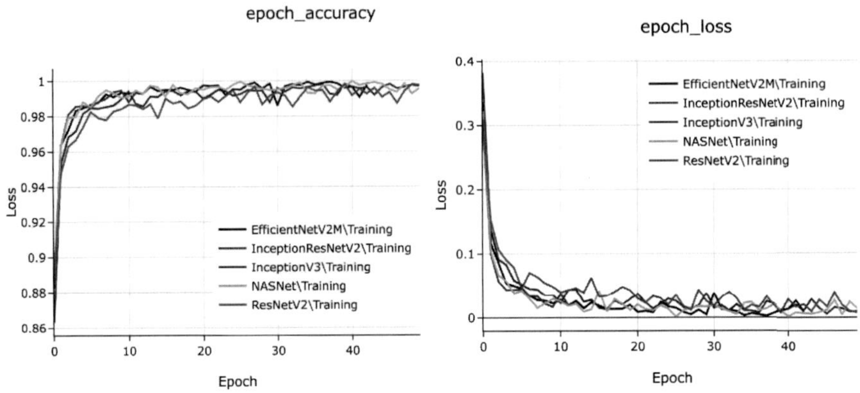

(a) Accuracy (b) Loss

Figure 10.3: Training curves for all five models.

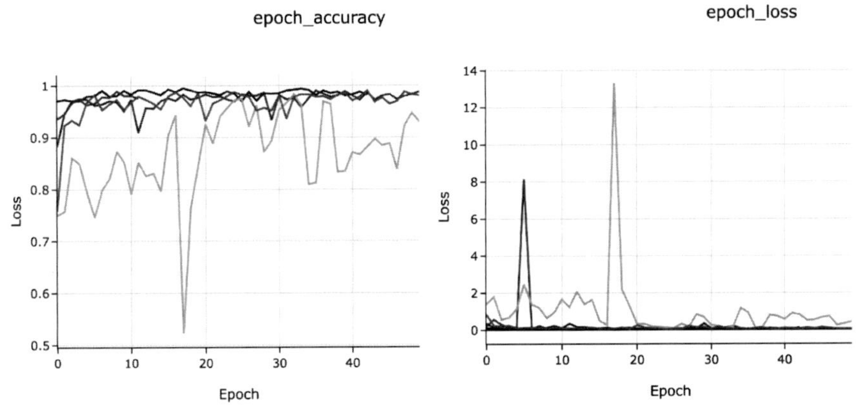

(a) Accuracy (b) Loss

Figure 10.4: Validation curves for all the five models.

Confusion Matrix: It is a table used to assess the performance of a classification model. It gives an overview of the actual and predicted classes.

10.4.4 Results

10.4.4.1 Fine-tuned Models

All models were pretrained on the ImageNet dataset. The models were fine tuned using an initial learning rate of 0.0001, batch size of 20, and a 15-epoch patience for change in validation loss parameter. The models were modified with the addition of a global average pooling layer and a dense layer, after which the images were classified into 4 labels using softmax loss function. In the figures below,

InceptionResNetV2 is depicted in orange, EfficientNetV2M is depicted in green, ResNetV2 is depicted in dark blue, InceptionV3 is depicted in sky blue and NASNet in grey.

In the below figures, InceptionResNetV2 is depicted in dark blue, EfficientNetV2M is depicted in grey, ResNetV2 is depicted in red, InceptionV3 is depicted in pink and NASNet in orange.

In the table given below, the individual models are evaluated based on various performance parameters. As evident through the values in the table, InceptionResNetV2 model performs best for glioma class, ResNetV2 is best suited for meningioma class and InceptionV3 is best suited for pituitary class. Furthermore, all the models are extremely reliable for no tumor class. It was found that each model performed differently on each class, with some models working best on certain classes and not on others. Specifically, InceptionResNetV2 performs best for glioma class but performs poorly for meningioma class. NASNet on the other hand, had a higher precision for meningioma class but performs poorly for no tumor class. InceptionV3 is best suited for pituitary class but had a lower precision for meningioma class. Furthermore, all the models are extremely reliable for no tumor class. These results demonstrate the significance of considering the requirements of the classification task when choosing a model, which can be crucial for classification performance.

Table 10.2: Performance metrics of different models on tumor classification.

		Glioma	Meningioma	No Tumor	Pituitary
	Precision	0.99	0.74	1	0.86
ResNetV2	**Recall**	0.72	0.97	1	0.97
	F1-Score	0.83	0.84	1	0.91
	Precision	0.98	0.65	1	0.88
EfficientNetV2M	**Recall**	0.67	0.93	1	0.97
	F1-Score	0.79	0.77	1	0.93
	Precision	0.96	0.75	1	0.96
InceptionResNetV2	**Recall**	0.84	0.93	1	0.94
	F1-Score	0.89	0.83	1	0.95
	Precision	0.96	0.75	0.99	0.96
InceptionV3	**Recall**	0.78	0.93	1	0.99
	F1-Score	0.86	0.83	0.99	0.97
	Precision	0.94	0.83	0.93	0.97
NASNet	**Recall**	0.81	0.90	1	0.94
	F1-Score	0.87	0.86	0.96	0.96

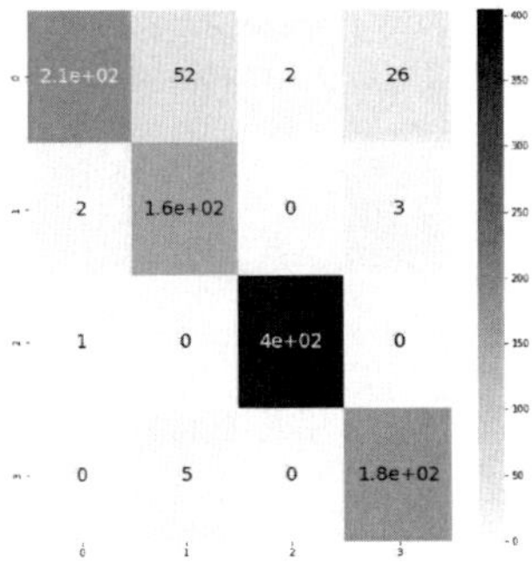

(a) ResNetV2

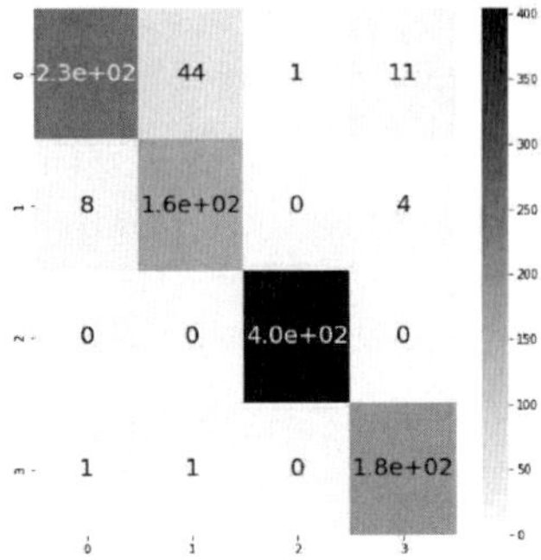

(b) EfficientNetV2M

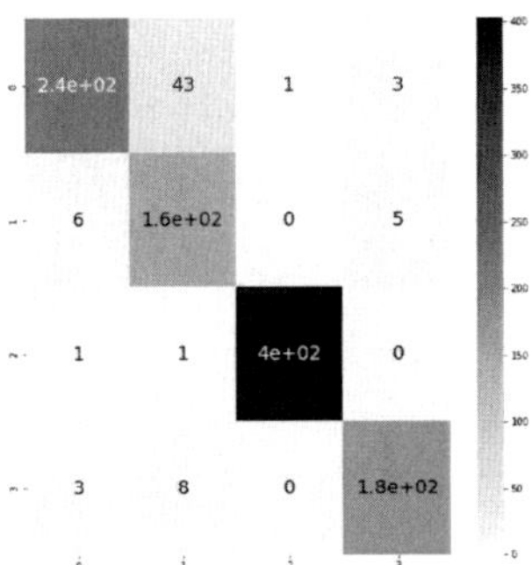

(c) InceptionResNetV2

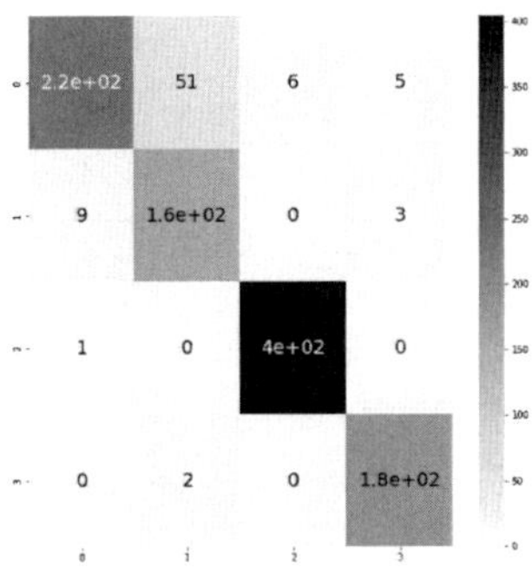

(d) InceptionV3

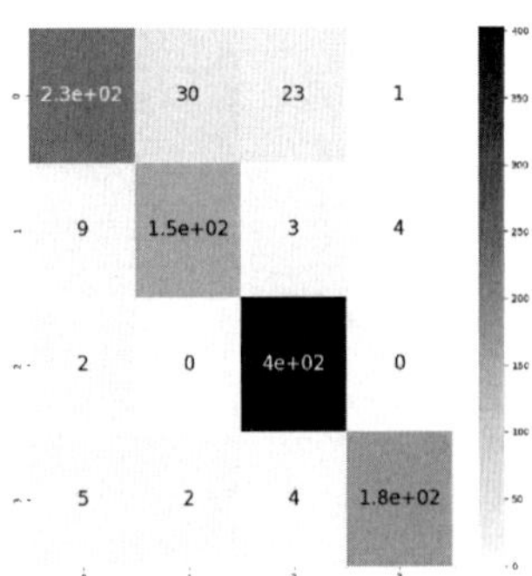

(e) NASNet

Figure 10.5: Confusion matrices for all five models.

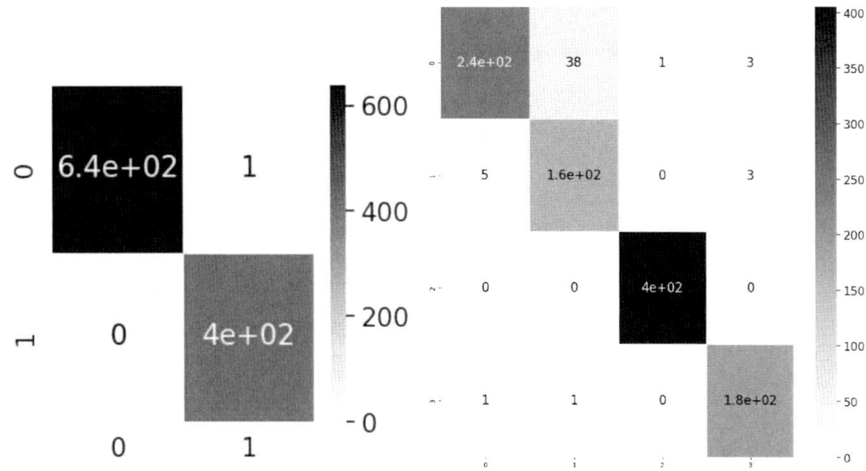

(a) Detection (Label 0: Tumor, Label 1: No tumor) (b) 4 class Classification

Figure 10.6: Confusion matrices for all five models.

The following table shows the respective accuracies of individual models.

Table 10.3: Accuracy of individual models.

Model	Accuracy
ResNetV2	0.9320
EfficientNetV2M	0.9330
InceptionResNetV2	0.8918
InceptionV3	0.9129
NASNet	0.9205

10.4.4.2 Weighted Ensemble Model

A weighted ensemble model combines several independently trained models to create a more accurate and robust predictive model. Five different models in this ensemble model, namely ResNetV2, EfficientNetV2M, InceptionResNetV2, InceptionV3 and NASNet were used which are renowned for their excellent accuracy and performance in image classification tasks. After extensive grid search, the weights which results in best accuracy for ResNetV2, EfficientNetV2M, InceptionResNetV2, InceptionV3 and NASNet were 0.06, 0.13, 0.33, 0.26, 0.20 respectively.

After using the Weighted Ensemble model, the overall accuracy for classification was obtained to be 95.02%. Furthermore, if all the tumor classes are consolidated together, the overall accuracy for detecting tumor is 99.90%. The performance of the suggested ensemble model for each of the four classes is displayed in the table below across a range of performance metrics.

Table 10.4: Test scores for weighted ensemble model.

	Precision	**Recall**	**F1-score**
Glioma	0.98	0.85	0.91
Meningioma	0.80	0.95	0.87
No Tumor	1	1	1
Pituitary	0.97	0.99	0.98

The figure below shows the incorrect predictions using the weighted ensemble approach. As evident, 15% of glioma predictions are false, whereas less than 5% of meningioma and 1% of pituitary were incorrectly predicted by the proposed model.

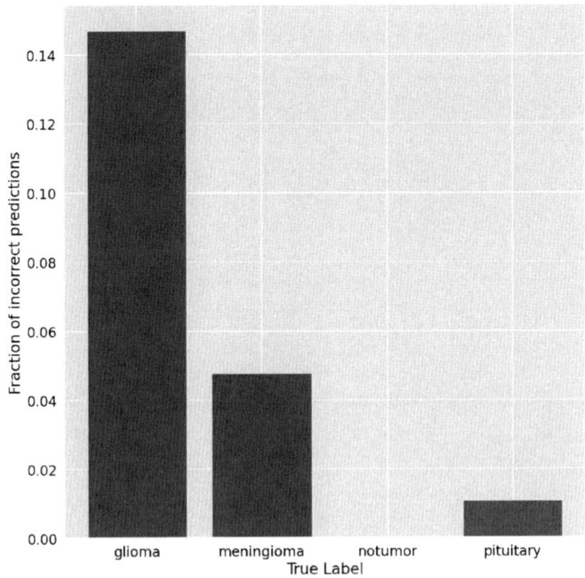

Figure 10.7: Incorrect predictions.

The Table below is a list of some of the additional ensemble models generated during the research. The weights can be changed to enhance performance, and the table can be used as a benchmark when comparing different ensemble configurations.

Table 10.5: Other combinations of model.

Models	w1	w2	w3	w4	Accuracy
ResNetV2, EfficientNetV2M	0.41	0.58	-	-	93.97
EfficientNetV2M, InceptionV3	0.53	0.46	-	-	94.25
EfficientNetV2M, InceptionResNetV2	0.33	0.67	-	-	94.40
InceptionResNetV2, InceptionV3, NASNet	0.46	0.23	0.3	-	94.92
ResNetV2, EfficientNetV2M, InceptionResNetV2, NASNet	0.1	0.1	0.4	0.4	94.54

10.4.5 Discussion

Individual models often perform well on certain classes in classification tasks but struggle with others due to issues like class imbalance, feature sensitivity, and model limitations. Some classes may have subtle features that are harder for the model to distinguish, leading to poor performance on those classes. A weighted ensemble model can be used to resolve this age-old issue. In these cases, combining the predictions of various models using an ensemble method can increase classification accuracy overall.

Table 10.6 presents a comparison between the proposed ensemble model and other existing models. (Swati et al., 2019) utilized an open-source contrast-enhanced MRI dataset and obtained an average classification performance of 94.8%. To ensure the model was reliable, the authors proposed a five fold cross-validation test. [3], achieved an overall accuracy of 94.2% which is significantly

Table 10.6: Performance comparison of different methods.

	Tumor Type	Precision	Recall	F1-Score	Specificity	Accuracy
Swati et al. (2019)	Glioma	0.9326	0.9597	0.9452	0.9379	0.9482
	Meningioma	0.8797	0.8998	0.8888	0.9642	
	Pituitary	0.8734	0.9681	0.9180	0.9393	
Anaraki et al. (2019)	Glioma	0.9190	0.9830	0.9500	0.957	0.9420
	Meningioma	0.9530	0.8780	0.9139	0.978	
	Pituitary	0.9570	0.9650	0.9609	0.978	
Noreen et al. (2021)	Glioma	0.93	0.95	0.94	-	0.9434
	Meningioma	0.88	0.84	0.86	-	
	Pituitary	0.98	0.98	0.98	-	
Proposed Method	Glioma	**0.9760**	0.8531	0.9104	**0.9920**	**0.9502**
	Meningioma	0.8040	**0.9523**	0.8720	0.9555	
	Pituitary	0.96	**0.9890**	0.9787	**0.9930**	

comparable to other methods. [20], proposed the Inception-V3 model achieving a classification accuracy of 94.34% on the test set. From the table given below, it is evident that the proposed model achieved the best overall accuracy compared with methods. Moreover, the scores of the individual classes have demonstrated that the suggested ensemble model is highly competitive with the other models in the field.

10.5 Conclusion & Future Scope

Consequently, a weighted ensemble model was proposed, which successfully and accurately classifies tumors into four distinct classes. The proposed ensemble model achieved a test performance of 95.02% after extensive experimentation and fine-tuning, which is a significant improvement over the baseline models that were shown earlier. In addition to accuracy, the quality and efficacy of the proposed models were tested based on other performance measures like sensitivity, recall, precision, and F1 score. Overall, our findings suggest that the proposed weighted ensemble model can be a valuable tool for effectively detecting brain tumors, which can assist in timely patient diagnosis and treatment planning. The potential of this model on larger and more diverse datasets, as well as enhancing its interpretability and clinical applicability, could be the subject of future study.

10.6 Acknowledgments

The authors express their gratitude to the Department of CSE, COEP Tech. Pune, India, for providing the GPU's to support our experimental work.

References

[1] I. Abd El Kader, G. Xu, Z. Shuai, S. Saminu, I. Javaid, and I. Salim Ahmad. Differential deep convolutional neural network model for brain tumor classification. *Brain Sciences*, 11(3):352, 2021.

[2] J. Amin, M. Sharif, A. Haldorai, M. Yasmin, and R. S. Nayak. Brain tumor detection and classification using machine learning: A comprehensive survey. *Complex & Intelligent Systems*, pages 1–23, 2021.

[3] A.K. Anaraki, M. Ayati, and F. Kazemi. Magnetic resonance imaging-based brain tumor grades classification and grading via convolutional neural networks and genetic algorithms. *Biocybernetics and Biomedical Engineering*, 39(1):63–74, 2019.

[4] B. Anilkumar and P.R. Kumar. Tumor classification using block wise fine tuning and transfer learning of deep neural network and knn classifier on mr brain images. *Int. J. Emerg. Trends Eng. Res*, 8(2):574–583, 2020.

[5] M. Arif, F. Ajesh, S. Shamsudheen, O. Geman, D. Izdrui, and D. Vicoveanu. Brain tumor detection and classification by mri using biologically inspired orthogonal wavelet transform and deep learning techniques. *Journal of Healthcare Engineering*, 2022.

[6] W. Ayadi, W. Elhamzi, I. Charfi, and M. Atri. Deep cnn for brain tumor classification. *Neural Processing Letters*, 53:671–700, 2021.

[7] Y. Bhanothu, A. Kamalakannan, and G. Rajamanickam. Detection and classification of brain tumor in mri images using deep convolutional network. In *6th international conference on advanced computing and communication systems (ICACCS)*, pages 248–252. IEEE, 2020.

[8] N. M. Dipu, S. A. Shohan, and K. M. A. Salam. Deep learning-based brain tumor detection and classification. In *2021 International Conference on Intelligent Technologies (CONIT)*, pages 1–6. IEEE, 2021.

[9] F. J. Díaz-Pernas, M. Martínez-Zarzuela, M. Antón-Rodríguez, and D. González-Ortega. A deep learning approach for brain tumor classification and segmentation using a multiscale convolutional neural network. *Healthcare*, 9(2):153, 2021.

[10] S. Gull, S. Akbar, and K. Safdar. An interactive deep learning approach for brain tumor detection through 3d-magnetic resonance images. In *International Conference on Frontiers of Information Technology (FIT)*, pages 114–119. IEEE, 2021.

[11] K. He, X. Zhang, S. Ren, and J. Sun. Identity mappings in deep residual networks. pages 630–645, 2016.

[12] T. Kalaiselvi, S. T. Padmapriya, P. Sriramakrishnan, and K. Somasundaram. Deriving tumor detection models using convolutional neural networks from mri of human brain scans. *International Journal of Information Technology*, 12:403–408, 2020.

[13] J. Kang, Z. Ullah, and J. Gwak. Mri-based brain tumor classification using ensemble of deep features and machine learning classifiers. *Sensors*, 21(6):2222, 2021.

[14] R. L. Kumar, J. Kakarla, B. V. Isunuri, and M. Singh. Multi-class brain tumor classification using residual network and global average pooling. *Multimedia Tools and Applications*, 80:13429–13438, 2021.

[15] H. C. Megha. Evaluation of brain tumor mri imaging test detection and classification. *International Journal of Research in Applied Science and Engineering Technology*, 8(6):124–131, 2020.

[16] S. Montaha, S. Azam, A. R. H. Rafid, M. Z. Hasan, A. Karim, and A. Islam. Timedistributedcnn-lstm: A hybrid approach combining cnn and lstm to classify brain tumor on 3d mri scans performing ablation study. *IEEE Access*, 10:60039–60059, 2022.

[17] H. Mzoughi, I. Njeh, A. Wali, M. B. Slima, A. BenHamida, C. Mhiri, and K. B. Mahfoudhe. Deep multi-scale 3d convolutional neural network (cnn) for mri gliomas brain tumor classification. *Journal of Digital Imaging*, 33:903–915, 2020.

[18] D. R. Nayak, N. Padhy, P. K. Mallick, M. Zymbler, and S. Kumar. Brain tumor classification using dense efficient-net. *Axioms*, 11(1):34, 2022.

[19] A.A. Nayan, A.N. Mozumder, M. Haque, F.H. Sifat, K.R. Mahmud, A.K.A. Azad, and M.G. Kibria. A deep learning approach for brain tumor detection using magnetic resonance imaging. *arXiv preprint arXiv:2210.1388.*

[20] N. Noreen, S. Palaniappan, A. Qayyum, I. Ahmad, and M.O. Alassafi. Brain tumor classification based on fine-tuned models and the ensemble method. *Computers, Materials amp; Continua*, 67(3):3967–3982, 2021.

[21] L. Pavuluri and M.K. Nath. Classification of brain tumor mr images using transfer learning and machine learning models. pages 1–9, 2022.

[22] P. S. Raja. Brain tumor classification using a hybrid deep autoencoder with bayesian fuzzy clustering-based segmentation approach. *Biocybernetics and Biomedical Engineering*, 40(1):440–453, 2020.

[23] A. Rani, S. Gupta, S. Tripathy, and S. Sahu. Convolutional neural network based approach for automated brain tumor detection and classification in mri images. *Journal of King Saud University-Computer and Information Sciences.*

[24] A. Rehman, M. A. Khan, T. Saba, Z. Mehmood, U. Tariq, and N. Ayesha. Microscopic brain tumor detection and classification using 3d cnn and feature selection architecture. *Microscopy Research and Technique*, 84(1):133–149, 2021.

[25] T. Sadad, A. Rehman, A. Munir, T. Saba, U. Tariq, N. Ayesha, and R. Abbasi. Brain tumor detection and multi-classification using advanced deep learning techniques. *Microscopy Research and Technique*, 84(6):1296–1308, 2021.

[26] A. M. Sarhan. Brain tumor classification in magnetic resonance images using deep learning and wavelet transform. *Journal of Biomedical Science and Engineering*, 13(06):102, 2020.

[27] M.I. Sharif, M.A. Khan, M. Alhussein, K. Aurangzeb, and M. Raza. A decision support system for multimodal brain tumor classification using deep learning. *Complex amp; Intelligent Systems*, pages 1–14, 2021.

[28] M. Siar and M. Teshnehlab. Brain tumor detection using deep neural network and machine learning algorithm. pages 363–368, 2019.

[29] C. Szegedy, S. Ioffe, V. Vanhoucke, and A. Alemi. Inception-v4, inception-resnet and the impact of residual connections on learning. 31(1), 2017.

[30] T. Tazin, S. Sarker, P. Gupta, F. I. Ayaz, S. Islam, M. Monirujjaman Khan, S. Bourouis, S. A. Idris, and H. Alshazly. A robust and novel approach for brain tumor classification using convolutional neural network. *Computational Intelligence and Neuroscience*, 2021.

[31] H. Ucuzal, Ş. Yaşar, and C. Çolak. Classification of brain tumor types by deep learning with convolutional neural network on magnetic resonance images using a developed web-based interface. In *3rd international symposium on multidisciplinary studies and innovative technologies (ISMSIT)*, pages 1–5. IEEE, 2019.

[32] Y. Xie, F. Zaccagna, L. Rundo, C. Testa, R. Agati, R. Lodi, D. N. Manners, and C. Tonon. Convolutional neural network techniques for brain tumor classification (from 2015 to 2022): Review, challenges, and future perspectives. *Diagnostics*, 12(8):1850, 2022.

[33] B. Zoph, V. Vasudevan, J. Shlens, and Q.V. Le. Learning transferable architectures for scalable image recognition. pages 8697–8710, 2018.

Chapter 11

Glioma Brain Tumour Grade Detection using Clinical Feature, Molecular Feature and ConvLSTM Network

Aleena Swetapadma,[a,*] *Nalinipravа Behera,*[a] *Brijesh Raj Swain,*[b]
Anil Kumar Swain,[a] *Anjali Vaish*[a] and *Satya Subham Nayak*[a]

Abstract

Nearly 90,000 people are affected by brain tumors each year, with gliomas being the most severe. Proper grading of gliomas increases patient survival rates. Clinical and molecular markers are crucial for tumor grade detection. This work uses ConvLSTM deep learning for glioma grade detection with a dataset containing 3 clinical and 20 molecular features. Random forest method has been used for selecting appropriate features from 23 features. Out of all features, 17 were selected

[a] School of Computer Engineering, KIIT deemed to be University, Bhubaneswar, India.
[b] PG Department of medicine, IMS & Sum Hospital, SOA University, Bhubaneshwar, India.
* Corresponding author: aleena.swetapadma@gmail.com

DOI: 10.1201/9781003531043-15

as optimal for designing the grade detection module using the ConvLSTM network. Optimal hyperparameters include 64 neurons, a sigmoid activation function, Adam optimizer, and a batch size of 10. The proposed method achieved 99.40% accuracy and an F-score of 0.993, outperforming existing methods. It effectively identifies glioma grades for appropriate patient treatment.

11.1 Introduction

Brain tumors have become one of the most frequently diagnosed cancers in recent decades, with gliomas among the most severe types. These tumors, originating within the brain, can be classified as benign or malignant and are categorized by type—such as meningioma, pituitary, and glioma—and by grade, which indicates their aggressiveness, ranging from Grades I to IV. Lower-grade tumours (Grades I and II) are generally less aggressive, whereas higher-grade tumours (Grades III and IV), including gliomas, pose significant health risks. Accurately identifying tumor grade is crucial for determining the appropriate treatment strategy. Numerous techniques have been developed for detecting, classifying, segmenting, and grading brain tumors, as outlined below.

For instance, a combination of deep learning models like DenseNet-169, Inception V3, and ResNeXt-50 with an SVM classifier using an RBF kernel has been utilized to classify brain tumors, as mentioned in [6]. Other studies have proposed models employing CNN architectures for brain tumor segmentation and classification, such as in [4]. The VGG16 model was used in [1] to differentiate between normal and tumorous brain MRI images, achieving a classification accuracy of 97.33%. A different approach, using EfficientNet versions B0 to B4 for transfer learning, classified brain tumors into glioma, meningioma, and pituitary categories, achieving 98.86% accuracy, 98.65% precision, 98.77% recall, and an F1-score of 98.71% [17]. Additionally, a CNN-based technique combined with U-Net for segmentation reached classification and segmentation accuracies of 98.7% and 98.8%, respectively [5].

Research focusing on the classification and grading of low-grade gliomas (LGGs) based on MRI radiomic features has been conducted [9]. In [8], segmentation and classification techniques were explored to facilitate early detection and grading of brain tumors. Furthermore, a machine learning approach using a genetic algorithm with extreme gradient boosting achieved 69.05% accuracy in classifying LGG subtypes [7]. Another model used U-net for segmentation and VGG16 for grading LGG tumors, achieving a Dice Similarity Coefficient of 0.84 and an overall tumor detection accuracy of 92% [10]. A hierarchical model combining feature selection and ensemble learning achieved 87.606% and 79.668% accuracy on the TCGA and CGGA datasets, respectively, for glioma grading using clinical and molecular features [16].

Several studies have emphasized the use of CNNs in glioma classification and segmentation, highlighting a growing focus on segmentation over classification [2]. Some methods, like the CNN-SVM model using firefly optimization for segmentation and grading gliomas, achieved an accuracy of 99.98% [14]. Other methods used gradient-based MRI features to capture subtle glioma variations, enabling effective classification and grading [13]. A review of machine learning applications in neuroimaging found advancements in tumor diagnosis, grading, and progression tracking, including glioma-specific transformations like the Non-Subsampled Contourlet Transform [3].

All these methods aim to detect brain tumor types and grade gliomas. However, some existing techniques for tumor grading lack sufficient accuracy for clinical reliability. Thus, this work employs a ConvLSTM method to enhance the grade detection of glioma brain tumors. This paper is organized as follows: Section 11.2 details the techniques used, Section 11.3 presents the proposed technique, Section 11.4 outlines the results, Section 11.5 discusses the findings, and Section 11.6 concludes the study.

11.2 Techniques Used

The proposed glioma brain tumor grade detection method uses the random forest method for feature selection and ConvLSTM for grade detection. These techniques are discussed below.

11.2.1 Random Forest

Decision trees are widely used in engineering applications for solutions [11]. Due to the overfitting issue of DT, ensembles like the random forest method have been designed. Random forest, an ensemble learning method, is used for classification and prediction tasks by combining the outputs of multiple decision trees. Averaging technique determines the final output. In this work, random forest selects appropriate features for glioma brain tumor grade detection.

11.2.2 ConvLSTM

Neural networks are among the best adaptive learning techniques for solving engineering problems [12]. Deep neural networks provide solutions in various fields. Recurrent neural networks like LSTM are commonly used for classification. This study employs ConvLSTM, which incorporates a recurrent layer similar to LSTM but replaces internal matrix multiplications with convolution operations. This allows ConvLSTM cells to maintain input dimensionality. ConvLSTM is used here for glioma tumor grade detection.

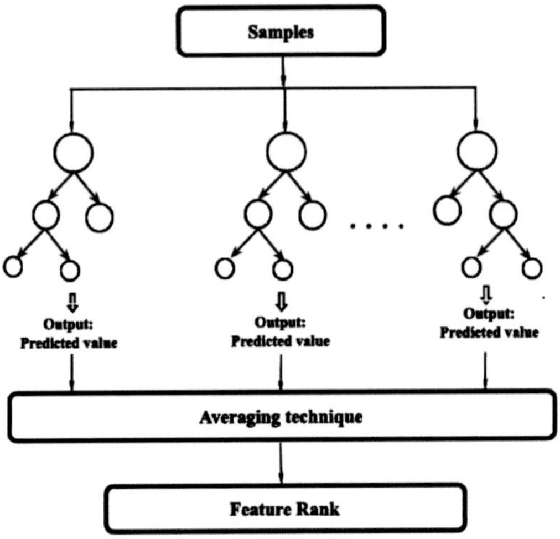

Figure 11.1: Random forest method.

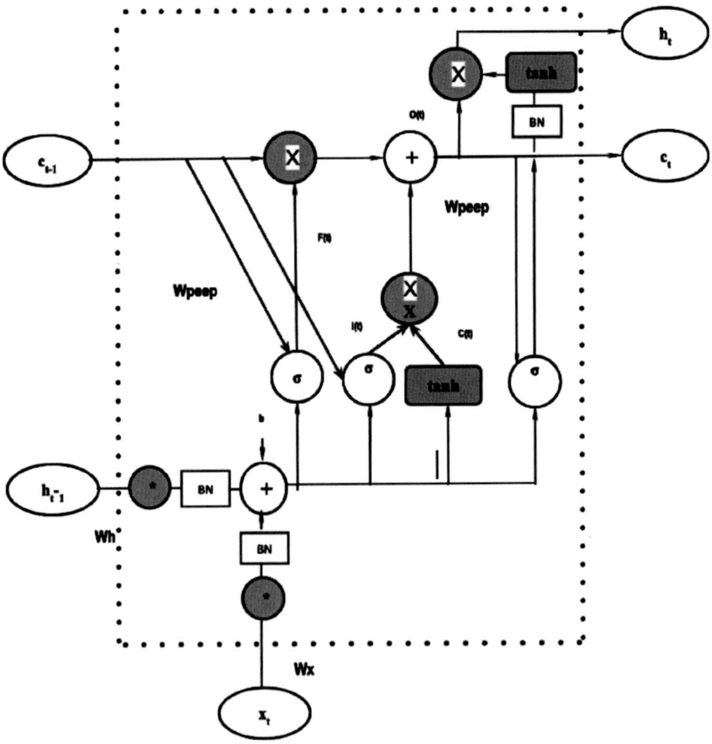

Figure 11.2: ConvLSTM network structure.

11.3 Proposed Method

The proposed glioma brain tumor grade detection methods have been implemented in Python. The method has been implemented on a system with processor of 12th Gen Intel(R) Core(TM) i7-1255U 1.70 GHz, 16GB RAM. The glioma brain tumor grade detection method follows various steps as shown in Figure 11.3. The details of each of the steps has been discussed in this section.

11.3.1 Inputs Used

The inputs for validating the proposed work were taken from the UCI repository [15]. The dataset includes the top 20 most frequently mutated genes and three clinical features from the TCGA-LGG and TCGA-GBM brain glioma projects. It is used to predict whether a patient has LGG or GBM based on clinical and molecular/mutation characteristics. The dataset consists of three clinical inputs and 20 molecular inputs, with the target being glioma brain tumor grade determination. The inputs are processed, and appropriate features are selected.

11.3.2 Feature Ranking

The inputs are processed to determine the most contributing features. The random forest algorithm with 100 trees is used for feature ranking. The top features include: 1-Gender-0.02159375, 2-Age-0.3358982, 3-Race-0.02387854, 4-IDH1-0.26684667, 5-TP53-0.02340488, 6-ATRX-0.03762281, 7-PTEN-0.0585407, 8-EGFR-0.02385998, 9-CIC-0.04813492, 10-MUC16-0.01303904, 11-PIK3CA-0.01503836, 12-NF1-0.01578687, 13-PIK3R1-0.01042765, 14-FUBP1-0.01143 -145, 15-RB1-0.01588744, 16-NOTCH1-0.01050188, 17-BCOR-0.00729296, 18-CSMD3-0.00483543, 19-SMARCA4-0.0062214, 20-GRIN2A-0.00578215,

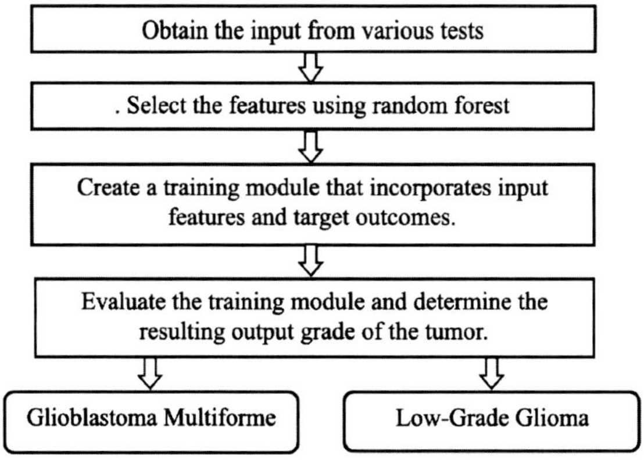

Figure 11.3: Flowchart of the method.

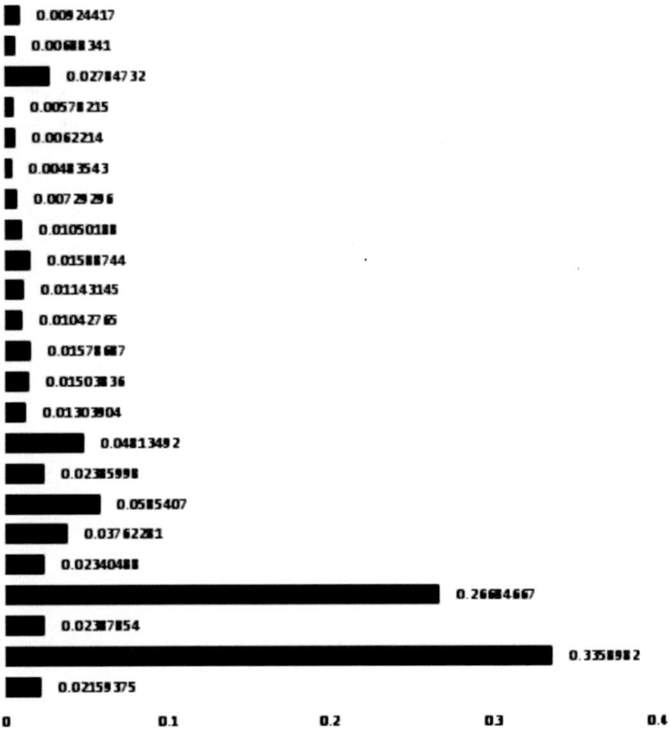

Figure 11.4: Feature importance.

21-IDH2-0.02784732, 22-FAT4-0.00688341, 23-PDGFRA-0.00924417. Some molecular features contribute less than 1% to glioma brain tumor grade detection: PGDFRA, FAT4, GRIN2A, SMARCA4, CSMD3, and BCOR. Hence, 3 clinical features and 14 molecular features are chosen as optimal.

11.3.3 Grade Detection Method

The glioma brain tumor grade detection method includes training and testing phases. In the training phase, input features and targets are used to design the ConvLSTM training module, with varying parameters. Optimal parameters, training accuracy, and loss are shown in Table 11.1 and Figures 11.5 and 11.6. The network with 64 LSTM units achieved 100% accuracy with 400 epochs. After training, the module is tested with new samples. Results are discussed in the next section.

Table 11.1: Parameters used in training phase.

Features Used	Network Structure	ConvLSTM Unit	Epochs	Training Accuracy	Training Loss
All	Dense(2), Activation=Sigmoid, Optimizer=Adam, Batch size=10	16	300	70.447%	0.531049
			400	78.955%	0.441302
			500	86.716%	0.296422
		32	300	78.507%	0.422243
			400	81.492%	0.352028
			500	89.199%	0.259347
		64	300	98.955%	0.053937
			400	99.850%	0.017640
			500	100.00%	2.484e-05
With >1% contribution		16	200	69.253%	0.576561
			300	69.253%	0.496663
			400	74.477%	0.486666
		32	200	65.522%	0.618863
			300	92.985%	0.188920
			400	98.059%	0.068837
		64	200	89.850%	0.210270
			300	99.850%	0.009792
			400	100.00%	0.000211

11.4 Result

The proposed glioma brain tumor grade detection method has been tested, and results are provided in this section. The method's performance has been analyzed using precision, recall, F-score, AUC, and accuracy.

$$\text{Accuracy} = \frac{\text{TP}+\text{TN}}{\text{TP}+\text{TN}+\text{FN}+\text{FP}} \times 100 \tag{11.1}$$

$$\text{Precision} = \frac{\text{TP}}{\text{TP}+\text{FP}} \tag{11.2}$$

$$\text{Recall} = \frac{\text{TP}}{\text{TP}+\text{FN}} \tag{11.3}$$

$$\text{F1-Score} = \frac{\text{TP}}{\text{TP}+\frac{1}{2}(\text{FN}+\text{FP})} \tag{11.4}$$

11.4.1 Performance with all Features

The proposed glioma brain tumor grade detection method has been tested considering all the features. The result obtained has been tabulated in Table 11.2 for

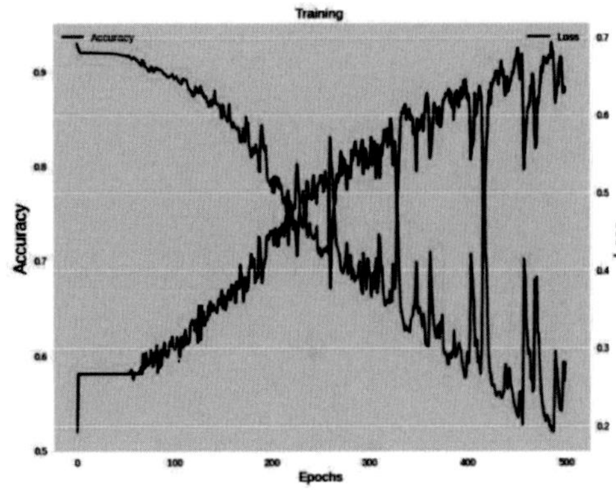

(a)

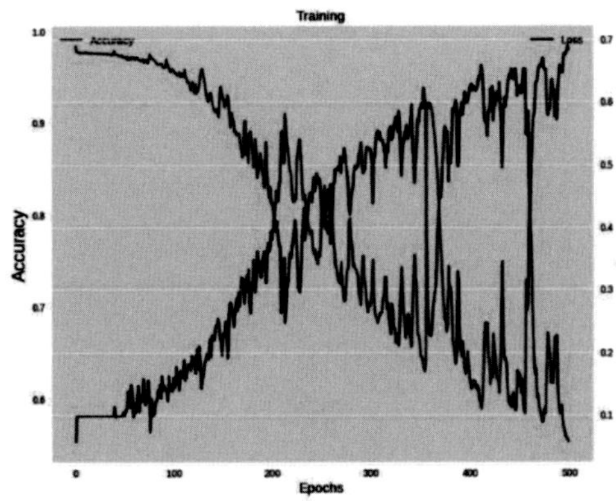

(b)

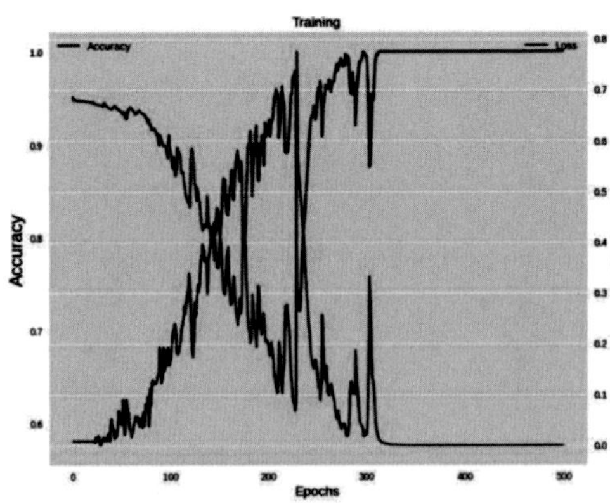

(c)

Figure 11.5: Performance of training modules for all features in terms of accuracy and loss (a) 16 (b) 32 (c) 64 ConvLSTM unit.

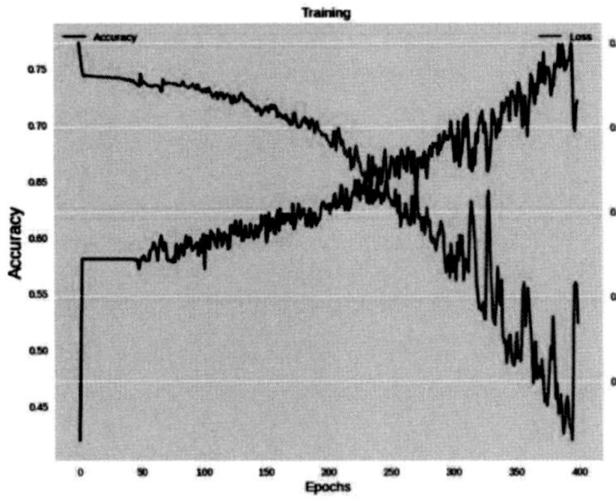

(a)

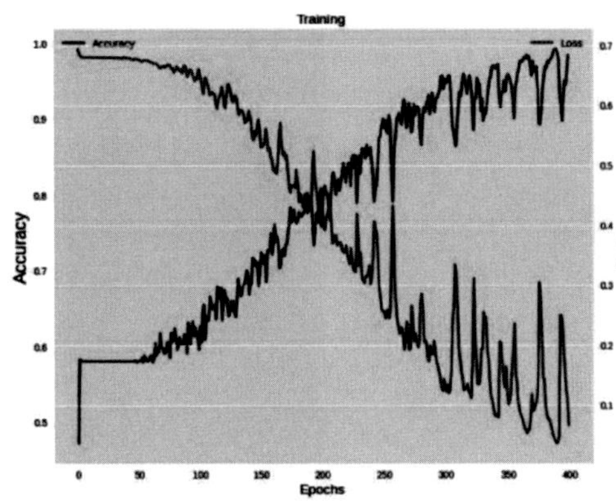

(b)

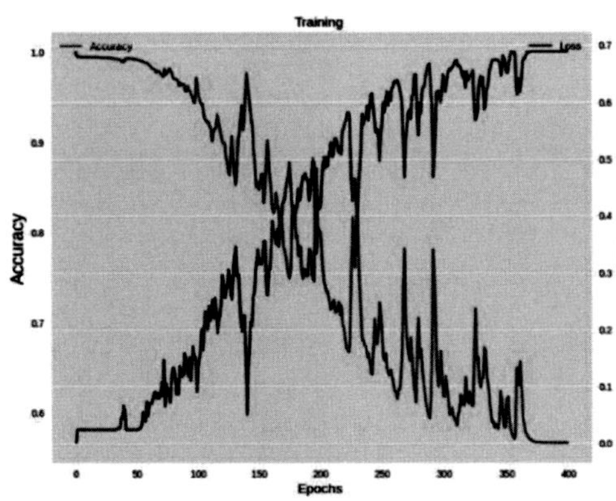

(c)

Figure 11.6: Performance of training modules for features having >1% contribution (a) 16 (b) 32 (c) 64 ConvLSTM unit.

Table 11.2: Performance of the method with all features.

ConvLSTM Unit	Precision	Recall	F-score	AUC	Accuracy
16	0.844	0.915	0.878	0.878	89.29%
32	0.925	0.704	0.799	0.831	85.12%
64	0.876	1.00	0.934	0.948	94.05%

glioma brain tumor grade detection using all features. The highest accuracy obtained for the proposed method is 94.05% for the network with 64 LSTM unit. The highest F-score obtained is 0.934. Figure 11.7 shows the AUC of different network. Although the method is giving good performance with all features, it can be checked for better performance with less features.

11.4.2 Performance with Selected Features

The glioma brain tumor grade detection method has been tested with selected features whose contribution is more than 1%. The result of the proposed method has been tabulated in Table 11.3 for glioma grade detection using selected features. The highest accuracy obtained is 99.40% for the network with 64 neurons. The precision obtained is 0.984 and the recall in 1.00. Figure 11.8 shows the AUC of different network with selected features. It can be observed that the selected feature accuracy is more than all feature accuracies. Hence, it can be chosen for glioma brain tumor grade detection.

11.5 Discussion

The results of the proposed glioma brain tumor grade detection method are provided in the previous section. Table 11.4 shows the overall performance with different features. The precision with selected features is 0.986, higher than with all features. The F-score is 0.993, also higher. The AUC for selected features is higher too. The highest accuracy with all features is 94.05%, and with selected features is 99.4%. Thus, the method can be effectively used in hospitals to assist doctors.

The proposed glioma brain tumor detection method has been compared with existing methods based on datasets, detection methods, tumor detection, tumor

Table 11.3: Performance of the method with selected features.

ConvLSTM Unit	Precision	Recall	F-score	AUC	Accuracy
16	0.783	0.915	0.844	0.864	85.71%
32	0.983	0.830	0.900	0.910	92.26%
64	0.986	1.000	0.993	0.994	99.40%

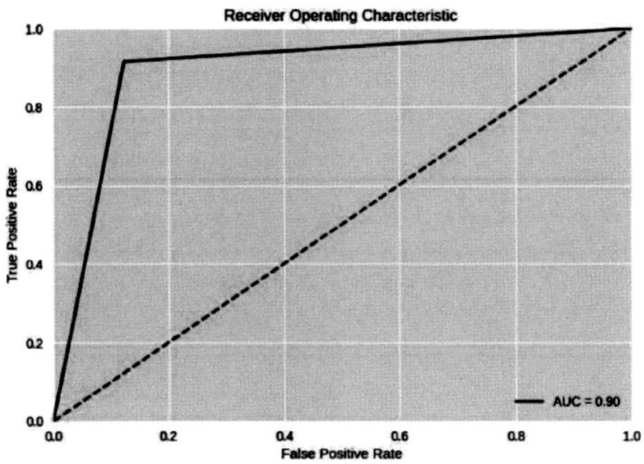

(a)

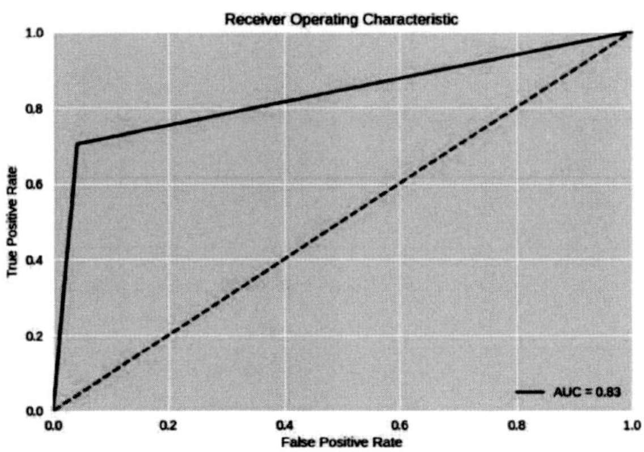

(b)

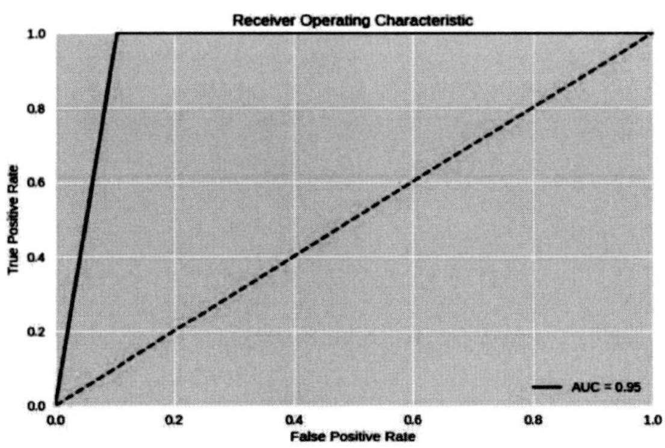

(c)

Figure 11.7: Performance in terms of AUC (a) 16 (b) 32 (c) 64 ConvLSTM unit.

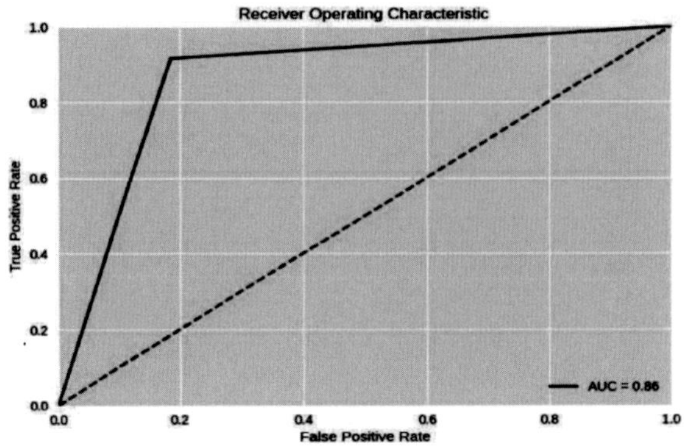

(a)

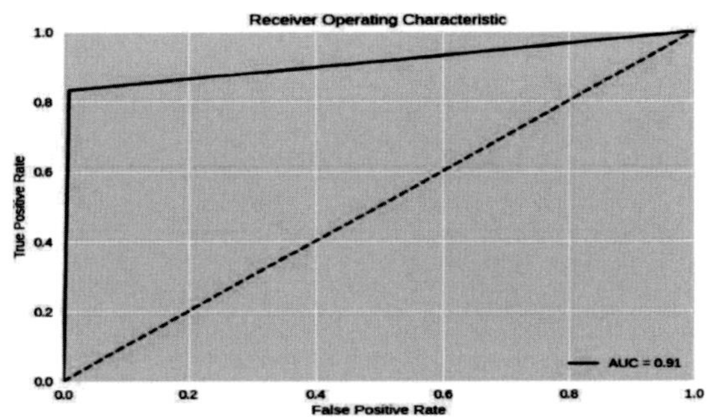

(b)

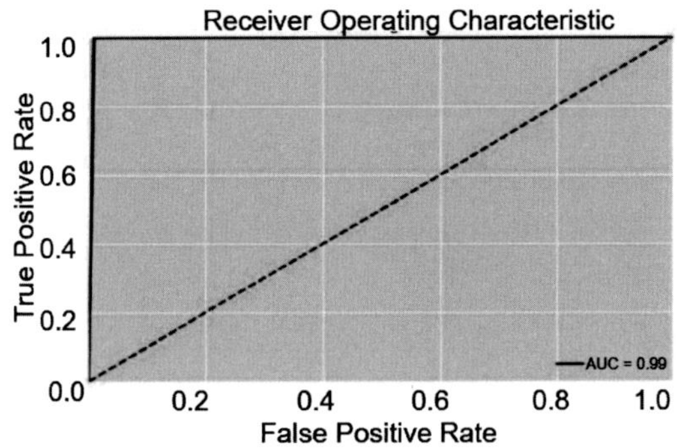

(c)

Figure 11.8: Performance in terms of AUC (a) 16 (b) 32 (c) 64 ConvLSTM unit.

grade detection, and accuracy (Table 11.5). Some methods classified the tumor but not the grade, while others found the tumor grade. The proposed method shows superior accuracy of 99.4% for detecting glioma brain tumor grades compared to other methods.

Table 11.4: Overall performance.

Features	Precision	Recall	F-score	AUC	Accuracy
All	0.876	1.000	0.934	0.948	94.05%
Selected	0.986	1.000	0.993	0.994	99.40%

Table 11.5: Comparison.

Authors	Data-set	Methods	Tumour detection	Grade detection	Highest accuracy
[1]	Kaggle	LRP on VGG16	Yes	No	97.33%
[17]	figshare	EfficientnetB0 - B4	Yes	No	98.86%
[5]	figshare SARTAJ Pradeep Sherif	VGG16 VGG19 EfficientNetB0 EfficientNetB7 ResNet152V2	Yes	No	98.70%
[10]	TCIA	U-Net and VGG 16	No	Yes	95.00%
[16]	TCGA	Ensemble Learning Model Scheme	No	Yes	87.60%
Proposed method	TCGA	ConvLSTM	No	Yes	99.40%

11.6 Conclusion

The proposed method uses ConvLSTM for glioma brain tumor grading, utilizing clinical and morphological features. Random forest feature selection identifies 17 out of 23 features with at least 1% contribution. These features are inputs for ConvLSTM in glioma grade detection, achieving 99.40% accuracy. This method can serve as a reference for developing efficient glioma brain tumor detection methods and effectively assist doctors.

References

[1] F. Ahmed, M. Asif, M. Saleem, U. F. Mushtaq, and M. Imran. Identification and prediction of brain tumor using vgg-16 empowered with explainable artificial intelligence. *International Journal of Computational and Innovative Sciences*, 2(2):24–33, June 2023.

[2] Mateusz Buda, Ashirbani Saha, and Maciej A. Mazurowski. Association of genomic subtypes of lower-grade gliomas with shape features automatically extracted by a deep learning algorithm. *Computers in Biology and Medicine*, 109:218–225, 2019.

[3] T. Chen, F. Xiao, Z. Yu, M. Yuan, H. Xu, and L. Lu. Detection and grading of gliomas using a novel two-phase machine learning method based on mri images. *Frontiers in Neuroscience*, 15:650629, 2021.

[4] F. J. Díaz-Pernas, M. Martínez-Zarzuela, M. Antón-Rodríguez, and D. González-Ortega. A deep learning approach for brain tumor classification and segmentation using a multiscale convolutional neural network. *Healthcare*, 9:153, 2021.

[5] A. Akter et al. Robust clinical applicable cnn and u-net based algorithm for mri classification and segmentation for brain tumor. *Expert Systems with Applications*, 238:122347, 2024.

[6] J. Kang, Z. Ullah, and J. Gwak. Mri-based brain tumor classification using ensemble of deep features and machine learning classifiers. *Sensors*, 21:2222, 2021.

[7] L. H. T. Lam, D. T. Do, D. T. N. Diep, D. L. N. Nguyet, Q. D. Truong, T. T. Tri, H. N. Thanh, and N. Q. K. Le. Molecular subtype classification of low-grade gliomas using magnetic resonance imaging-based radiomics and machine learning. *NMR in Biomedicine*, 35:e4792, 2022.

[8] G. Mohan and M. M. Subashini. Mri-based medical image analysis: Survey on brain tumor grade classification. *Biomedical Signal Processing and Control*, 39:139–161, January 2018.

[9] S. Munquad, T. Si, S. Mallik, A. Li, and A. B. Das. Subtyping and grading of lower-grade gliomas using integrated feature selection and support vector machine. *Briefings in Functional Genomics*, 21:408–421, 2022.

[10] M. A. Naser and M. J. Deen. Brain tumor segmentation and grading of lower-grade glioma using deep learning in mri images. *Computers in Biology and Medicine*, 121:103758, 2020.

[11] S. Pathak, I. Mishra, and A. Swetapadma. An assessment of decision tree-based classification and regression algorithms. In *2018 3rd International Conference on Inventive Computation Technologies (ICICT)*, pages 92–95, 2018.

[12] N. Saha, A. Swetapadma, and M. Mondal. A brief review on artificial neural network: Network structures and applications. In *9th International Conference on Advanced Computing and Communication Systems (ICACCS)*, pages 1974–1979, 2023.

[13] S. Shargunam and G. Rajakumar. An efficient glioma classification and grade detection using hybrid convolutional neural network-based svm model. *The Imaging Science Journal*, 72(1):1–22, 2023.

[14] G. Song, G. Xie, and Y. Nie. Noninvasive grading of glioma brain tumors using magnetic resonance imaging and deep learning methods. *Journal of Cancer Research and Clinical Oncology*, 149:16293–16309, 2023.

[15] E. Tasci, K. Camphausen, A. V. Krauze, and Y. Zhuge. Glioma grading clinical and mutation features. `https://doi.org/10.24432/C5R62J`, 2022.

[16] E. Tasci, Y. Zhuge, H. Kaur, K. Camphausen, and A. V. Krauze. Hierarchical voting-based feature selection and ensemble learning model scheme for glioma grading with clinical and molecular characteristics. *International Journal of Molecular Sciences*, 23(22):14155, 2022.

[17] F. Zulfiqar, U. I. Bajwa, and Y. Mehmood. Multi-class classification of brain tumor types from mr images using efficientnets. *Biomedical Signal Processing and Control*, 84:104777, 2023.

Chapter 12

Machine Learning for Ocular Disease Detection in Fundus Images

*Harish Gavel** and *Chandrashekhar Azad*

Abstract

Medical imaging is critical in modern healthcare, delivering essential information about human anatomy and disease. However, the exponential rise of medical images creates storage, processing, and interpretation issues. This research investigates the relationship between medical imaging and bioinformatics, which combines biology, computer science, and information technology. We look at how bioinformatics provides researchers and doctors with enhanced approaches for pre-processing, analyzing, and interpreting medical images. Feature extraction, statistical analysis, and machine learning algorithms uncover the potential of quantitative data buried within images, resulting in faster diagnoses, more personalized treatment plans, and better patient outcomes. Case studies reveal the revolutionary impact of this collaboration in fields such as cancer diagnosis, neurological problems, cardiovascular illness, and retinal disease detection. We

Department of Computer Science and Engineering, National Institute of Technology, Jamshedpur, India.

* Corresponding author: harishgavel@gmail.com

DOI: 10.1201/9781003531043-16

examine the difficulties of data security, privacy, interoperability, and algorithmic bias, emphasizing the necessity for strong frameworks and ethical concerns. Finally, the study discusses future medical imaging and bioinformatics prospects, emphasising the promise of AI, cloud computing, radiomics, and explainable machine learning models. By embracing these innovations, we can fully realize the potential of data-driven healthcare and transform patient care.

12.1 Introduction

The human body remains a captivating mystery, a symphony of complicated systems hidden under a layer of skin. For centuries, physicians depended on intuition, observation, and basic equipment to diagnose and cure disorders. However, the introduction of medical imaging has transformed healthcare by offering a non-invasive view of the body's interior workings. From the skeletal clarity of X-rays to the comprehensive visualizations of interior organs by CT scans, these technologies have enabled healthcare practitioners to make diagnoses more informative, resulting in more effective treatment strategies for better patient outcomes.

In the modern digital era [9], among the several medical imaging modalities, diabetic retinopathy (DR) screening has proved to be an excellent example of this transformational potential. Diabetes-related microvascular complications quietly damage the retina, the crucial light-sensitive layer for vision at the back of the eye. Uncontrolled blood sugar levels in one's body can damage the retina's fragile blood vessels, causing leaks, haemorrhages, and irregular vessel development. If not recognized and treated, DR can gradually degrade eyesight, eventually leading to blindness. However, early identification is critical for preventing visual loss. Fundus or retinal photography, a non-invasive imaging technology that produces detailed retina photographs, is the foundation of DR screening programmes.

However, the effectiveness of fundus photography modalities depends on a complex web of interconnected components known as a cyber-physical system (CPS). CPS combines physical equipment, such as fundus cameras, with software applications and communication networks. These cameras take high-resolution pictures of the retina, which are then securely communicated across a network to a Picture Archiving and Communication System (PACS), a centralized archive of medical images. Healthcare practitioners may retrieve these high-resolution pictures via diagnostic workstations, allowing them to examine the retina for symptoms of DR. The smooth interplay of these physical and technological components are very critical to the workflow's overall success.

However, the intrinsic strength of CPS is coupled with some clear vulnerability: security. The delicate nature of patient data obtained by fundus imaging needs stringent security measures throughout the procedure. Personal health information (PHI), especially retinal scans, is extremely valuable. Malicious actors might exploit flaws in the CPS to get unauthorized access to this information, resulting in a severe violation of patient confidentiality. Corrupted systems can alter or delete medical data, including fundus images, hindering accurate diagnosis and delaying treatment for DR patients. Ultimately, a security compromise in a DR screening CPS might result in quality loss of images and may cause lasting harm to numerous people.

The spectre of security risks in medical imaging CPS drives us to further research and explore their terrain. This chapter will examine the main medical imaging modalities and their uses in healthcare diagnostics. We will next delve into the complexities of DR, its pathogenesis, and the essential role that fundus photography plays in the early diagnosis of different diseases. The potential devastation caused by security breaches necessitates a proactive approach to securing DR screening CPS. This chapter advocates for a multi-disciplinary approach, recognizing that robust security demands collaboration. Ophthalmologists, healthcare IT professionals, cybersecurity experts, and device manufacturers must come together to identify these weaknesses and implement robust security measures.

Medical imaging CPS is a dynamic field that constantly changes in tandem with technological advances. The growing role of artificial intelligence (AI) in medical imaging, particularly in automated DR categorization, will be examined in this chapter. AI presents new security problems and enormous potential to increase screening accuracy and efficiency.

The chapter is organized as follows: We will discuss the research on classical machine learning (ML) and deep learning (DL) techniques in the next section. We'll detail the techniques and algorithms used in our enhancement strategy. The "Results and Discussions" section will present and analyze our findings. Finally, the "Conclusion" will highlight our work's significance and potential implications in retinal imaging.

In summary, our research represents a major step forward in the continuous pursuit of better retinal imaging and classification of disease to comprehend the origins and management of conditions connected to the eyes. By employing different AI Techniques in retinal images, we can enhance our ability to see and interpret the intricate characteristics of the human retina.

12.2 Related Works

Fundus image analysis is one of the crucial fields of study for computer-aided diagnosis (CAD) of ocular diseases. In this section, we will look into earlier research that has substantially impacted this field, going beyond the limitations of the IDRiD dataset and various machine-learning techniques for classification.

We will explore several topics, including classical machine learning and deep learning methods, image processing techniques, various datasets, and disease detection and segmentation applications.

12.2.1 Early Works and Traditional Machine Learning Approaches

Pioneering work in machine learning-based approaches has concentrated on manually constructed feature extraction methods. To extract features like blood vessel crossings and bifurcations research by [24] and [14] used techniques like Gabor filters and mathematical morphology. These efforts prove to be producing promising results in blood vessel segmentation and diabetic retinopathy (DR) diagnosis.

As research progressed, statistical and machine learning algorithms gained popularity. Researchers [21] showed the potential of machine learning [6] for automated analysis by using a support vector machine (SVM) classifier for diabetic retinopathy screening on the DRIVE dataset. Similarly, [22] showcased the adaptability of different ML techniques, using Naive Bayes (NB) and Decision Tree (DT) classifiers for glaucoma detection.

Automated Diabetic Retinopathy Grading using Support Vector Machines (SVM) [4] and Local Binary Patterns (LBP) for feature extraction, LBP [11] are used in this work by [17]. The Local textural information in the image is captured by LBPs, which can be useful in identifying features related to DR, such as haemorrhages and microaneurysms. An SVM classifier is then provided with the collected features to grade the degree of disease (no disease, mild, moderate, severe). This method produced an encouraging outcome, which shows machine learning's promise for automated DR analysis on the IDRiD dataset.

Exudate detection is crucial in diabetic retinopathy analysis. [25] utilized wavelet transform and support vector machine for classifying diabetic retinopathy images. Exudates, or fatty deposits that seep from retinal blood vessels are characteristic of diabetic retinal disease. The author has used Wavelet transforms to extract features, breaking the image down into several frequency bands so that high-frequency information (like microaneurysms) and low-frequency information (like background light) can be captured. An SVM is then trained with the retrieved features to identify DR images as normal or containing exudates. This work highlights the significance of feature extraction methods designed to extract particular DR-related attributes.

Retinal image preparation and Machine Learning Techniques, highlighted by [5] uncover the importance of image preprocessing for enhancing classification performance. Before employing Gabor filters for feature extraction, they investigated different preprocessing methods, such as noise reduction and contrast enhancement. Blood vessel anomalies in DR images can be detected using Gabor filters, which capture specific orientations and frequencies. Decision trees and k-nearest Neighbors (kNN) algorithms then classify these features. This work emphasizes the importance of proper data preparation for effective machine learning analysis.

[15] proposed a Fuzzy-SVM method for grading diabetic retinopathy in the IDRiD dataset, integrating fuzzy logic into the SVM framework. Fuzzy logic addresses the variability in retinal images by describing the uncertainty in feature values. This work demonstrates how fuzzy logic enhances the robustness of machine learning algorithms for DR grading.

12.2.2 Diverse Datasets and Multimodal Analysis

Recognizing the limitations of single datasets, researchers extended their work beyond the IDRiD dataset by [20]. The MESSIDOR dataset was then introduced by [13], focusing on identifying diabetic macular edema (DME). The REFUGE dataset, containing a wider range of retinal diseases, was presented by [19]. These initiatives enhanced the discipline by facilitating the creation and assessment of algorithms on a wider range of retinal diseases.

Multimodal analysis, which combines data from different sources, has proven useful. Author [8] paired fundus images with optical coherence tomography (OCT) images for glaucoma diagnosis, achieving better performance. This demonstrates how adding supplementary data from different modalities can enhance accuracy.

12.2.3 Deep Learning and Convolutional Neural Networks (CNNs)

The introduction of deep learning, particularly convolutional neural networks (CNNs), has revolutionized the field. Using the Messidor-2 dataset, [23] demonstrated that CNNs effectively identify diabetic retinopathy, outperforming human specialists.

Specialized CNN architectures for processing retinal images have been proposed. Using a U-Net-based architecture, [12] achieved state-of-the-art blood vessel segmentation. To detect microaneurysms, [1] introduced a deep residual network (ResNet), demonstrating the efficiency of deep learning models in identifying key diabetic retinopathy markers.

12.2.4 Segmentation, Registration, and Interpretability

Research has expanded towards segmentation tasks, even while classification tasks such as identifying diseases remain important. [16] used deep learning to segment the optic disc and cup, which is crucial for glaucoma investigation. A framework for vessel segmentation by [10] and diameter estimation was described by [18]. These studies underscore the significance of precise segmentation for the quantitative examination of retinal structures.

Image registration techniques have gained popularity. [7] introduced a deep learning-based vessel registration method, facilitating longitudinal data analysis. This is essential for monitoring disease progression and treatment effectiveness.

Research on the interpretability of DL models, also known as explainable AI, is now ongoing. Methods for elucidating CNN models' predictions in the classification of diabetic retinopathy were investigated by [2]. Gaining trust and guaranteeing dependable clinical applications requires understanding how these models make decisions. These are often significant for clinical validation and acceptance for use in clinical settings.

12.3 Methodology

The block diagram in Figure 12.1, provides a high-level overview of the machine learning process, outlining three stages: data preprocessing, model selection, and performance evaluation.

The leftmost block, labeled "Database," represents the raw data used to train the model, which can be multi-labeled or singly labeled. It then undergoes various pre-processing techniques, including data cleaning, normalization, handling missing values, histogram equalization, and resizing, as indicated by the "Pre-Processing Techniques" block.

The center block, labeled "Machine Learning Models," represents 12 different algorithms for training a model, including Logistic Regression (LR), Random Forest (RF), and Support Vector Machines (SVM). The choice of algorithm depends on the input data and desired outcome.

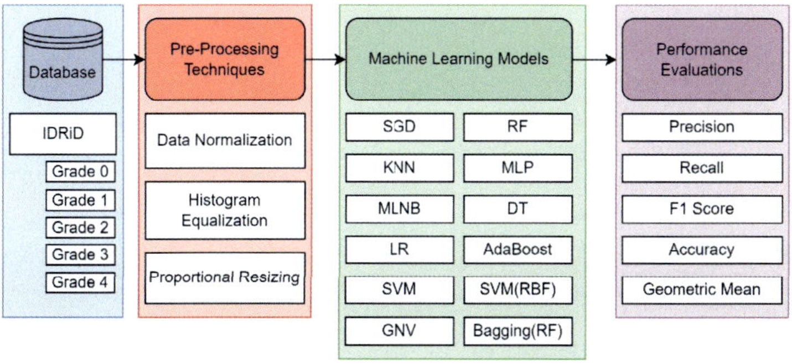

Figure 12.1: Flow Diagram depicting common methodology for classification of DR.

The final or rightmost component, "Performance Evaluations," deals with evaluating a machine learning model's performance. Usually, to accomplish this, the dataset is divided into two sections: the training set, which is usually larger, and the testing set, which is usually smaller. The testing set is used to assess the model's performance after it has been trained on the training set. Accuracy, F1 score, precision, and recall are some of these performance metrics. We will explore them in greater detail in the next section.

12.3.1 Dataset Description

The Indian Diabetic Retinopathy Image Dataset (IDRiD) [20] is a publicly available dataset of retinal images with annotations for diabetic retinopathy. The Topcon TRC NW400 non-mydriatic retinal camera was used to take the 516 colour fundus images with a size of 4288x2848 pixels. Two experienced ophthalmologists rated each image's diabetic retinopathy and diabetic macular oedema according to the International Clinical Diabetic Retinopathy Severity Scale. The dataset consists of 413 training images and 103 testing images, with grades ranging from Grade 0 (DR absent, as shown in Figure 12.4) to Grade 4 (DR positive, as shown in Figure 12.5). The grade distribution is depicted in Figure 12.2. The training set includes annotations for the positions of the optic disc and the fovea centre and annotations for diabetic retinopathy and diabetic macular edoema.

Figure 12.2: IDRiD datasets distribution of DR Grades.

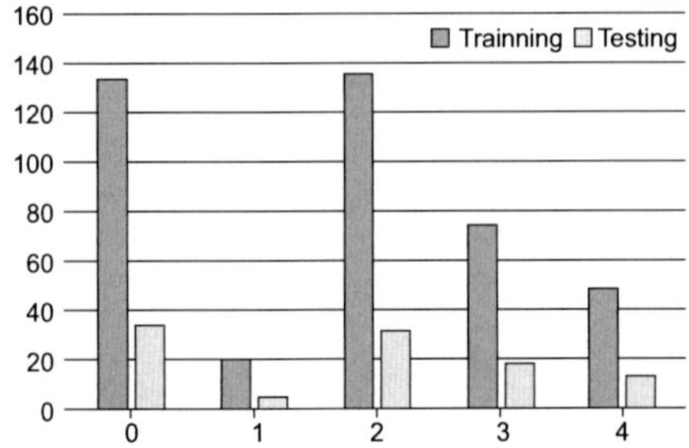

Figure 12.3: Distribution of Idrid dataset w.r.t. their grade in training and testing set.

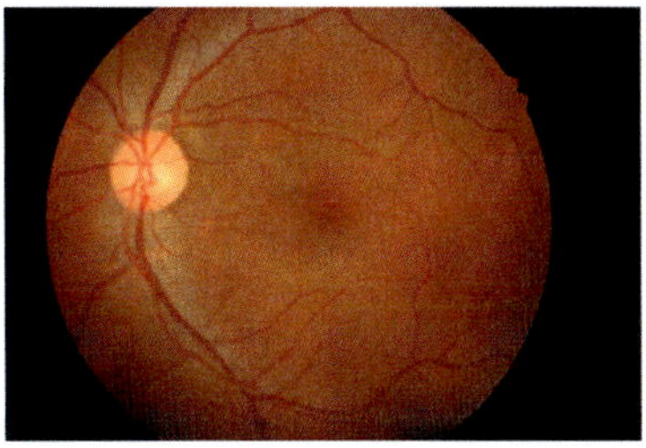

Figure 12.4: Sample Non-DR images from IDRiD dataset.

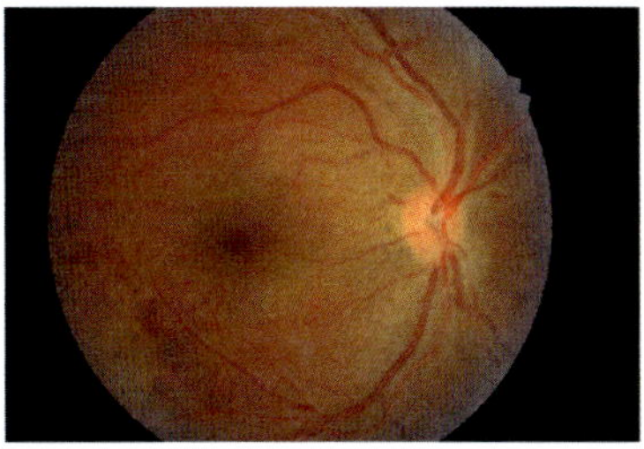

Figure 12.5: Sample DR images from IDRiD dataset.

12.3.2 Pre-Processing

Fundus images, capturing the intricate details of the retina, are invaluable tools for ophthalmologists diagnosing eye diseases like diabetic retinopathy and glaucoma. However, some essential pre-processing steps are crucial before unleashing machine learning algorithms' power on these images. These techniques act like preparing a canvas for a painting – ensuring optimal conditions for accurate analysis. We explore three key preprocessing techniques for fundus image analysis: data normalization, contrast enhancement (Histogram Equalization with CLAHE), and proportional resizing.

1. **Data Normalization**

   Fundus images can show variations in intensity due to factors like camera settings and illumination conditions. Data normalization tackles all these challenges by scaling the pixel intensities in the image to a specific range. This ensures that all images are represented on a common scale, promoting consistency and improving subsequent processing steps' effectiveness. Commonly, these normalization techniques consist of min-max scaling, where pixel values are mapped to a range between 0 and 1, and z-score normalization, where values are centred around the mean with a standard deviation of 1. After establishing a standardized intensity range, this normalization allows algorithms to focus on the image's underlying information rather than brightness variations.

2. **Histogram Equalization with CLAHE**

   Fundus images often contain important features like blood vessels and microaneurysms (tiny bulges in blood vessels). However, uneven illumination or inherent limitations in image acquisition can lead to low contrast, making these features difficult to identify. Histogram Equalization (HE) addresses this issue by redistributing the pixel intensities across the entire range. It stretches the histogram, increasing the contrast between foreground and background features. This can be particularly beneficial for highlighting subtle abnormalities in the retinal vasculature. However, traditional HE can often amplify noise in the image. Here's where CLAHE comes in – Contrast Limited Adaptive Histogram Equalization. CLAHE performs HE on localized or small regions of the image instead of the entire image. This approach enhances contrast in specific areas while minimizing noise, resulting in a balanced improvement in detail visibility.

3. **Proportional Resizing**

   Fundus images can vary in resolution based on the data acquisition device. While HE and normalization address intensity variations, proportional resizing is crucial. Maintaining the original aspect ratio (width to height) prevents distortion of anatomical structures, ensuring accurate analysis and measurements of retinal features.

In conclusion, Data normalization, Histogram equalization with CLAHE, and Proportional resizing are essential pre-processing techniques for fundus or retinal image analysis. By addressing the variations in intensity, contrast, and image size, these techniques show the way for robust and accurate analysis of retinal features, empowering researchers and clinicians to unlock the full potential of these images in diagnosing and managing eye diseases.

12.3.3 Machine Learning Models

In the expanding world of machine learning, classification algorithms are powerful tools for organizing and understanding data. They analyze data points with defined features and assign them to specific categories. For instance, a classification algorithm can automatically categorize seashells by analyzing their shape, size, and color. This chapter delves into popular classification algorithms, exploring their strengths, weaknesses, and decision-making processes.

1. **Decision Trees (DT)**

   Decision Trees (DT) [3], resemble a tree structure, starting with the root node representing the entire dataset. Subsequent nodes represent features, and branches represent possible feature values. As data points move through the tree, they reach a leaf node that determines the final class. Decision trees are interpretable, allowing us to understand the classification process by following the branches. They handle categorical and continuous data and are less sensitive to outliers. However, decision trees may overfit, meaning the model performs well on training data but poorly on new examples. The tree's depth and complexity are directly linked to its performance.

2. **Support Vector Machines (SVM)**

   SVMs use a geometric approach for classification, identifying the hyperplane that maximizes the separation between two classes in a higher-dimensional space. Support vectors, the data points closest to the hyperplane, are crucial in establishing this margin. SVMs handle high-dimensional data well and resist overfitting but can be computationally expensive, especially for large datasets. They excel in binary classification and need modifications for multi-class problems.

3. **k-Nearest Neighbors (kNN)**

   kNN is a simple yet powerful classification method. It classifies a new data point by majority vote from its k closest neighbors in the training data. Imagine you're at a party and can't decide which group to join—kNN would analyze those nearest to you and categorize you based on the dominant group. It's easy to implement and requires minimal training data but can be computationally expensive for large datasets. The choice of k value greatly impacts performance, and kNN can be sensitive to irrelevant features in the data.

4. **Random Forests (RF)**

   RFs utilizes the power of ensemble learning. First, we construct many decision trees trained on a subset of features and datapoints. Each tree casts a classification vote for a given data point, and the final prediction is the class that has won most of all votes. This method prevents overfitting and generally performs better than individual decision trees. Random forests are resistant to outliers and can handle the combination of categorical as well as continuous data efficiently. However, they can be less interpretable compared to single decision trees, as the reasoning behind a specific classification can be complex and hidden within the ensemble. Additionally, training random forests can be computationally expensive due to the multiple trees involved.

5. **AdaBoost**

   AdaBoost, another ensemble learning method, takes a staged approach. It starts by training a weak learner, a classification model with slightly better than random performance. Then, it focuses on training examples that were misclassified by the previous model. This process creates a series of increasingly accurate weak learners, which are then combined through a weighted voting scheme to form a stronger final model. AdaBoost is very useful for dealing with unbalanced datasets in which one class has many fewer data points than the others. However, AdaBoost is sensitive to noisy data, which might overfit if not properly calibrated.

6. **Stochastic Gradient Descent (SGD)**

   SGD is a fundamental optimization approach used to train a variety of machine learning models, such as classifiers. It works by adjusting the models parameters iteratively to minimize a loss function. SGD adjusts the parameters using a tiny fraction of the training data (a stochastic step) rather than learning the complete dataset. This approach can be computationally efficient for large datasets, especially when dealing with complex models. However, SGD can be sensitive to the learning rate, a hyperparameter controlling step size during training. A large learning rate may cause the algorithm to oscillate or miss the minima, while a very small rate leads to slow convergence.

7. **Multi-Layer Perceptron (MLP)**

   MLPs are a classical type of artificial neural network (ANN). They consist of interconnected layers of nodes, each using a non-linear activation function on the weighted sum of its inputs. This structure allows MLPs to learn complicated nonlinear correlations amongst features and target variables. MLPs work really very well in pattern recognition and can be powerful tools for various classification tasks. However, they may become computationally costly to train, particularly for big datasets with numerous features. Additionally, MLPs can suffer from overfitting if not regularized appropriately. Furthermore, MLPs are more likely to overfit if not properly regularized. Regularization techniques impose constraints so that the model becomes less able to simply memorize and gain high variances specific to training data.

8. **Gaussian Naive Bayes (GNB)**

   GNB is a probabilistic classifier that assumes a conditional dependence between features. It computes the likelihood of a data point belonging to a specific class using the individual probabilities of each feature value within that class. GNB is well-known for its simple, efficient, and effective categorical features. It works effectively even with insufficient training data. However, the assumption of conditional independence of characteristics may not always hold true in real-world data, which may influence model accuracy. Additionally, GNB may not be suitable for handling complex non-linear relationships between features.

9. **Bagging (Random Forest)**

   While Random Forests were previously discussed, it's worth delving deeper into the specific implementation of bagging used within Random Forests. Bagging is an ensemble learning technique employed to reduce variance. It involves generating multiple models from randomly selected subsets of the training data and aggregating their predictions. This implies that certain data points may be included in many training sets, whereas others may be excluded outright. Bagging helps to deal with both as it averages predictions made by a number of individual trees which reduce the variance and make outputs more robust compared those from a single decision tree. A random forest is nothing but a bagged version of an ensemble model which uses decision trees as the base learners. It is a highly and very effective classification technique, but as mentioned earlier, when built into an ensemble it is challenging to interpret due to its complex nature.

After training and testing each classifier, their performance is evaluated to determine the best-suited ML algorithm for the specific use case.

12.3.4 Performance Metrices

This section describes the performance matrices for classification and image enhancement, along with their respective mathematical formulas.

1. ***Accuracy (ACC):*** It is a statistical measure indicating a prediction or classification model's correctness. It is calculated by dividing the total number of correct predictions by the total number of predictions made by the model. Mathematically, it can be written as;

   $$ACC = \frac{p+q}{p+q+r+s} \tag{12.1}$$

   p, q, r, and s represent the model's overall amount of true positive, true negative, false positive, and false negative samples.

2. ***Precision (PR):*** It shows the share of true positives out of all positive predictions produced by a classification model. We can also say that it assesses how well the model recognizes positive samples. Mathematically, it can be written as;

   $$PR = \frac{p}{p+r} \tag{12.2}$$

3. ***Recall (RC):*** It assesses how effectively the model identifies each of the positive samples. The RC is the ratio of the number of true positives to the

total of TP and FN. Mathematically, it can be written as;

$$RC = \frac{p}{p+s} \tag{12.3}$$

4. ***F1 measure (F1):*** It is referred to as the F1 score, which combines PR and RC to produce a single result. F1 is particularly useful in scenarios with an imbalance between positive and negative samples, as it considers both true positives and true negatives. Mathematically, it can be written as;

$$F1 = \frac{2*PR*RC}{PR+RC} \tag{12.4}$$

5. ***Geometric Mean (GM):*** It is used for finding the average value of a collection of numbers. It can be computed as the nth root of the product of n numbers, with n being the total number of values in the collection. When dealing with uneven data, the geometric mean is commonly employed to assess overall performance. In unbalanced datasets, when one class has significantly more samples than the other, accuracy might be a deceptive indicator. A high geometric mean indicates that the model performs well in identifying positive samples and accurately rejects negative samples.

$$GM : \sqrt{\frac{\mathrm{p}}{\mathrm{p+s}} \cdot \frac{\mathrm{q}}{\mathrm{q+r}}} \tag{12.5}$$

12.4 Results and Discussions

Table 12.1 compares various machine learning algorithms on Precision, Recall, Accuracy, F1-score, and Geometric Mean (product of all four metrics). The table highlights the best and second-best performing classifiers in bold and bolded italics, respectively. Figures 12.6, 12.7, 12.8, 12.9, and 12.10 illustrate the performance of different ML classifiers for each metric.

The table shows that the AdaBoost classifier achieves the best overall performance based on the GM with a score of 0.6494. This indicates that AdaBoost performs well across all four individual metrics. However, examining each metric individually, we see that SGD achieves the highest precision of 0.6542, while DT achieves the highest recall of 0.6196. For accuracy, MLP achieves the highest score (0.6699), followed closely by AdaBoost (0.6796) and RF (0.6602). Finally, DT achieves the highest F1 score (0.6186), followed by AdaBoost (0.5308) and SGD (0.4372).

These results suggest that there is no single best-performing classifier across all metrics. The best classifier depends on which performance metric is most important for the specific task. For example, SGD might be a good choice if precision is most important. On the other hand, if recall is the most important factor, then DT might be a better choice.

Table 12.1: Performance of different machine learning algorithms in IDRiD Dataset.

Classifier	Pr	Re	Acc	F1	GM
SGD	**0.6542**	*0.5867*	0.4563	0.4372	0.5464
RF	0.5626	0.5226	0.6602	0.4857	0.6095
KNN	0.5799	0.5831	0.6214	*0.5809*	0.6002
MLP	0.3350	0.5000	*0.6699*	0.4012	0.4737
DT	0.6179	**0.6196**	0.6602	**0.6186**	*0.6387*
LR	0.5502	0.5382	0.6311	0.5340	0.5893
MLNB	0.5462	0.5384	0.6214	0.5368	0.5825
SVM	0.5434	0.5307	0.6311	0.5231	0.5856
SVM(RBF)	0.5157	0.5083	0.6311	0.4839	0.5704
GNV	0.4590	0.4721	0.5825	0.4538	0.5171
Bagging(RF)	0.6006	0.5597	*0.6699*	0.5510	0.6343
AdaBoost	*0.6206*	0.5520	**0.6796**	0.5308	**0.6494**

[1] Bold text indicates the greatest value.
[2] The italicised underline represents the second-best value.

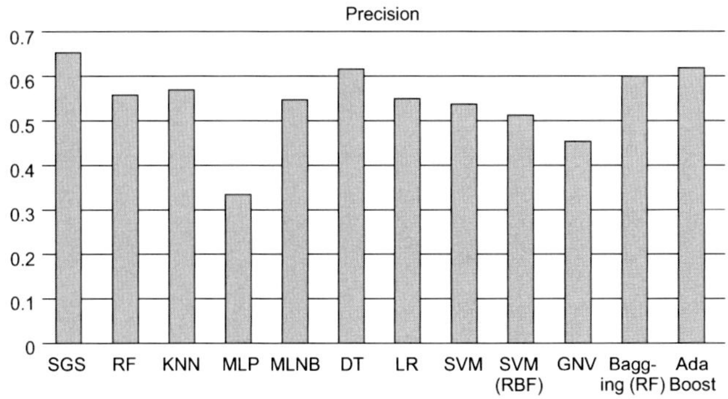

Figure 12.6: Bargraph representation in terms of Precision.

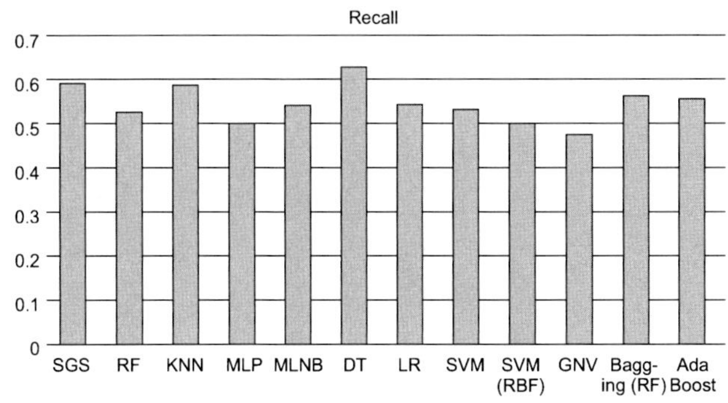

Figure 12.7: Bargraph representation in terms of Recall.

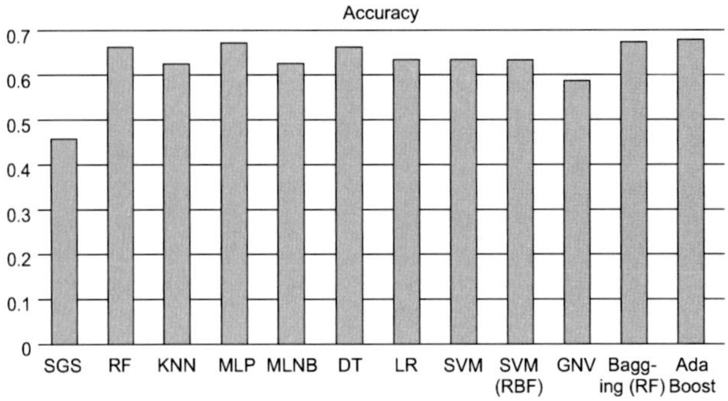

Figure 12.8: Bargraph representation in terms of Accuracy.

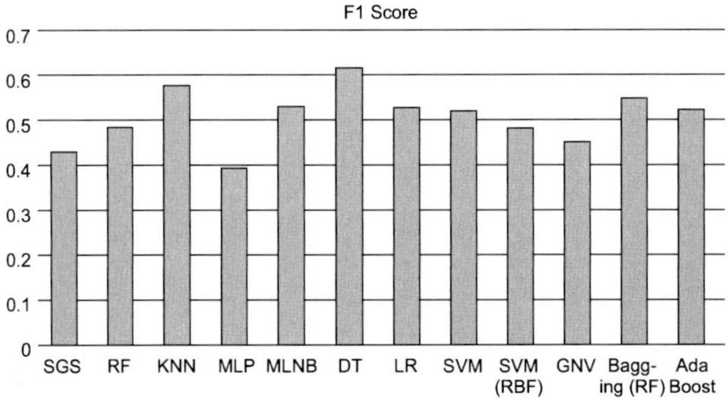

Figure 12.9: Bargraph representation in terms of F1Score.

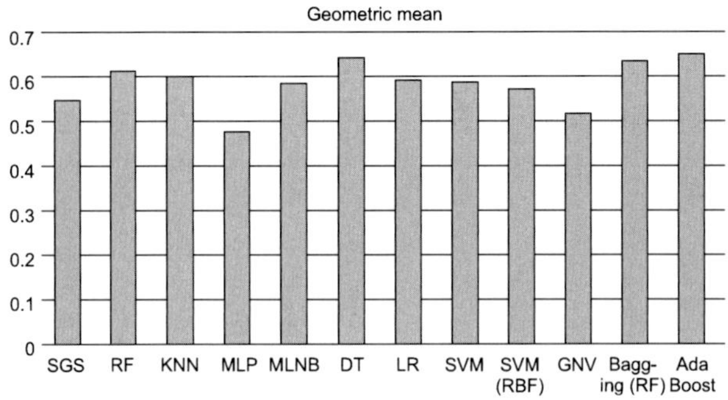

Figure 12.10: Bargraph representation in terms of Geometric Mean.

Here's a more detailed breakdown of the performance of each classifier:

- **SGD:** Achieves the highest precision (0.6542) but has a lower recall (0.5867) and F1-score (0.4372).

- **RF:** Has a moderate performance across all metrics (Pr = 0.5626, Re = 0.5226, Acc = 0.6602, F1 = 0.4857).
- **KNN:** Has a moderate performance across all metrics (Pr = 0.5799, Re = 0.5831, Acc = 0.6214, F1 = 0.5809).
- **MLP:** Achieves the highest accuracy (0.6699) but has a lower precision (0.3350) and F1-score (0.4012). This suggests that MLP might be a poor choice for tasks where precision is important.
- **kMeans:** Has a low performance across all metrics (Pr = 0.4640, Re = 0.4595, Acc = 0.4757, F1 = 0.4530). This suggests that kMeans is not a suitable classifier for this task.
- **DT:** Achieves the highest recall (0.6196) and a high F1-score (0.6186), but has a moderate precision (0.6179) and accuracy (0.6602).
- **LR**: Has a moderate performance across all metrics (Pr = 0.5502, Re = 0.5382, Acc = 0.6311, F1 = 0.5340).
- **MLNB:** Has a moderate performance across all metrics (Pr = 0.5462, Re = 0.5384, Acc = 0.6214, F1 = 0.5368).
- **SVM:** Has a moderate performance across all metrics (Pr = 0.5434, Re = 0.5307, Acc = 0.6311, F1 = 0.5231).
- **SVM(RBF):** Has a moderate performance across all metrics (Pr = 0.5157, Re = 0.5083, Acc = 0.6311, F1 = 0.4839).
- **GNV:** Has a low performance across all metrics (Pr = 0.4590, Re = 0.4721, Acc = 0.5825, F1 = 0.4538). This suggests that GNV is not a suitable classifier for this task.

On the downside, the table doesn't reveal the hyperparameters used for each algorithm. Hyperparameters are settings that control the training process of a machine-learning model. Tuning these hyperparameters can significantly impact the algorithm's performance. Note that other factors such as computational cost and training time are not taken into account here. This table highlights the performance of algorithms based on metrics like precision, recall, and accuracy. However, some models can be computationally expensive and time-consuming to train.

12.5 Conclusion

The performance of different machine learning classifiers in classifying a binary test for diagnosing diabetic retinopathy shows SGD and DT classifiers achieved the highest accuracy (66.02%). Notably, Random Forest achieved the highest F1 score (0.5809), indicating a better balance between precision (true positives vs.

false positives) and recall (correctly identifying all true positives). This suggests that RF might be less prone to misclassifications than SGD and DT, which might prioritize accuracy at the expense of missing some true positive cases.

Looking beyond accuracy and F1 score, the table also includes metrics like sensitivity (recall) and specificity. A high sensitivity is crucial for diabetic retinopathy screening, as missing a positive case can lead to delayed diagnosis and vision loss.

In conclusion, the table suggests that SGD, DT, and RF might be promising candidates for diabetic retinopathy detection. However, a more comprehensive analysis considering all performance metrics alongside factors like dataset characteristics and computational efficiency is necessary for a definitive conclusion. Finally, it appears likely that more sophisticated algorithms and patterns for feature engineering might also improve overall performance in diabetic retinopathy classification with machine learning

Disclosure Statement

The authors disclose no competing interests.

References

[1] S. N. Ahmed and P. Prakasam. A systematic review on intracranial aneurysm and hemorrhage detection using machine learning and deep learning techniques. *Progress in Biophysics and Molecular Biology*, 2023.

[2] João P. Amorim, Pedro H. Abreu, Alberto Fernández, Mauricio Reyes, Jorge Santos, and Maria Helena Abreu. Interpreting deep machine learning models: an easy guide for oncologists. *IEEE Reviews in Biomedical Engineering*, 16:192–207, 2021.

[3] C. Azad, B. Bhushan, R. Sharma, A. Shankar, K. K. Singh, and A. Khamparia. Prediction model using smote, genetic algorithm and decision tree (pmsgd) for classification of diabetes mellitus. *Multimedia Systems*, pages 1–19, 2022.

[4] C. Azad, A. K. Mehta, D. Mahto, and D. K. Yadav. Support vector machine based ehealth cloud system for diabetes classification. *EAI Endorsed Transactions on Pervasive Health and Technology*, 6(22):e3–e3, 2020.

[5] S. Bapatla and J. Harikiran. Diabetic retinopathy classification using hybrid optimized deep-learning network model in fundus images. *Journal of Electronic Imaging*, 32(6):063011–063011, 2023.

[6] A. Bhowmick, K. D. Mahato, C. Azad, and U. Kumar. Heart disease prediction using different machine learning algorithms. In *2022 IEEE World Conference on Applied Intelligence and Computing (AIC)*, pages 60–65. IEEE, 2022.

[7] X. Cao, Y. Wang, X. Li, and S. Zhang. Retinal vessel segmentation using deep convolutional neural network. In *Computational Intelligence and Neuroscience*. 2017.

[8] Z. Chen, X. Zheng, H. Shen, Z. Zeng, Q. Liu, and Z. Li. Combination of enhanced depth imaging optical coherence tomography and fundus images for glaucoma screening. *Journal of Medical Systems*, 43:1–12, 2019.

[9] A. Choudhury, S. Roychowdhury, B. K. Singh, and T. P. Singh. Introduction to digital society: An overview. In *Evolution of Digitized Societies Through Advanced Technologies*, pages 1–6. 2022.

[10] P. Dhal and C. Azad. A novel approach for blood vessel segmentation with exudate detection in diabetic retinopathy. In *2020 International Conference on Artificial Intelligence and Signal Processing (AISP)*, pages 1–6. IEEE, January 2020.

[11] H. Gavel and A. K. Mehta. A novel approach of multi-objective based feature selection method for face recognition. In *2021 2nd Global Conference for Advancement in Technology (GCAT)*, pages 1–6. IEEE, 2021.

[12] M. E. Gegundez-Arias, D. Marin-Santos, I. Perez-Borrero, and M. J. Vasallo-Vazquez. A new deep learning method for blood vessel segmentation in retinal images based on convolutional kernels and modified u-net model. *Computer Methods and Programs in Biomedicine*, 205:106081, 2021.

[13] L. Giancardo, F. Meriaudeau, T. P. Karnowski, Y. Li, S. Garg, K. W. Tobin Jr, and E. Chaum. Exudate-based diabetic macular edema detection in fundus images using publicly available datasets. *Medical Image Analysis*, 16(1):216–226, 2012.

[14] S. Gross, M. Klein, and D. Schneider. Segmentation of blood vessel structures in retinal fundus images with logarithmic gabor filters. *Current Medical Imaging*, 9(2):138–144, 2013.

[15] M. Imran and S. A. Alsuhaibani. A neuro-fuzzy inference model for diabetic retinopathy classification. In *Intelligent Data Analysis for Biomedical Applications*, pages 147–172. Academic Press, 2019.

[16] A. Kovács-Valasek, T. Rák, E. Pöstyéni, A. Csutak, and R. Gábriel. Three major causes of metabolic retinal degenerations and three ways to avoid them. *International Journal of Molecular Sciences*, 24(10):8728, 2023.

[17] S. Kranthi, Kiran, A. Sivasangari, P. Ajitha, T. Anandhi, and K. Indira. Identification of diabetic retinopathy and myopia using local binary pattern with machine learning. In *Advances in Systems, Control and Automations: Select Proceedings of ETAEERE 2020*, pages 347–357. Springer Singapore, 2021.

[18] S. Moccia, E. De Momi, S. El Hadji, and L. S. Mattos. Blood vessel segmentation algorithms—review of methods, datasets and evaluation metrics. *Computer Methods and Programs in Biomedicine*, 158:71–91, 2018.

[19] J. I. Orlando, H. Fu, J. B. Breda, K. Van Keer, D. R. Bathula, A. Diaz-Pinto, ..., and H. Bogunović. Refuge challenge: A unified framework for evaluating automated methods for glaucoma assessment from fundus photographs. *Medical Image Analysis*, 59:101570, 2020.

[20] Prasanna Porwal, Shubham Pachade, Rahul Kamble, Manesh Kokare, Gautam Deshmukh, Vasundhara Sahasrabuddhe, and Fabrice Meriaudeau. Indian diabetic retinopathy image dataset (idrid): a database for diabetic retinopathy screening research. *Data*, 3(3):25, 2018.

[21] S. Purusharthi and B. Kurhade. Identification of diabetic retinopathy in retinal images using support vector machine. *International Journal of Computing and Technology*, 1(2), 2014.

[22] S. Ravishankar, A. Jain, and A. Mittal. Automated feature extraction for early detection of diabetic retinopathy in fundus images. In *2009 IEEE Conference on Computer Vision and Pattern Recognition*, pages 210–217. IEEE, 2009.

[23] S. Sharma, S. Maheshwari, and A. Shukla. An intelligible deep convolution neural network based approach for classification of diabetic retinopathy. *Bio-Algorithms and Med-Systems*, 14(2):20180011, 2018.

[24] J. V. Soares, J. J. Leandro, R. M. Cesar, H. F. Jelinek, and M. J. Cree. Retinal vessel segmentation using the 2-d gabor wavelet and supervised classification. *IEEE Transactions on Medical Imaging*, 25(9):1214–1222, 2006.

[25] B. Venkaiahppalaswamy, P. P. Reddy, and S. Batha. Hybrid deep learning approaches for the detection of diabetic retinopathy using optimized wavelet based model. *Biomedical Signal Processing and Control*, 79:104146, 2023.

Index

L

M

O

P

Q

R

S

T

U

V

W

Made in the USA
Columbia, SC
17 September 2026

3e019f55-e218-4d36-8df7-18f43afaf7b6R01